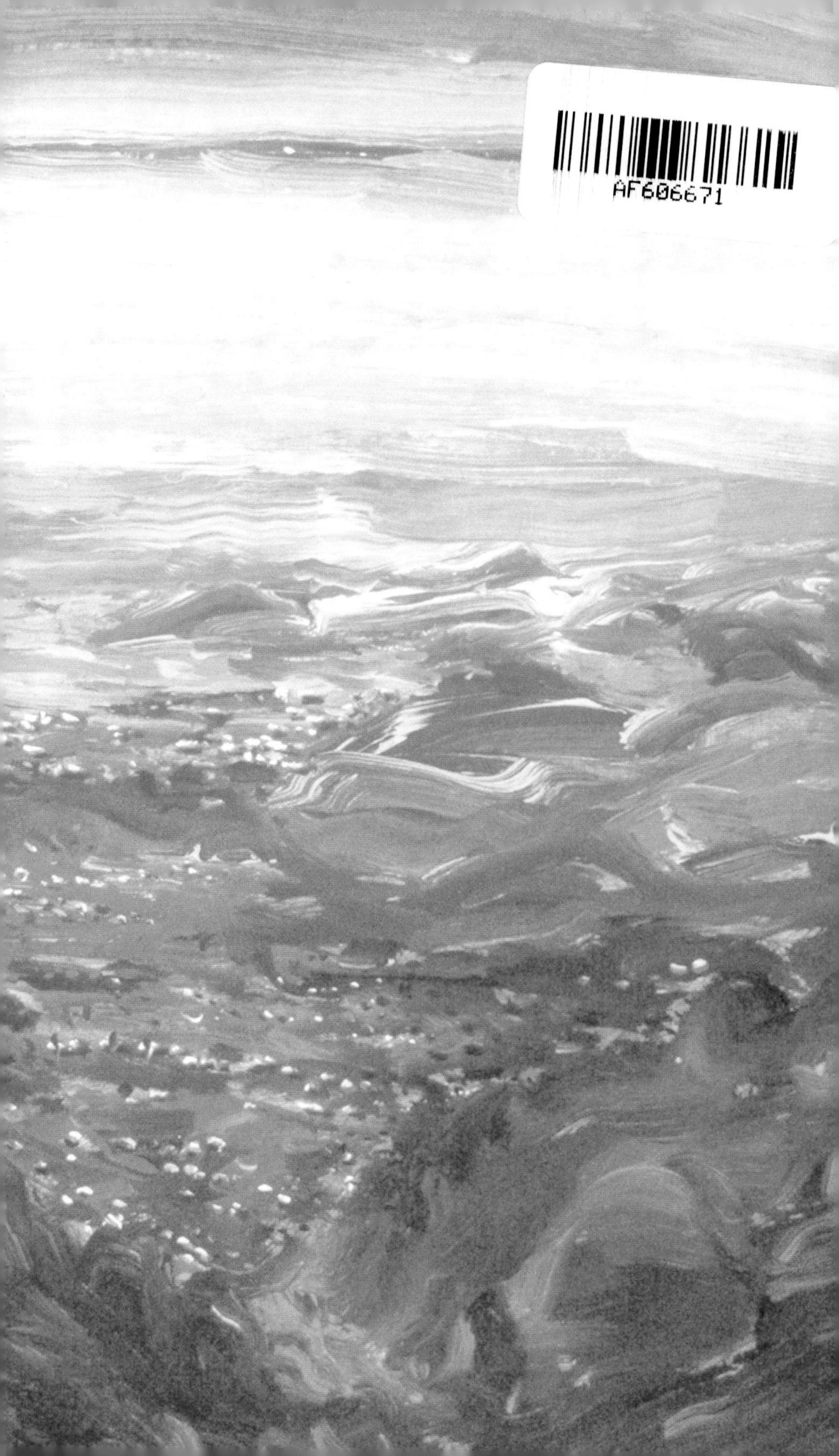
AF606671

AMERICAN JOURNEY

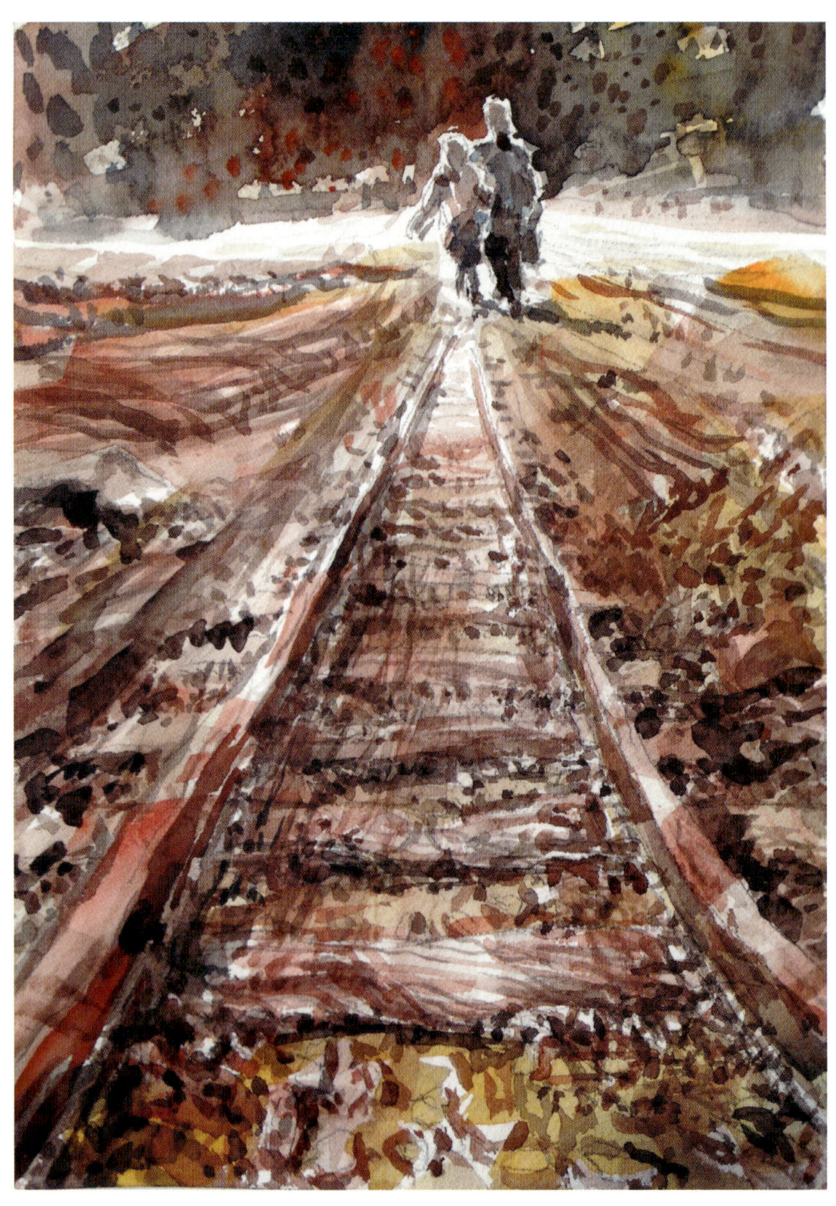

AMERICAN JOURNEY

MY LIFE IN ART

MARCO SASSONE

WITH PETER CLOTHIER

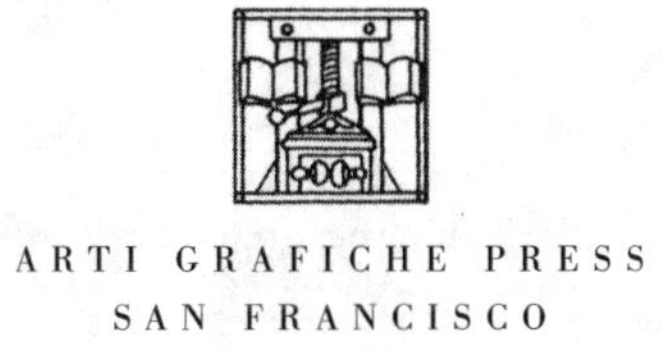

ARTI GRAFICHE PRESS
SAN FRANCISCO

Published by Arti Grafiche Press

Cover design by Annie Cormier

Publication managed by AuthorImprints

Artwork photography by Rick Lang, Ian Lefebvre, Richard Paradowski, Robert Ratkowski and Sean Weaver

Jacket cover: *Emilia* by Marco Sassone, oil on canvas, 2008. © Marco Sassone

Frontispiece: *Viaticus* by Marco Sassone,
watercolor on paper, 2017. © Marco Sassone

Publisher's Cataloging-In-Publication Data

Names: Sassone, Marco Massimo, 1942- author. | Clothier, Peter, 1936- author.

Title: American journey : my life in art / Marco Sassone, with Peter Clothier.

Description: First edition. | Florence ; San Francisco ; Toronto : Arti Grafiche Press, [2022] | Includes index.

Identifiers: ISBN 9780935194159 (hardcover) | ISBN 9780935194166 (ebook)

Subjects: LCSH: Sassone, Marco Massimo, 1942- | Painters--Italy--Biography. | Italian American artists--Biography. | LCGFT: Autobiographies.

Classification: LCC ND623.S312 A3 2022 (print) | LCC ND623.S312 (ebook) | DDC 759.5--dc23

Printed in the United States

maybe two, three girlfriends, then getting married, have children. No. That wasn't for me.

It was all somehow so innocent. Even the sex, so innocent. And so easy. But I'll come to that.

And in the meantime, here she comes, this young, blond gallery lady, knocking at my studio door. And I'm thinking, *Jesus Christ!*

* * *

Who am I? Where do I come from? Where am I going in my life? These are the questions that vex me, late at night, when I'm finally alone in my studio . . . You take a person of twenty-four years, you disrupt his life, and he becomes an American. And then one day he finds he's not accepted in either place. I even chose American citizenship. I have the passport to prove it. But am I an American? Am I an Italian? Perhaps I'm more on the Italian side, since I was born and raised there. But when I go back home they treat me like an American. So I end up feeling like I am somewhere in between, or on the edge.

* * *

It's a lively district, the Fillmore area of San Francisco, where I have had my studio these past fourteen years. Lots of restaurants with tables out on the street, on a sunny day. Lots of bars and boutiques. Lots of people, bustling, jostling. Lots of life. It reminds me sometimes of Italy.

But now, at ten thirty at night, even Fillmore Street is quiet as I drive home. I reach for the garage door opener, click open the automatic door, and squeeze the yellow Jag in—listen, at one time, I was at the top of this game, I was making more money than I ever knew existed in the old days—through the

Lonely? Yes, I'm lonely.

So here comes this nice, attractive woman and I'm thinking, Yes, why not admit it? I could use some taking care of. And what's wrong with that? I'm an artist, no? I need time in the studio. I need time to paint.

And that's it, right there. The studio. My refuge. My protection. And my jail.

So I want to tell her, "Yes." One whole part of me wants to tell this woman, "Yes, come in, the door is open. Take care of me." Right? But there's another whole part of me that wants to say, "Stay out of here. I need my silence, I need my time. Not another complication. Not another person in my life that I'll end up taking care of." I'm looking at this woman, this art person, who can help me, who says she can open doors for me, with the galleries, the business, all that stuff. And she's young, attractive, blond, and not-Italian.

And I'm thinking, *Jesus Christ!* I've been here before, haven't I?

So many women, none of them Italian. That's strange. It's not normal. But that's how it has always been from the start, those days in Florence as a young guy, very young, eighteen, maybe twenty, working summers at the Uffizi market. Not the Galleria, understand. Not the famous Uffizi Galleria, home of the great masterpieces of the Renaissance, which is the reason tourists go to Florence. No, this was the market right below it where I was working. And at the end of the day, I'd have two or three dates—remember?—it was always so easy back then. They were always foreign women, none of them Italian. Not like a normal young Italian guy, with a nice Italian girlfriend, galleries, the dealers, the finances, the paperwork. All my life, I end up taking care of things for other people. That's been my story. There are my parents to worry about, over in Italy; my assistant, Lee, here in San Francisco; the people I work with; and my son, though he's past most of his problems now. He's setting himself up nicely down in Southern California, where he grew up. He has a good job in the Italian food business.... Even Deborah. I end up taking care of things for Deborah too. When we first got together, I thought this would be someone who could help take care of things for me. She's smart; she understands where I'm coming from. She knows what I need. She has a great job at the San Francisco Opera House. She's a terrific woman, unlike many of the others. Deborah has substance; she is a strong woman.

And look what happens. I end up taking care of things for Deborah too. She comes back to the studio one day a year ago and says, "Marco, I lost my job." Then we travel together to Italy and while we're there I help her find a job. And now she wants to stay there. She's living in my house in Tuscany, she's driving my car, and she loves it so much she wants to stay there. Great! And I can't help thinking, what's in it for me? Here I am, back in San Francisco, living in my studio. I hardly get to see her. My studio work is based more in America than in Italy, and I feel that something's happening over here right now. Nothing tangible, nothing specific coming up. Yet it's a feeling that something's happening in my life and work. And I have to follow that feeling, even though I know I need to spend more time in Italy. Perhaps this is selfish, perhaps I should be in Italy with my aging parents, taking care of them. Besides, my two sisters are living there in Florence. And yet...

1

SAN FRANCISCO: THE STUDIO

SPRING 2003

So here I am in the studio, painting, and along comes this woman knocking at the door. She says, "Marco"—she's a gallery person, this one, she knows the art world—"I know you. I knew you even before I met you, from your paintings." She continues, "You're an artist, and you're not getting the support you need. You need someone to take care of things for you while you're in the studio, working." And I'm thinking, *Jesus Christ.*

I'm thinking, She's right, this woman. Why not? I do need someone to take care of all those other things for me. Here I am, already past my sixtieth birthday, looking ahead to the last productive years of my life. And what do I need more than anything? I need time in the studio to paint. I need time to work. And always there have been these other things, the distractions that devour my time. The bullshit things—the

CONTENTS

To my collectors all around the world whose support nurtured my life and sustained my journey.

Thank you.

narrow tunnel that leads to the underground parking spaces below my building.

It's dark in here. A cave. With parked cars, a junked old Volvo, packing cases, and stuff that's been stored here on jittery racks for more years than I can remember. The place echoes with silence.

I have painted pictures like this in my time. Dark pictures, junkyards, scenes of downtown desolation, and apocalypse. Tunnels, canals, all leading nowhere. It speaks to me, this darkness. You might not guess it, if all you knew about me were those bright land and seascapes, glittering with Southern California light, that I did all those years ago when I first came to America. People loved those pictures. They made me good money. I did sellout shows. I remember once, in New York, I arrived early for one of my openings at the Wally Findlay Gallery on 57th Street and saw a crowd of people outside on the street. So I asked Wally, when he buzzed me in, "What are all those people doing out there on the street?" And he laughed and said, "They're here for you, Marco. They're waiting for the door to open so they can be the first to buy a painting."

Those paintings made me a reputation, too. Those days, the name "Sassone" had cachet. Oh, they all pronounced it wrong, with the emphasis on the "o"—"Sass-oh-nay"—where it should be on the "a," with a soft musical "o" and "e" behind it. But the name had cachet. I left that all behind years ago, when I left Laguna Beach and headed north to San Francisco. I chose to leave it behind, because some voice within was telling me I'd somehow taken the wrong path. None of it gave me what I wanted. Not the money. Not the fame. But here's the truth: the new Sassone still hasn't found what he is looking for.

Still hasn't found that place, as a painter, that he longs for. That other Uffizi. Dreams of greatness. Dreams of immortality.

I make my way out through the garage and up the narrow concrete stairway leading to the studio. Walls. Concrete walls. The basic architecture of this utilitarian building. I pause in the corridor at the little hole I've always jokingly called my "window"—a small, 4-inch circular hole, drilled through the concrete—and stoop down to peer out to the street. A glimpse of the world out there, in darkness. And the joke comes back at me now as I wonder what it says about me, this hole. This window. Is this as much as I allow myself to see of the world, these days? Is this as much as I allow the world to see of me?

And heading on down the corridor to my studio, another curious little mockery: at the dead end of the hall, where the corridor turns, lies a pile of studio trash and, balanced on top of it, a small metal sign that says, FIRE ESCAPE, with an arrow pointing away from the studio toward, another dead-end wall. Tonight, it reads like some ironic metaphor for the way I've chosen to live my life. With a fire within me, and dead end walls surrounding me.

I unlock the studio door and enter through the hallway with its Sassone paintings. I walk past racks and print drawers stuffed with works from every period of my life and finally enter the large, cluttered area of the studio itself. The smell of oil paint—so familiar now that I barely notice it anymore. The shadowy skeletons of easels, standing upright in the semidarkness. Worktables, laden with cans and tubes, palette knives and brushes. And paintings everywhere. And drawings, watercolors, and pastels. On the walls, on the floor. Some old, some new. Some small, some huge. A good number of them still in progress, waiting for me to find the time to get back to them.

My creatures as I call them. Sleeping, somehow, until I get the lights turned on. Then they come alive. They crowd around me, calling for attention. During the day I have been going through all sorts of stuff which can be more or less irritating. These are things that I'd be delighted to have taken care of for me. The business things. Late at night, it's a different story. I start reflecting on the work, and then find myself lately going into these monologues. I drift off a bit into memory land.

So what's that about, I wonder? And where is it all taking me? I don't know. Right now, I don't know.

I look around, coming back for the thousandth time to one of the pastel drawings laid out on the floor. Venice. There has always been this obsession with Venice, even from this distance, from my California studio. Venice, with its long canals crowded in on either side by buildings. Its water. I have always painted water. It has always been a hallmark of my work, one of my major themes. Water surrounding me and leading nowhere. Water has really become an identity with myself, not just because it runs wild and free, but because it is liquid, fluid, like life itself. And dark, mysterious, dangerous. Here I am, today, still caught up in the same obsessive imagery. I have been told by people close to me that I am stuck in the mud, and I tell myself I don't know what they are talking about. But maybe that's not completely true. Maybe I do know on some deeper level. Or, maybe I'm just beginning to understand what they mean.

This particular pastel is a dark one. It has all the Venetian elements that I like so much, and the gestural quality of the medium. It's less resolved than the other pastels, too, and that's another part I like. It feels like I'm going in there and don't know where I am going. So I like what I see, because I don't quite know what is going on. I just know the canal leads into that familiar tunnel, a place where there's no forward, no return. I've been stuck on that canal for a long time now.

So many canals… I've made them in watercolor, ink and charcoal, and in paint. It's all about Venice. And the banks of those canals were not altogether so friendly. They were always difficult. Always dark. One of my friends suggested that they have the feel of the birth canal, and I know what he meant. It's like I am trying to go somewhere, trying to get out, but I am somehow still stuck. I feel that when I come here late at night. Stuck in my cave.

I like to tell myself I am free like the water, but in truth I still don't feel free. At times, I wish my life and my art were not so connected. That way I might feel freer. I often think other people—normal people—have more freedom than I do. I tell myself they have the freedom and flexibility to move forward. For me, I'm always trying to be the artist, not wanting to give an inch of myself to another person. With the result that I sacrifice my personal life for art, protecting the studio at all costs in order to live my art. It's not just the painting, the practice of the skills, the time devoted to the profession. It's the living and being in the work, in each and every stroke of paint. It's the eating and working. It's the waking up and looking at the work in progress before your morning cappuccino. It's the feeling of being numb to anything else, the feeling of never having the space for a social life.

This is the sort of madness that becomes a kind of affectionate companion, while painting itself is your lover—your special lover. It's your entire persona, the essence of who you are—such a pain, and such a pleasure. And how can you possibly ask the woman in your life to support all this? I chose never to ask. I always preferred to assume that it was something evident to everyone on the outside looking in and seeing, a precise and delicate border, an imaginary line defining the possibility of a relationship, unspoken words in a beautiful silent dialogue.

But I was wrong. It does needs to be spelled out. It needs to be part of a mutual understanding. Perhaps that's why a lasting relationship still eludes me.

And here I am in the stomach of the whale, in my studio, with my works surrounding me like live creatures, speaking to me, giving me suggestions, seeking to spread their energy beyond the walls of my personal confinement. As a young painter, beginning to feel the pull of art, you somehow believe that hard work alone will be enough to get you what you're looking for. But as you mature, you discover that, no matter where or how far you travel, you're always still at the beginning.

I have been deep, chasing shapes on a canvas as though hunting a beast whose smell I hardly know. I aim for targets that are always shifting, never predictable, with no natural gifts other than this amazing obsession with art. And in this darkness, I am still negotiating my existence. I have never lied or tried to save myself by choosing an easier path. When the world speaks, whether those voices are of blame or praise, whether they come from friends or enemies, they sound like ghosts. Still, they have the power to provoke real suffering. Hence, that penetrating ache at the depth of my soul—not even willpower seems to have the strength to alter the root from which we grow.

And all this agony, for what? I haven't been showing at the Museum of Modern Art or the Met. But I have the sense that something is moving, and I am happy about that. Perhaps after all this work of forty years or more, something is happening. There is always something that keeps me going, something that keeps me painting. A little satisfaction. And maybe with something moving like this, I need to go back. It's time to drift back into memory land. Time to take a look at where I've been and where I've come to. And where I need to go from here.

2

CAMPI BISENZIO, MY BIRTHPLACE

1942–1952

"Massimo! Massimo!"

It's my grandmother, Nonna, calling me from the ancient walls of Campi Bisenzio, a small town in Tuscany, not far from Florence.

"Massimo!"

My grandmother had decided, for some reason, to call me by my middle name when I was born. My full name is Marco Massimo Sassone. It's only since I came to America that people call me Marco. In Italy, in the family, it's still Massimo, to this day. The Greatest. They must have had high expectations for their son.

"Massimo," she calls. "Get moving! You're late for dinner!" Late as usual. And Papa will be mad, as usual. I can still feel the smart of his hard palm on my backside.

"Got to go," I shout to my friend Sanzio. "Ciao. See you later." And I run toward my grandmother's voice, heart beating, knowing for sure that Papa will be mad at me. Again.

* * *

Imagine a brilliant day in this village a few miles outside of Florence. I come here almost every afternoon, to the parched Campo Santo, where my friends and I play *bocchi* with little glass balls on the gray, compacted dirt, or toss coins with nickel liras still embossed, in those days, with the image of Il Duce on one side and the Fascio Littorio—the fascist emblem—on the other.

"Come on," calls Nonna, "hurry!"

Nonna was a slender woman of a nonetheless imposing presence. A tough Italian matriarch. Nonna was the only one of all of us to resist typhoid fever when it struck the family one year after the war, sending us all to the hospital. She was also as sharp as anyone I ever knew but always sparing with her words. Nonna was the one who always took care of me when I was a little boy and who was always there to protect me from Papa's anger.

She has come halfway to meet me and takes my hand as she whisks me back toward my mother's family home, where we all live with Nonna Maria and Grandpa Giuseppe—Nonno, as we children called him. Nonno walks on crutches. He had polio when he was little. The "cure" in those days, so I heard as a child, was to take him to the slaughterhouse from time to time and close him up in the carcass of a slaughtered animal. It didn't work; Nonno lost the use of both his legs for his entire life. He died eventually in his wheelchair, hit from behind in the dark by a scooter as he was returning home through the city streets of Florence. But I still remember those beautiful hard wooden crutches that he walked with. Nonno was strong in his body though and as voluble as his wife was quiet. He had a large forehead, an expressive face with kind brown-green eyes, and a bushy black mustache. Despite his disability, he managed to produce five beautiful children, two boys and three girls—my mamma and my aunts Fiorella and Liliana, all of whom still lived with Papa and me in the family house in Campi. It was only later, after the war, that my little sisters, Milly and Patrizia, were born.

I was born the year before the Allied invasion of Italy, on July 27, 1942, at the family house in Campi, but I was too young to remember much more of the war than the anxiety and fear amongst the grownups. And, soon after the war ended, the lines for scarce food and rationed bread, known as *pane a tessera*, began. And the black market, for those who could afford it.

But I'll never forget Papa's anger at the dinner table. He was a man of medium height and a slender body, but also powerful and handsome. *Ti ho detto di ritornare a casa prima della cena, capito?* he yells. "Didn't I tell you to get back home before dinnertime?" *Non si ritorna a quest'ora, hai capito?* "You cannot get back at this hour, do you understand?" My father never called me names. He never swore. But he would scream and yell when he was angry, and that was almost every day. And he'd follow it up with a good spanking on the backside, or a slap across the face. I guess he considered it his right as father of the family. That's how it was, in those days. Bless you, Nonna, for stepping in to calm him down. *Va bene, via, basta.* "It's okay," she'd say, soothingly. "Enough." *Il bambino ha capito.* "The bambino got the message."

So we'd sit down for dinner, the whole family around the big marble slab table in the kitchen, for the evening ritual. It was Nonna who did the cooking for us. Even now, across the years, I can still smell her roasted chicken with roasted potatoes. And her *Ribollita*, a thick, sweet-smelling Tuscan soup with cannellini beans. And sometimes, if she could find them at the market, she'd cook Florentine steaks. It must have been from my Nonna that I learned my love of cooking, of good Italian country food, for I still eat nothing else to this day.

And when Papa's anger was gone—he was a man of quickly shifting moods—the grownups would argue over dinner about politics and art, the daily squabbles between the Christian Democrats and the Communist Party, each with their own local headquarters in town. Or, Nonno would hold forth with his usual easy eloquence on the virtues of his favorite composer, Giuseppe Verdi, whose powerful style he touted over the romantic melodies of Puccini. Papa shared with Nonno his intense love of music. The family was proud of his beautiful tenor voice—a voice that he might have used professionally, had the circumstances of history not stood in his way. Renowned for his natural talent at interpreting the great Neapolitan songs with a delivery at once graceful and poetic, Papa often took to the stage at the local Teatro Dante, where he was the artistic director in the years following the war.

But I think he lacked the belief in himself that could have made him a successful performer. He sabotaged himself in many ways—as an artist, as a singer, as a man. He never thought of himself as good enough. He had a friend, Narciso Parigi, who turned professional as a singer and became a big name, not only in Italy but all over the world. Years later Narciso came to my art openings and my mother was always so pleased to see him; I felt his presence reminded her of my father's inability to pursue his own career.

Don't misunderstand me, though. I loved my Papa, and no matter his human weaknesses, he had some wonderful qualities. He could be handing out a terrible spanking at one moment, and at the next be sitting me on his knee and promising some special treat: *Domani ti porto sul Bisenzio con l'aquilone*, he'd say. "Tomorrow we'll go down to the Bisenzio river with the kite, and in the evening we'll all go together with la mamma to get a gelato at La Bella Mora or at Pacchino." And he'd give me a kiss and a pat on the head, and all would be well again.

Perhaps it was by way of compensation for his disappointment as a singer that Papa turned his creative passion to painting. Even today, I am not quite sure how good he thought he was, nor how seriously he took it. I'm no judge of my father's work. I guess I'm biased. I recall as a child, though, that other people admired his special talent with watercolors. But the ingredient that failed him was the same as with his singing: he lacked a core belief in his own talent. Still, his love of painting was often a topic at the dinner table, and he would hold forth at length on the style he loved the best, Impressionism, and particularly the Italians who worked in this way, known as the Macchiaioli. Papa judged them as being less commercial and more poetic than their French counterparts. Poetry, too, was important in his life, and he was always ready with a quote from his favorite poet, Gabriele D'Annunzio.

Did he dream of being a professional artist? Maybe, but it never happened for him. He did sell paintings, later on, in Florence, and participated in group shows put on by art associations. He was pleased, one year much later, during the '70s, when he won first prize at the Il Cenacolo art association show in Florence. The family had always hoped that he could turn his talents—whether as a singer or a painter—into something, but for whatever reason, the opportunity passed him by. He was certainly a truly gifted man, good at everything in the arts—writing, singing, directing, painting—but master of none. Of course, during the post-war period it was difficult, but he somehow lacked the strength and willpower to make it happened and had to look for stupid day jobs to keep the family going.

Papa had his own traumas, of course. His father—the governor of a region in Italy and a man of considerable wealth and fame in his own time—had died when Papa was only fourteen years old. Following her husband's death, his mother formed a relationship with another man, whom she never married for fear of losing her widow's pension. With him, she produced two more children. I think Papa always saw this as something of a betrayal, or at least a step down for his mother, and he cared little for the man whom he considered an intruder. By the time he was drafted at nineteen, he never wanted to go back to his native Naples—just as I later left Florence and never lived there again. All his wonderful memories of his father and grandparents—the Sassone Family was a noble family—were somehow spoiled for him. His mother was incapable of keeping the estate, and my father felt the repercussions of all this as he grew up. This was perhaps the source of his own inner conflict, for he always talked about his father. It was after the draft, when he was stationed near Campi Bisenzio that he walked into my grandfather's shop one day and met my mother. As Papa told the story, he was riding his bicycle along the main street when a beautiful girl with dark hair appeared in a shop window. He jerked on the brakes so suddenly that he almost fell off his bike! He didn't have the nerve to step into the shop right then, he had to regroup and go back the next day under the pretense that he was shopping.

I think there was much about his life that Papa regretted, and in later life he looked back on it all with a kind of wisdom that he shared with me in some memorable letters. I remember once I'd written him, using the metaphor that all my windows were shut, and I didn't want to open them. I had been feeling a bit disgusted with the way my life was going and had decided that my mission was my art and that I'd settle for that. And Papa wrote back to say, what are you talking about? Your windows need to be open, always. You made your own decisions, and you were lucky to have the choice to make the ones you did, you chose to be who you are. You chose to leave Florence, you chose to live in the United States, you chose to get married, you chose to get divorced. You made all these decisions, no one forced you. So don't go talking about closed windows. In my own case, he wrote, I didn't have the luxury, to making my own decisions. They were made for me. I didn't choose to have my father die.

I guess that tells me a lot about my Papa and his weaknesses and a lot about myself, when I think about it. I see him as both a model and a mirror in my life. He was my best admirer, when I began to paint. He really thought he had something with this kid, and he gave me all the encouragement I needed when I started entering competitions. "I'm thinking of sending in this one," I'd tell him, as I showed him a painting: "What do you think?" And he'd look at the painting, look at me, and say, "One of these days you're really going to show them, Massimo. You're really going to show them how it's done." I often think that he longed for me to be the success he never quite managed to be. I'm grateful to him, too, for dragging me off to museums as often as I'd let him, as a child: I went to the Uffizi with my father many more times than I can remember.

So Florence and the art of the Renaissance was another topic at the dinner table, with Papa expounding on how he found contemporary elements in Giotto's paintings, or swooning over the unbelievable draftsmanship of Leonardo. By dinner's end, sleepy, I'd be watching Mamma, expecting her at any moment to pack me off to bed. Instead, she'd give a little laugh and announce that, sadly, she still had not been able to find coffee in the shops. "It's terrible," she'd say with a regretful shrug. "But what do you expect, it's wartime. How about a cup of my special brew instead? It's the best that I can do." Her "special" was a concoction of *vinaccioli*, grape seeds that she would toast, grind, and brew into a hot substitute for coffee that the family agreed was really not too bad.

Mamma was beautiful with her perfectly proportioned face and figure, and an inner strength that conveyed serenity and calmness. She knew who she was, where she came from, and was proud of it. She was the reason, I suspect, that my father decided not to return to Naples after the war. Even though he tried for two years to find a job there to support the family, it was a half-hearted effort, he knew Mamma was not happy with the thought of living there. She had big, lovely eyes and resplendent skin, and I always knew she had this special feeling for her only son. My sisters were too young to be jealous of me while we were children, but later, as adults, they'd joke about it: "Look at Mamma," Patrizia would say, "Massimo's in Florence, and no more headaches, no more problems—a miracle!"

As for me, I was a rebellious kid in my own way. Not that I'd dream of talking back to Mamma or Papa—I knew better than that. But I always had an independence spirit that would get me into trouble. I was rash, foolhardy and unaware of consequences. Like the time I borrowed Papa's bicycle. I'd been forbidden from riding it alone, because I was not too steady on it yet, but I took it without asking and rode all the way out to the Villa Rucellai to visit friends. So far so good. But on the way back I crashed into one of those three-wheeler motor scooters and smashed the front wheel. I walked back home in a state of shock and dread, expecting the worst when I had to face Papa with my crime. But for once he was too upset to even punish me.

Another incident that reflected my spirit of independence and foolhardiness was when I met a homeless man lying on the sidewalk on my way home from school. His name was Dona. I was nine years old, and while my friends were scared at the sight of this filthy man, I helped him get up off his feet and managed to bring him home to the amazement of my parents and grandparents. I remember Nonna cleaned him up and fed him, then he went back on the streets. Also, this time I got lucky—I was only scolded and told not to bring these kinds of people to the house ever again!

I loved to run, too. I often think today that I've been running all my life. I remember how much I loved it already at the age of five, the sense of freedom the movement gave me. And later, in school, I was an ace at the 800 meters, the 1500 meters, and the mile. Always running, always going, always moving.... Until I ran away from Florence at the age of twenty-four.

But I am already getting ahead of myself.

* * *

My grandfather was the pillar of the family, both emotionally and financially. He owned the house where we all lived, along with the adjacent millinery shop on the Corso Santo Stefano, the main street of Campi Bisenzio. He sold beautiful Borsalino hats, beautiful umbrellas... all kinds of things. A tough old guy despite his disability, he was the one shop owner in Campi who, with his son Giordano, resisted an order from the retreating German troops to open up all the shops, so they could help themselves to whatever they chose to take with them as they fled. Nonno and Uncle Giordano slammed down the iron window shutters in defiance, but the Germans wrecked the place anyway, smashing through the storefront with a tank and destroying everything inside. My grandfather had to start over, and he did.

A meticulous man, Nonno kept everything in order in this well-lit, spacious shop where I was always welcomed as a child. To me it was a very special place, whose light and airy atmosphere reflected the generous nature of its owner, a gregarious man who was never without a cheerful word or a joke for his customers: "An umbrella, signora? Of course, of course. But are you sure you want to use it right this moment? I see it's raining really hard outside. It could get wet." I remember making gummed tape with him—this was long before the days of ready-made Scotch tape—on the meter-long rolls of brown paper that he used to wrap his customers' purchases. I remember the neat display cases, the filled shelves, the floor with its gleaming yellow Tuscan tiles.

This was our world, along with the adjacent house that was our home. And no matter the hardships of the post-war world, it was a safe and loving environment where our family lived in as much harmony as any other family we knew. Until the day Nonno decided to sell everything, the house and the shop, and move north with my Nonna and my aunt Liliana, to where his sister, Fiorella, was now living with her husband.

I was ten years old.

"We're going to live in Florence," Mamma told me, when she broke the news. Florence. The capital of Tuscany. It sounded big and distant. It sounded like anything but home.

"You'll like it there, I promise," my mother said. "And the schools are better, too," my father added. "You'll get a much better education."

But even at that young age, I knew this move would change my life forever.

3

FLORENCE: THE UFFIZI MARKET

1953–1967

What a palace Papa found for us that first year in Florence! I could hardly believe my eyes when we arrived for the first time one summer afternoon. The villa looked majestic as we walked up to it, dwarfed by the classical stone pillars of the main gate. Rows of tall, dark cypresses framed the driveway to the mansion with their slender silhouettes while sunlight flooded the faded Tuscan yellow facade. I was overwhelmed by the grandeur of it all in those first few moments, and it took me weeks more to explore the gardens with their huge clay pots of lemon trees. Papa turned the heavy key to let us into our new quarters, and what a sight was there to greet us! This was no ordinary entry—it was a 2000-square-foot reception hall with soaring ceilings, towering windows, and a large balcony!

We stood there, open-mouthed, gaping at the opulence. So this was the new home for the Sassone family? Understand, this was a time when previously wealthy families who had owned villas before the war could no longer afford to maintain them, so they began to subdivide their huge estates. The Villa Schneiderf, where Papa had found our palatial residence, was situated on a hillside about fifteen minutes outside Florence, and Papa had picked out what must have been the best apartment in the entire complex in his desire to make the move to the city a pleasant one for the family. We were right in the center of the building, and from our balcony we could see a panorama of the entire city of Florence and the Arno River. There must have been at least three bedrooms, since I remember my sisters shared one and I had my own. And there was a very large living room downstairs and a huge kitchen. The place was still luxuriously decorated, with furnishings that must have been kept here since the old days, before the conversion. The great fireplace in the hall was decorated on either side with ornate paintings of harvests and vines, and a splendid Venetian glass chandelier was suspended from the beams above a magnificent antique table. For a little boy, it was grand beyond anything I had ever dreamed of.

We lived in the Villa Schneiderf for the year I went through the fifth grade, and it was a wonderful time for me. We used to take the shortcut to school and home again through narrow country lanes, a good twenty minutes down the hill from the villa to the little town of Candeli. The teacher liked me because I was more outgoing than some of the other kids. Full of life already, I had begun noticing the girls in an innocent kind of way, and sometimes they'd come home with me to do their homework. It was while we were living in the villa, too, that I met my first American girl—the daughter of a writer who rented an apartment in the villa while he worked on a research project. I remember being fascinated with this little girl, so blond, so blue eyed, and a little bit wild—not the least bit like any of my school friends. She always had me charging around the table in the great hall, riding piggyback on my shoulders, and shouting at me, "Faster, faster!" What a prescient image, I now realize, of my later life! Even her name seemed exotic: Anne Louise. She liked me a lot, I knew, and I liked her.

Papa found a job working for the city and spent long days out in the field working on road construction projects as a *capo cantiere*, a road gang foreman in charge of a large crew of workers who resurfaced old roads and built new ones. He worked on construction projects, too. I recall being especially proud of him one year when he supervised the building of a *campo sportivo*, a sports complex with dozens of tiers of concrete seating all around the field. Looking back with the perspective of time, I know how much he must have sacrificed his creative energies in the process, yet he seemed happy enough with his job. I had the impression, as a child, that he was simply satisfied knowing he was taking care of his family and that we were settling into this new life without Nonno's support. But I can't help but wonder how it affected him deep down in his artistic soul.

What I remember most about this period was how he kept after me about my school work. "If you want to make something of your life, *caro* Massimo," he was always telling me, "you need an education." I'm sure he felt his own had been neglected, and that he attributed his current situation to that fact. No matter how hard it might have been for him, I also have wonderful memories of Papa coming home from work around seven or eight in the evening, and the sense that the whole family came back together when he walked in the door. Sometimes I would wait for him, squatting high up on those pillars at the front gate until I spotted him in the distance striding up the hill. Papa walked faster than anyone else I ever knew. Then I'd jump down and run to meet him. He'd pick me up and give me a big kiss before walking the rest of the way with me, hand in hand.

And then, more often than not, he'd find the time for family. Unlike many papas I knew back then, he wasn't a big drinker, except for a glass of wine with dinner. So instead of settling down in an armchair with an aperitif when he got home, he'd get down on the floor and play with me, my sister Milly, and my friend Anne Louise, until Mamma finally broke up the fun with her familiar summons: *Si mangia, a tavola!* "Dinner time, take a seat, and hurry the American *bambina* home." And then, in her usual teasing way, she'd add, "Don't they eat dinner in America?"

It was a wonderful life. But even as a child, I was aware that our new grandiose residence at the Villa Schneider was way beyond our family's means. Papa was not the most practical of men when it came to cold hard money. I learned much later that my grandfather, who had been the sole supporter of the family up until then, had divided the proceeds from the sale of his properties amongst his children to ease their transition to a new way of life. Thanks to his generosity, my parents were left with a year's financial support, to cover our living costs and rent while we relocated. We had only one year to adjust to independence.

We managed to maintain the fantasy for exactly a year. I knew it was coming to an end when Papa announced one day that one of his workers had told him about an apartment for rent in Florence, *di la d'Arno*, across the Arno, on the left bank. *Non si puo' andare avanti qui,* he told us sadly. "We can't go on living here. We have to move to Florence anyway for my job and the city schools." I don't think Mamma was too unhappy with the idea that she would see more of my father; he could now come home for lunch each day, whereas at the villa she saw him only in the morning and at dinner time. As for me, I suppose I accepted the move as just another one of those inevitable facts of life, but I was also sure in my heart that our next home could not possibly compare to the villa.

I was right. When we made the move to Florence, life changed completely, only this time it was not for the better. Suddenly, there was less time for the family, less money, and less food on the table. After a year in the villa, our new apartment seemed small and gloomy, not much more than two rooms in all. No magnificent panorama. In fact, no view at all. To me, the place felt like a prison in the middle of a concrete jungle. The world outside the building was just as bad: the street was too steep for us to even play. And the neighborhood was noisy from first light, when we'd be woken every day by the baker's man: *Polacche briosce!* His morning yell would echo up and down the street. "Polish brioches!" My sisters and I hated living there.

So for the family, these were years of learning how to be content with less and adjusting to city life. We had to learn how to make do with restricted space and a tight financial situation, much as Italy herself was forced to do as she recovered from the war.

Still, by compensation, this was also the time that I began to find an escape in art. I discovered pleasure in drawing and painting. Perhaps "discover" is not the right word; it implies that there was something, a new world, waiting to be found. If there was a secret love or talent for painting hidden within me, I was unaware of it at the time. It would be more accurate to say that I painted because in doing so I found ecstasy. The discovery of my talent came later. In the beginning there was no such thing. I simply found that painting made me happy. That was the important part.

One evening, many years later, I asked Papa how he came to recognize my talent. "You did a landscape with a cloud formation," he told me, "and I could only see the clouds because they were real." It was not really an answer to my question, but I loved the story and was more than happy to believe it. I'm sure clouds were not an unusual accomplishment for an eleven-year-old boy. What I do know is that Papa had his own talent—for believing in his soul that anything his son did was extraordinary. His attitude was infectious, and I, too, came to believe in myself as unusually artistic.

So whenever I felt inspired, I would make a few pictures. Paper, pencils, and pens were always available. I kept drawing, and when it came time to show off my pictures, my first choice was Papa. He always gave me the sort of response I wished for, by first examining the drawing with astonishment and appreciation that never failed to amaze me, and then offering me his interpretation. "Look how beautifully you caught the way this pathway moves towards the horizon." After which I would rush to draw another picture. It was in this way that I learned how to accept praise. When I showed the picture to La Mamma, though, I would tell her proudly, "Look what I did."

"That's interesting, Massimo," she would say. "But what about your homework?"

One day after I had done a drawing at school, everyone crowded around me to see it. My teacher, who wore her red hair in a bun, decided to pin it to the wall. I felt like a wizard! All I had to do was draw these marvels, show them off, and bask in the praise. And by now I was becoming skilled enough to claim some talent. For inspiration, I spent hours poring over Papa's art books in the house, but what I loved best was to sketch from life.

Proud of my creations, I would study my drawing and linger over some particular detail before standing back to take it all in. Yes, I told myself, here was a thing of beauty and I'd made it. No, it wasn't perfect, but still I had drawn it and it was just fine. It had been a joy to create, and now it was a joy to stand back and pretend that I was someone else admiring my picture. Not much has changed to this day!

Occasionally, looking at my drawing through someone else's eyes, I would notice there was something else to add. Or, perhaps, I would be overcome with the urge to prolong the satisfaction I had felt while drawing it, so I would add another cloud, more highlights in the foreground, more touches. In later years, there were times when I thought I had ruined my drawings with these further touches; but working on them never failed to bring me back to that initial moment of euphoria, so I found it impossible to stop myself.

As I put a little distance between myself and the child that I once was, I can recall the reasons for the pleasure I felt. Drawing allowed me to create instant wonders that everyone around me could appreciate. Even before I was done, I was already looking forward to the praise and love my drawing would elicit. As this expectation deepened, it became part of the act of creation and part of its pleasure. After a time, my hand became as skilled as my eyes. If I was drawing a boat in the Arno River, it felt as if my hand were moving without conscious direction on my part. As I watched the pencil move confidently across the paper, I would look on in stupefaction, as if the drawing were the evidence of the presence of another being, as though someone else had taken up residence inside of me. As I marveled at "his" work, aspiring to become "his" equal, another part of my brain was busy inspecting the reflections in the water and the composition as a whole, while still aware that I had created this scene on a blank piece of paper. I was acting before I could think, and at the same time I could take stock of what I had already done. My ability to analyze the progress aroused in me the pleasure of discovery, of fearlessness, of freedom. The coordination between mind and hand, the sense that my hand was acting on its own, had something of the sensation of release into the world of dreams. I made no secret of my drawings. Rather, I showed them off to everyone, anticipating praise and taking pleasure when it came. To draw was to discover a parallel world—one without embarrassment or shame. The things I drew were real, and I felt as though I owned everything I drew.

I also loved the smell and visual appeal of paper, pencils, paints, and other materials. I loved the sensuality of blank drawing paper. I liked to keep my drawings; I liked them for their material presence.

Discovering all these simple pleasures, I dared to believe myself different, even special. I was hesitant to be a show-off, but I definitely wanted my drawings to be seen. The world I was creating enriched my life and gave me a legitimate escape from the humdrum of everyday life. Art became my great savior, and my youthful passion.

The Via Costa San Giorgio, where our apartment was located, had the one advantage of leading directly to Forte Belvedere and then on to Via San Leonardo, an ancient cobblestone street so beautiful that it offered countless picturesque corners to paint. It was a perfect invitation to start painting on location. I made numerous pilgrimages to that street and came back home with an armful of watercolors. It was here, too, that I met my first mentor. Ottone Rosai was a well-known Florentine painter who had made it his life's mission to paint the Via San Leonardo. You could just feel his love for that poetic byway in his pictures. The notion of rendering an illustration was secondary to him; what he created were lyrical visions in paint, capturing the mood and spirit of the place with a paradoxical blend of soft coloration and bold delivery. You can still see much of what I learned from Rosai in my paintings even today, some forty years later. But for him, this was every painter's obsession, correlative to his sensibilities, the pure projection of himself.

I first met Maestro Rosai when I suddenly became aware of a presence behind me, watching me as I worked. When he spoke, I was at once both flustered and annoyed. *Va bene*, he urged softly. "Keep working. Keep working while the paper is still wet." Then I realized what he meant and kept on painting. God knows, since then I've always kept the paper wet, right up to my most recent series of Venice watercolors.

Thank you, maestro, for your guidance. After our first meeting, I used to run to the maestro often on the Via San Leonardo, and he was always ready with a word or two of encouragement and a compliment on my earliest efforts. His support was a very special gift.

Moving on to high school at this time, I was beginning to take my art classes seriously, too, especially the drawing class taught by a man named Ugo Maturo. Having started out with a woman who was a nice, gentle teacher, I remember the shock when a large, scary bearded character first strode into the room. He was huge, as big and round as an opera singer, and the class was petrified of him, including me. But I soon got used to him. He taught us for two hours every week. In Italy, art was as serious a subject as literature or history, and you could easily be flunked for failing the class. This guy loved my life drawings, though. They were all still lifes of vases, vases, and more vases. Professor Maturo insisted that they be rendered in chiaroscuro, meaning with the proper shading. "They must be round," he'd tell us. "They must be three dimensional; the eye must travel all the way around the object, no?" Then he'd pick up one of my drawings and hold it up for the class to see. "This is the way you draw," he'd say. I couldn't believe it. I glowed, of course, with pride and pleasure, but the tasks he set were not a big deal for me.

I was not too good in my other classes, except for physical education, but in art I'd not only finish my own drawing, but I'd have time to draw another one for someone else as well.

And my classmates always seemed to appreciate the help. It was quite something, helping those brainy types who were at the top of the class in every other subject, but hadn't the first idea how to make a charcoal drawing. It was fun to be good at something. But I never gave it much serious thought, and it certainly never crossed my mind that someday I'd be an artist.

Working on wood panels I began to paint mostly local landscapes out of my special love for Florence. I had a desire to portray my native city in vistas from the surrounding hills, as well as its narrow cobblestone streets and the alleyways of the historic center. I could never forget that I was painting views of the world-famous Florence, but I also never felt that I had to live up to the many Tuscan artists who had painted the same scenes before me. My involvement was total. I would put together my materials as fast as I could, but even as I assembled my paints and brushes with the wood panels, I often had no idea what I was going to paint. That didn't matter. I was simply eager to get on with the process.

It was around this time that I began to use dots and flecks of paint in the manner of the Macchiaioli painters, leaving the wood itself visible in places—a practice that in essence resulted in creating a more cohesive overall effect. To lose myself in the particulars of a skyline silhouette, to evoke the shapes of cypresses and country roads in precise details, to dwell insistently on the domes, the bridges over the river, and the men fishing from the shores—all this was to feel as if I were wandering among the very things that I was painting. The elation that I felt upon finishing a piece was so great that I felt the urge to touch it, pick out some detail to delight in, even take it in my mouth, bite into it, consume it.

My choice of subject was as equally important as my style or technique; most of all, I wanted my art to be a spontaneous expression of something inside me. I loved to paint houses and village roads receding into the distance, obeying the rules of perspective I had just recently mastered. If I liked the results, a haze of pleasure and security would settle over me; in my mind, I had succeeded gloriously in capturing the poetry of my land.

Part of what excited me, I'm sure, had to do with the fact that I was growing and developing physically, and beginning to feel the power of the attraction to the female body. And happily there was soon someone on hand who gave me plenty of those body images to feast my eyes upon. Silvio Loffredo was teaching at the Galileo Galilei Institute in Florence, where I enrolled to study architectural drafting. I was amazed to find a gestural painter teaching at this primarily technical school, and we struck a bond immediately since neither of us, teacher nor student, cared much for all of those pitiless architectural straight lines. Instead, I started going more and more to his private studio and eventually dropped out of the Galilei Institute altogether—much to my father's dismay.

Loffredo was a crazy man, and I loved it. He taught me the freedom to express myself, the freedom to think for myself, and see with my own eyes. Something he had learned well at the "School of Seeing" of Oskar Kokoschka, the great Austrian master and his teacher during the early 1950s in Salzburg. Loffredo's art was clearly making a break from the old respected traditions of Tuscan painting, and I liked that, too. I'd rush up a dark, narrow stone stairway to his fourth floor studio and find him working there. From the windows you could almost reach out and touch the Baptistery, the Brunelleschi dome, or the Giotto bell tower. And if the view outside was spectacular, the interior of the studio was equally incredible to me. There were paintings stacked up everywhere, open cans of oil paint with color spilling down the sides, and brushes sticking out every which way. The place was completely cluttered, and I found it unbelievably beautiful and seductive. And not least, over in a special corner, reclining on a faded purple velvet couch, would be one of Loffredo's many models, all sensual and naked! Incredible! Silvio would be chattering away as he painted: "Come in," he'd tell me. "Get to work! Grab a piece of charcoal. Help yourself to the paints. Whatever you want."

To this day, I cannot adequately describe the profound emotions I felt every time I entered Loffredo's studio. He was one of the major Tuscan painters in the expressionist tradition of the 1900s. Yet the humility with which he approached his work proved to be contagious, a liberating force for the entire period of my apprenticeship in his studio. When I worked with him, I never failed to sense the value of this extraordinary experience, which was a much needed and timely addition to my traditional academic studies. It was no longer a matter of the basics—color wheels, gray scales, one-point perspective, and the like. Here it became a profoundly personal journey into the gestural and technical skills that led me to develop and define my own natural artistic expression.

Loffredo would never impose his method of painting on anyone. Indeed, it was a mark of his sensibility and his ability as a teacher that he always encouraged his students to pursue their own vision. I was amazed watching the fluid brushwork with which he could manipulate form, color, and light to intensify the subtleties of emotional and expressive effects, and it was this aspect of his work that I would seek to assimilate into my own painting.

He was open to everything and welcomed the use of fractured color that I embraced out of love for the "Macchiaioli" painters of the mid-nineteenth century, especially its younger members. Mario Puccini and Ulvi Liegi, for example, were notably more concerned with the effects of fragmented color used to approximate the effects of natural light on the two-dimensional surface of a canvas, than were the older artists of the group. They painted on unprimed wood panels to which they directly applied color—an approach that I continued to practice during the early years of my life in Southern California. It was later that I decided to return to the more conventional support, laying down a toned ground on the stretched canvas in order to simulate the solid surface of the wood panel, before moving on to evolve a sequence of tints appropriate to the painting's subject.

I had time to test out my technique under Loffredo's guidance, painting hundreds of figures on the surfaces he himself preferred, the *cartoni telati* or canvas covered boards, that he kept everywhere in great numbers, stacked up against the walls. I still treasure one of the portraits on canvas board by the hand of this master painter, received as gift from him in Florence in 1972. It is a beautiful reminder of those glorious formative years, so essential to the evolution of the autonomy of my painting style today.

My parents must have been aware that their teenage son was developing into manhood, but we never talked about such things as a family. I think Papa was inclined to leave these things for me to discover for myself. He was probably too shy to tell me anything about the facts of life, and back then sex education classes were unheard of. I ended up with all the usual adolescent inhibitions, not to mention the restrictions imposed by my tyrannical Papa. He was a controller in every conceivable way. I'd be in big trouble if I came home after my curfew. And smoking—never! I'm grateful now, but I remember the humiliation of being smacked across the face one day when I came home with my clothes smelling of tobacco smoke. I had been hanging out in a coffee bar with friends, but Papa was outraged. *Hai fumato?* He yelled at me. "Have you been smoking?" "No, Papa." *No, é vero.* "No, I promise you." But he still reached out and slapped me hard across the face.

At the time, I was always furious at Papa for being so strict about every little thing. Not only was smoking out of the question, but he demanded absolute correctness in the way I spoke and presented myself to others in every detail of personal and public etiquette, from the way I dressed to table manners. So I was raised quite differently than most of my friends. I learned to be articulate, polite, and well-spoken. I never resorted to using everyday street language. And I realize now that these things have been important to me in my life.

So *grazie*, Papa. For everything.

* * *

If I learned about manners from Papa, I learned about life from the "Uffizi School," as my father referred to it with disdain. And he didn't mean anything that had to do with art. The Uffizi was an open market with dozens of stalls located right below the famed Galleria to attract tourists. During the summer months, I used to work there at a stall owned by a

Mrs. Corsi, selling leather goods—wallets, briefcases, boxes of all sizes, small items such as key chains, belts, and bookmarks, along with all kinds of beautifully-crafted leather bags, from casual to formal. I still recall vividly the smell of all that leather. We had to be there by eight in the morning to set up the stalls for business, and we stayed most days until eight in the evening to pack up our wares and store them for the following day. I proved to be an adept salesman in the several years I worked there, both before and after my military service in 1965. It was at the market that I learned English—and a whole lot more. I developed my social skills, learning how to put my native Italian charm to excellent use. I also discovered women.

Florence was an unbelievable place in the 1960s. Americans were flocking to Italy, and Florence was a major destination. They could buy anything with the U.S. dollar at the time, and I was a great pitch man. The art of selling, I discovered, was never to talk about the leather goods. I chatted instead about the museums, the art academy, and about my life as a struggling art student. I painted myself as a bohemian artist, selling my drawings and watercolors under the counter, as well as the leather goods. The tourists liked me. I gave one hundred percent of myself, and they were delighted to spend their dollars at Mrs. Corsi's stall. I was earning good money, too, and managed to contribute my share to the family finances, since I continued to live with them until I eventually left Florence in 1967. And I met wonderful people, not to mention plenty of girls to date in the evening hours.

Believe me, the "Uffizi School" offered a complete course in human sexual relations, and by the time I started working there, I was ripe for the education. My first experience had been with a Swiss girl, older than me. I was nineteen and she was twenty-six, an already mature woman with brown eyes and a sweet, appealing look. She came to the stall one day while I was working at my first job at the Straw Market, known as "Il Porcellino," where I worked one summer before moving on to the Uffizi. I was pretty nervous before we got together that evening, as I was so sure that this was going to be the night. And sure enough, everything fell nicely into place. I couldn't afford a hotel room, of course, so an hour before stopping to pick her up in the Piazza Stazione, I cunningly draped a blanket over the branch of a tree in the Carraia—a still-undeveloped area not far from the Piazzale Michelangelo. So we had a nice dinner at La Beppa, a trattoria that served casual Florentine cuisine on an outdoor patio and conveniently located on the way to the Carraia. Afterwards I took her to this open field, where I casually plucked down the blanket and spread it out under the tree.

Well, we fumbled around for a bit, and eventually I managed to make a clumsy entry into that most mysterious of all places. I recall she had a particular scent about her, and I can still see the mass of small hairs under her arms. But I have to say that it all seemed a bit disappointing, after my high expectations. I hardly knew the girl, and the whole thing happened so fast I scarcely felt it. Worst of all, I felt like a total amateur.

That changed rapidly with the first-class education offered at my new school under the Uffizi Galleria. Love and sex became a glorious addiction, and at that age, I admit, I found it difficult to tell the two apart. It was my Florentine version of *La Dolce Vita*, and for a while I lived that sweet life to the fullest. I'm not aggressive by nature, but my natural intensity and big warm smile were quite enough to do the work for me. This period in my life will likely not please many women in this day and age, but I'm trying to be truthful about my past. And the truth is that I was never short of girls who appreciated who I was and who shared my love of life. So the dates multiplied, followed soon by some full-blown romances. Since most of the women I dated were Americans, I'm sure these experiences contributed not a little to my first interest in traveling to the United States one day.

Take Barbara, for example. She was a lovely blond, maybe twenty-three years old, who stopped by my stall one day wearing jeans and an open-neck white shirt. As she inspected the row of handbags strung up on a rod along the awning at the front, there was no mistaking the energy she projected. I liked her from the start.

"Can I help you?" I asked casually. The deep brown tan against the white V-neck of her shirt looked warm and fascinating. She shrugged and gave me a tentative smile. "Oh, I don't know.... Guess I'm just window-shopping," she said. I returned her smile. "So where are you from?" I asked. "Have you been to the States?" She turned the question around on me, implying that I wouldn't know anyway, even if she told me. My turn to shrug. "Maybe, one day. Who knows?" She smiled again, relenting. "I'm from Santa Monica, California," she said. "You know where that is?" I shook my head. We both knew we were flirting, and enjoying it. "So what brings you to Florence then? From Santa Monica, California?" "Oh, I just needed to get away," she said, with a vague, disclaiming wave. "And I did this course in Renaissance art at college ..." "Ah," I said, grateful for the opening. It was all I needed. "So you're interested in art?" "Well, kind of," she conceded. And ten minutes later I'd talked her into taking a coffee break with me, and there we were sipping a cappuccino each at the Rivoire, the most elegant coffee bar in Florence, just a few steps from the Uffizi. I learnt a bit more about Barbara and made a date with her for that same evening.

That's how it always went. I'd show up prompt at nine o'clock at the hotel on my green Lambretta scooter, cleaned up and dressed for the occasion, heart racing with the anticipation of getting together with my date again. I might be wearing an elegant blue pinstripe suit, say, with a sharp cuff at the ankles and a clean, crisp white shirt, and loafers with white socks. And how beautiful they all looked, these girls, these women, out of their tourist casuals and dressed up for the evening! At times, I could hardly recognize my date, she looked so much more exciting at night than I had imagined during the day. More often than not, we would end up in bed that same night, and if not on the first night, then at least the second. Barbara, I remember, was more coy than some of the others: she dragged me up all those steps in the Giotto campanile, and through half the museums in Florence, before she felt we were well enough acquainted. But when we finally got to bed, she was amazing. And after that first time, we could hardly wait until the next. By the time she left, we were spending half our time in bed together.

But leave she did, of course, and went back to California. I missed her keenly for a couple of days, before another beautiful woman came along. And they kept coming. They came in a hundred different shapes and sizes, some younger, some my own age, and some older—blonde, brunette, tall, short, big, busty, and petite. Most of them seemed to come from California or the East Coast, and there was always a common denominator for their traveling to Italy. And no, it was not to visit the museums. It was not to explore the architectural splendors of the Renaissance. They came in droves to meet an Italian man who could cure them of whatever was ailing them. Their stories varied in the details, but underneath they were often all the same: they were taking time off to test their love for a boyfriend in America; or taking a trip before the engagement or the wedding; or wondering if what they had felt back home was "real love." Or, they had come to Italy after a breakup with a boyfriend, or a separation from a husband, or a recent divorce. The married women traveling alone seemed to need no special reason to meet a man, just being there was somehow synonymous with their needs.

And, of course, obliging young Massimo Sassone was always eager to be of help in their time of need. I was one of an elite group of young Florentine men who dated only foreign women. There were probably no more than a couple dozen of us engaged in this unusual activity, and we were always busy. As I've mentioned, I was not aggressive by nature, and women seemed to fall for this quality. One thing I learned early is that it is never we men who choose. The woman chooses. And I was fortunate in that many of them chose me. Some of my friends were jealous that Sassone always had a date, and I was quick to tell them that I never came on to women as Italian men are reputed to. No, no, no . . . I never liked to push people, especially women. And while my dates were frequent and short-term, I never failed to treat them with the utmost respect. I loved them all in the moment. We might be more or less involved, but I never thought of any single one of them as less than love affairs. And, in return, I was treated the same way.

We young men all knew each other at the Uffizi market. At the stalls in those years during the 1960s, there was a fine variety of characters in our inner circle. There was Bibi and his *barzellette*—his constant jokes. He was a handsome guy, your typical Italian male, and he had a good singing voice, which he showcased Saturday nights at the Fagiano restaurant on the Via de' Neri during dinner with a group of other musicians. There was Aldo, *Il Moro*, the "dark one," another tall and handsome man who could stack up against any of today's big-time movie stars. There was his brother, Alberto, *il nibbio*" the dreamer, who immigrated early on to Nebraska and married an American woman he had met at the market. He would send American care packages to his brother, who lives in Florence to this day. My friend Giancarlo, a few years older than me, was the one who really liked me and encouraged me to continue painting. He, too, had a great singing voice like Bibi. Then there was Rolando, still a good friend of mine, with whom I shared countless adventures. And Bruno, *Pennello*, the "paintbrush," so called for his long flowing hair, was a close friend and my partner in crime during our travels together in Greece and England. Bruno was a sweet, tall, and lanky fellow who sported an odd variety of clothes from army jackets with tattered labels to velvet-collared Edwardian coats from Portobello Road in London. People would stop and stare at him in Signoria Square, tourists and Italians alike. A strange bird, but together we made a fine couple.

Another major player was Paolo Catani, nicknamed "Sonny." With a contagious laugh, he always seemed to have some nefarious business going on. Aside from the work at the stall, he was often busy buying and selling local artists' paintings. Sonny lives in New York now, where he has become a major player in the art business, and he still has big deals going down. Franco and Massimo Vezzosi owned their own stand of *bigiotteria*, or trinkets. I worked for them for one season. Franco, a few years older than me, was the founding member of *I Pappagalli*, the Parrot Club, with full regalia and elaborate diplomas for any real pappagallo—an Italian gentleman devoted to the promotion of cultural relations amongst foreign women. *Newsweek* even published an article about him and his newly formed club in the early '60s! He passed away several years ago from a cerebral embolism. Massimo shared my name, of course, and was around my age. Once, during a party at La Beppa Trattoria near the ancient walls of Florence, just below the Piazzale Michelangelo, he decided to go home with a friend to pick up a record player. He never came back that evening. He and his friend had been in a crash with a motor scooter and Massimo had crushed his foot so badly that they had to amputate. I donated blood for him while he was in the hospital. He is fine these days and leads a normal life. And then there was Cico, one of a younger group of guys who hung around us, and who watched us closely to learn the ropes. The scion of the Giannini family that produced the famous Florentine stationery brand with the *fleur-de-lis* pattern, he now owns a chain of stores in Florence called II Papiro. Cico was a gentleman. He was the one who'd deliver a rose for me to girls with whom I had to break a date because of an overbooked schedule on any given evening. Trouble was, they tended to show up at the stall the following day, creating some interesting moments with those who had already arrived—some of whom I'd managed to keep my appointment with the previous night.

And so it went. The experiences multiplied, and the girls kept coming. I learned to read their "license plate," as we used to say, the moment they approached Mrs. Corsi's stall. Wilma, as I came to call her later in life, was constantly amazed by the comings and goings at her business. She told me once that my *pisello*—that operative part of the male anatomy—must have been made of solid gold, for all the attention devoted to it. But she tolerated it all so long as business was good, and it always was. I was at pains to make sure of that. I was the essential ingredient in the booming business that we did, and Wilma knew it. I was in London in May 1967, when I received a return ticket home from her by express mail. She was so panicked the tourist season in Florence would begin without me.

But that year was to be the last that I would work at the Uffizi market—the last year of a glorious, if sometimes misspent youth. It was the year that I left Florence for America.

4

THE GREAT FLOOD OF FLORENCE

1966

I was awakened by papa at quarter to six in the morning. It was November 4, 1966. I looked out the window and saw below a torrent of water flowing down the street. It had been raining heavily for the last two weeks in Florence. The night before I stood on the Ponte Vecchio, the "Old Bridge," with my friends Bruno and Rolando. The water level had risen so high we could almost touch it from the bridge. It was dark and eerie, yet we still could not have imagined what would come in the next few hours.

Florence was still asleep, while the most frightful drama of its history was, by this time, unstoppable. At four o'clock in the morning, at the threshold of the city, a monster wave, unloaded by the dams of Valdarno, was already cascading over and into the Arno River. I couldn't tell how many hours it took for the terrifying body of water to reach and destroy Florence, for its volume and power made a mockery of any normal sense of time. But perhaps even a few hours notice would have been enough to grasp the situation, to have used that dire suspension of time to choose between an orderly removal of one's valuable possessions and the chaos of attempting to escape by car only to be swept away.

It took only two hours, we later learned, for the fury of water to crash through the banks of the river and flood the streets of Florence. An ocean of muddy water cut the city in two and isolated it from the world, making it unreachable from either sky or ground. The first victims already lay beneath the mud. The sick, the elderly, the disabled, and dozens of tenants of low income housing, were screaming hopeless calls for help from the roofs of their homes. There were women crazed with fear, throwing things from their windows, imploring somebody to save their children.

Wherever the water flooded into basements, it shattered the central heating systems in the city buildings, leaving a river of viscous, flammable black oil mixed with the mud. An oily black line that would leave its mark on the walls for history to recall the level of the flood. It would be that foul black ooze to assault the masterpieces of Florentine art, forcing its way everywhere, into the heart of man as well as the finest creations of his ingenuity and knowledge. It was a punishment of humiliation and obliteration.

In Italy, November 4th is a national holiday—*Festa delle Forze Armate*—Armed Forces Day. The flags of Italy that graced palaces and public buildings were whipped by wind and rain, and the tragedy of Florence was already standing in the wings. But the fact that it was a holiday may have saved thousands of lives. Had it been a typical workday, many more would have found themselves like mice in a trap. Anyone going about their daily tasks would have been caught up in the avalanche of liquid fury along the banks of the Arno, which inundated so many places familiar to everyday life.

Soon the BBC in London was issuing a desperate alarm: "The world is losing one of its gems: Florence." Network television stations in New York broadcasted hourly on the city's fate.

Meanwhile, from the windows of our fourth floor apartment, it seemed as if we were doomed as the deluge continued its crescendo. Electricity, water, and gas were out. And the news was spreading—we did not know how—on that frightful night. It was as though we were all hallucinating. There were stories of people drowned like rats in the underpasses of the train station, stories of whole villages, of thousands of people, submerged in the flatland suburbs that surrounded the city.

My father's car, a yellow ocher Citroën, was parked on the street near the main entrance of our building. We could still see the roof of the car. On an impulse, I decided to risk a trip down the stairs armed with a thick rope, in an attempt to secure the car to the wall of the building. Once down, I immersed myself in the cold, muddy black water and tied the Citroën to a large iron ring on the wall that had been used during the Renaissance to tether horses. My attempted rescue later proved to have been a futile exercise.

The water kept surging, ripping trees from the riverbank and vehicles from the streets. It felt like the water level would soon reach the sky. It did not. But it reached eighteen feet in

Via de' Neri, our street, forcing our neighbors from the first and second floors to move to the upper floors. We were trapped for two days. Florence was devastated.

The morning of the 5th, we awoke to find that the water had retreated from the streets of the historic center, leaving the city enveloped in a repulsive quilt of mud and sludge.

"Where are you going?" asked my father as I put on my galoshes.

"I need to see," I replied as I went down the stairs of the building. Once out on the street, I started wading through slimy, sticky stuff and sinking in, the mud oozing halfway up my leg. There were men and women who had been out since sunrise fighting a river that was trying to rip the city from both its past and future.

The director of the Uffizi Galleria had started recovery operations immediately, organizing and moving some of the most invaluable artworks to safety, including Filippo Lippi's *Coronation,* a Madonna by Masaccio, two works by Simone Martini from the Berenson Collection, and a painting by Giotto. Also three hundred works from the Portrait Gallery, including Botticelli's *Coronation.* The director of the Science Museum had begun frantically to move all of the precious instruments to the upper floors, including Edison's phonograph and numerous scientific wonders from the 1700s. But the fury of the Arno River was relentless. The water continued to surge, now threatening to invade the second floor of the museum. *Allora mi feci coraggio*, the director recalled later: "I summoned the courage I needed and crawled out through a window on the second floor and around a cornice, reaching a window of the State Archives where I broke the glass. With the water continuing to rise, I was able to save several objects of exceptional historic value, including the binoculars of Galileo Galilei."

The friars at Santa Croce Church were terrorized. They ran into the Pazzi Chapel and pushed through to the threshold of the Cloisters, using wooden tables as floating devices. The spectacle that greeted them was a picture of desolation in the wake of an apocryphal deluge. Large dark pieces of flotsam were being whipped around in the swirling whirlpools. They were documents—invaluable manuscripts and papers of the National Library, adjacent to the Santa Croce Church—being swept out through a bottomless door the flood had created. Beyond that door, the waters were chewing up the inestimable wealth of the library. In the ancient refectory that housed the museum, the river had smashed a wonderful golden crucifix, the gem of Cimabue that marks the passage between the medieval art and Giotto's world. This would be the greatest of the city's artistic losses.

At the same time, the torrent of water, sludge, and tree trunks hit the Baptistery in the Cathedral Square, shattering the famous door by Andrea Pisano. One after the other, the bronze panels of the Doors of Paradise broke and sank beneath the mire. Fortunately, their weight and their protective gates held them in place. They would be recovered in the following days.

I slipped and fell a few times as I wandered through an immense dead city. The water had swept everything away. There was no food available for miles around. And there was panic. Where would our next meal come from? I was the first in my family to venture out onto the streets, and after hours of searching I finally came up with a small package of biscotti, which would be our dinner that night.

The panic lasted several days before help began to arrive, but when it finally came the response was great. Organization eventually replaced chaos. Soldiers, officials, police—anyone who was willing to work—helped out. Students, mostly Americans from Stanford, Syracuse University, and Smith College gave their precious time and effort to the city of Florence. Every day there was new light in the sky and even though there seemed to be very little progress, after two weeks we could see through to the surface of the streets.

One thing that really affected me during those first few days was the media coverage devoted to the tremendous loss of art in Florence, while the loss of human life and family security were sadly neglected. Even though art is my life, I felt it should take second place to human suffering. Still, once the immediate human problems were eased, we quickly moved on to the damage to the city's art and the miracle of Florence eventually took place. We all went to work in silence, with quiet dignity, equipped with only the most primitive of tools to save whatever was salvageable. No matter how different we might be as people, nor how quarrelsome or angry with the world, we found ourselves fraternally united in the great *Pieta* of Florence, washing and soothing the open wounds of the aching, lacerated body of a city brought to its knees. It is this vision I recall, as both spectator and emotional participant, as the most beautiful moment of an otherwise terrible and unforgettable event. I will always thank God for the privilege of having lived it.

In the years that followed, I carried this vision with me wherever I went. It was an experience that left indelible memories of darkness along with a feeling of helplessness—a new palette of colors I did not know existed. It was a vision that would surface unpredictably at any moment and provided the shadow that persists in my work to this day—the material for my dark series of paintings. And often, later, it would prove a difficult paradox for my faithful collectors accustomed to seeing my sunny landscapes.

After working on the streets of Florence for several weeks, Bruno and I left for Greece for two weeks. We needed some sun, some warmth, and decided to meet our friends, Cynthia and Diana Hirsch, on the island of Crete. Bruno had met the two sisters in mid-September at the Uffizi Market. We had enjoyed their company for a few days in Florence and then drove with them in their Rover to Naples and to the Amalfi Coast. The moment they heard about the events in Florence they began trying to reach us from England to make sure we had weathered the flood. Cynthia was finally able to connect with Bruno several days after the disaster. The girls suggested we take some time away from the stress of living in post-flood Florence and we happily accepted their proposal. The girls flew to Greece from London. For us, the trip was much longer, but we were still excited to catch the train to Brindisi, where we would take a boat to Athens, whence we could take another, overnight boat to Crete—a boat that we soon discovered was packed with locals and a menagerie of goats, squealing pigs, and squawking chickens.

Arriving at our destination, we settled with the girls on the eastern part of the island in the village of Saint Nicholas. This was never supposed to be a romantic getaway, but the accommodations at the inn were sparse and we had to settle for sharing a room between the four of us. Still, everyone seemed fine with that, and we managed to sort things out without undue embarrassment. The pale sun was a welcome change and the local colors inspired me to work on location, painting and drawing the landscape near the shores. It was a brief respite, during which I enjoyed the physical distance from Florence; but, at the same time, the vacation left me feeling guilty for having left my family in a Florence still inundated with mud. "Bruno," I said one morning while we were having breakfast with Cynthia and Diana, "I need to get back home." This was fine with Bruno, but not with the girls, and the conversation degenerated quickly into an argument right there at the table.

This did not stop us from packing our bags and getting on our way that same afternoon. In any event, it was just a few days earlier than our scheduled departure, since the ferry from Crete to Athens left only twice a week. So we set off on foot with our belongings, having barely said goodbye to our friends. However, only a few minutes later, the girls caught up with us and stopped us on the road. They found kind words for us, suggesting with persuasive affection that a few more days with them in Crete would leave us all with a better feeling than breaking up the vacation. We were both touched, and soon made up and returned with them to our residence, where the landlady seemed to acknowledge with a smile how pleased she was with our decision to stay on.

The next morning we learned how that decision proved wiser than we could ever have imagined. As the four of us were gathering as usual on the patio to discuss the plans for the day, our landlady came rushing up to our table. There seemed something sinister about the appearance of this woman in her black clothes against those brilliant surroundings, yelling excitedly and waving her arms in the air. And with good reason, as we soon discovered. The vessel which Bruno and I were supposed to have boarded the day before had sunk in the middle of the night halfway between Crete and Athens. None of the passengers or crew survived. Deeply shocked, we hugged the girls and thanked them for their incredible sixth sense.

I finally returned to Florence with Bruno, while Cynthia and Diana flew back to London to catch a plane home to New York. As I recall, we were both sad and strangely re-energized as we resumed cleaning up the streets of Florence. By this time, it seemed as if the entire world was at work; we were all there participating in the rebirth of the city from the mud. And it was here, on these dismal streets, that I one day ran into Charlotte Scudamore. Barely eighteen years old, with reddish blond hair—I used to tell her that it was the color of Titian Red—she had a smile that was as contagious as it was beautiful, and she inspired me from the moment I saw her.

How special it was to be with her in Florence at this time! I knew she had to go back to London soon, but I could not wait to see her each time we met. It was very innocent. I felt revived in her presence. She represented a world outside my own, a world that I had come to feel I needed to discover, and from there the events of my life seemed to begin unfolding of their own accord. I am quite sure that we are all assisted by a guiding light through various periods of our lives. We are assisted in the process of discovery—the discovery of ourselves. These things are not coincidences. They are subtle occurrences that lead us where we need to go. I still recall how touched my mother was when Charlotte brought her a bouquet of flowers in the middle of the day, walking through the muddy streets of Florence and up to the fourth floor of our apartment building. She was studying at a residential school for foreigners located near the Poggio Imperiale. Many times Bruno and I accompanied Charlotte and her friend Annabelle on their long walks back to the school through the Porta Romana, outside the ancient walls of Florence and up the hill through a beautiful boulevard leading to the Poggio Imperiale. This place was majestic, and we felt at peace here, away from the muddy streets of the historic center. On the way back to the center of Florence, Bruno and I were always busy talking, gesticulating, and discussing plans for our next trip.

5

FROM LONDON TO CALIFORNIA

1967

Immediately after the Christmas holiday, in January of 1967, Bruno and I boarded the night train from Florence to London. It was Bruno's second trip to London, but for me, it was my first. I found it exciting—and scary. Twenty hours later, as the train approached Victoria station, I was flooded with a new kind of excitement. This was London during the 1960s, in the middle of the music revolution, and I was filled with high expectations as soon as we arrived. How comforting it was to see Charlotte waiting to pick us up! She looked a perfect part of the scene. Bruno and I settled into a bed and breakfast on Earls Court Road, in a section of the city known for its affordable lodging. One pound per night provided us with a huge breakfast, something we were not accustomed to in Florence. However, the meal would provide us with sustenance for the rest of the day:

eggs, ham, cereal, and toast with butter and marmalade... and, of course, tea with milk.

A couple of weeks later, we moved to Fulham Road in South Kensington, in an apartment located right above a restaurant called Bacco. King's Road was a block away, where Mick Jagger and the Rolling Stones were often in the neighborhood. We shared this place with Johnny, a jovial English guy we met through friends. He would leave for work very early in the morning, and when Bruno found a job at a cafeteria near Piccadilly Circus, I had the apartment to myself. I could paint watercolors while listening to the Stones. There was one tune that I liked very much:

Who wants yesterday's papers
Who wants yesterday's girl
Who wants yesterday's papers
Nobody in the world

And truly, here, at this moment in time, yesterday did not count. I was always in forward motion, ready to discover, to make a new drawing, to capture the moment. I had dreams of staying, of exhibiting my work in London, something that never materialized. Fortunately, I was able to sell some of my works on paper on the streets. I recall that a sale would always come along at precisely the right moment, right when I was completely broke. The London scene was an experience, from the nightclubs of Carnaby Street to Portobello Road where we used to purchase old Navy clothes and Edwardian-style jackets. At this time London was the epicenter of the "swinging" popular culture: art, theater, literature, pop music, and fashion—these were all in creative turmoil. The miniskirts were very short. As for Bruno and myself, we enjoyed dressing the part of the English peacock. We went shopping together at the new boutiques sprouting along the King's Road in Chelsea; a special favorite was Granny Takes a Trip, established just the year before, in 1966, where the Beatles and the Rolling Stones bought their one-off groovy threads. Arriving at this boutique one day, we elbowed a path through the crush of celebrities at the entrance, inhaling the fumes of hashish that wafted through the air, and clapped eyes on some exquisite pairs of high-heeled snakeskin boots that were on display. Without a moment's hesitation, we lavished every last penny that we had, and each of us acquired a pair. These boots became my prized possession; they eventually traveled with me from Europe to California—and I still own them to this day.

When Charlotte came back from her parents' country house to their London flat, she noticed a transformation in the way I dressed, even though I recall that I still often liked to wear my Italian suits, tailor-made in Florence. I felt I was different in these clothes, that it was my Italian look that people responded to. Just as life was becoming intense in the city, Charlotte invited me out to the country to be her partner at a hunt ball. I took a train and after a couple of hours arrived in Hereford, where Charlotte and her mother picked me up. We drove for another hour and a half. I had no idea, of course, where we were going, but I realized from the landscape that this was not going to be a regular country house. When we finally approached the estate, I thought for sure we were going to drive right past it. But much to my amazement, we turned in through the huge entrance of a castle.

This was Charlotte's home, Kentchurch Court—in Herefordshire. I could hardly believe it! I was shown to my appointed bedroom, which I soon discovered was on the opposite side of the castle from Charlotte's bedroom! Fair enough, I thought. We had to draw a map so that I could see Charlotte late at night. I did make a few drawings. One showed, from a distance, the facade of the castle, and Charlotte's father bought it for a pound—an image that earned me a good deal of flattery. As the preparations for the ball started, I learned that the party was to take place at Croft Castle, an even larger estate. On the night of the event, cars were arriving from all directions, with ladies in ball gowns and gentlemen in tailcoats, some black, the others scarlet, as this was the Queen's Ball. I wore black tails and a white tie, compliments of Charlotte's mother. I thought I looked the part, and integrated well into this spectacular setting, but in fact I felt quite out of place, a young Italian amongst this multitude of the posh British elite, drinking champagne and chattering away without a thought for tomorrow. My language skills also proved to be quite limited, making conversation something of a challenge. I did enjoy the dancing, though. Charlotte looked stunning, a vision of beauty herself amongst what seemed like thousands of guests, and the festivities lasted throughout the night.

Shortly after, sadly, I lost contact with Charlotte. Her schoolwork kept her occupied, and her parents made sure that she stayed close to her books and far away from struggling Italian painters. But I would always be grateful for my brief interlude in a world so distant from everything I had known until that time—a world in which I clearly did not belong but which was certainly great to experience.

And the saga continued. One day, soon afterwards, Bruno and I ran into two girls as we were leaving a market in the middle of the day. They were pleasant, strikingly blond, and American; their names were Jill and Donna. I could not have known, at that moment, how this encounter would completely change my life. We had a coffee together, splitting up already into couples to chat. I was with Donna, Bruno with Jill. We made a date for a few days later, and they insisted on meeting again at the same corner where we originally met. They kept us waiting almost an hour and we were about to give up when they finally arrived, beautifully dressed. I had the impression they had been gossiping about us for some time, which was the reason for their being late. In fact, they admitted as much later. After dinner, they invited us to their apartment, and Bruno realized instinctively what was happening, slipping the word to me in Italian that we would do better to switch the girls. No resistance from me. I liked Jill from the moment I saw her. I felt that this was something special. We talked late into the night, and from that moment Jill and I were inseparable. We talked endlessly and she told me with much affection about her family in California. Her parents were divorced, and she lived with her mother and two sisters near Long Beach. Jill was in London on vacation.

As the month of May approached, I knew my time in London was coming to an end. The tourist season in Florence had already started, and the pressure to return was mounting. Mrs. Corsi, was waiting for me to get back to work at the Uffizi market, selling leather goods. Eventually, she sent me a ticket and that was it. I had to say goodbye to Jill. I told her I loved her and that, one day in the future, I would travel to California to see her.

Sad and lonely, I made my way back to Florence. I worked hard that summer and Mrs. Corsi was pleased. The encounters with other women were not in short supply that summer either, but the thought of Jill was never far from my mind.

One day, right at the end of that hot summer, I turned away from the stand after talking with clients to take a break and sit in my chair directly across the way. I could not believe my eyes: there was Jill, sitting on that same chair, in a mini skirt, legs crossed, with her long, beautiful blond hair draped partially across her breast. The afternoon light had just begun to suffuse through the arcades of the Uffizi, and Jill was the vision of a young modern Madonna. She smiled. "Massimo," she said, "you told me in London that you would come to California one day in the future. I want that day to be now." Her eyes searched deeply into my own, demanding a reply.

I paused to recover from the thrill of seeing her, and my words began tumbling out with no more than a semblance of coherence. "I'd really love to go with you, Jill. But what about my work? I have an exhibition in Florence in October that I just can't miss. Besides, I don't have the money. I might be able to afford a round trip ticket by the end of the year, but not before. And how would I be able to survive in California? You know what a struggle it was to last six months in London."

Thankfully, though, it turned out she was just happy to know that I wanted to go, so she decided to stay in Florence and wait for me.

The thought of going to America was exciting, to say the least. I was quite sure it would happen, but I had no idea how I would manage financially. October came, and my first one-person show opened at the Galleria d'Arte Mentana.

Maestro Loffredo helped me select sixteen paintings on wood. I just needed to sell a couple of these works in order to go to America. The attendance was good, and all of my friends and family showed up. Maestro Loffredo himself was there—but there were no sales except for a small watercolor purchased by a tourist, a piece that was not even part of the show. It was not enough. A few days later, Jill took me out to dinner and told me she had spoken with her mother in California. "Massimo is welcome to stay with us as long as he wants. No problems," her mother had said. "No problems." I thought to myself, either this woman is really something special, or she made this decision in order to get her daughter back to the States. Later, it proved to be both.

On November 4, 1967, the exhibition *Perché Non Si Dimentichi* (*So That We Won't Forget*) opened at the Lo Sprone Cultural Center in Florence. This was a group show commemorating the great flood of Florence, exactly a year before. It was a juried exhibition. I submitted one piece titled *San Remigio*, a monochromatic oil painting, with tones of gray, black, and brown. It was selected. My name appeared in the catalog along with all the known Florentine artists, including my own maestro Silvio Loffredo. That felt good, and I remember my father being happier even than myself, happy to have me in Florence and happy to have me painting. Little did he know, however, that I would soon be leaving again for the longest journey of my life. I had purchased my round trip ticket to America. It left me with no more than a few dollars to my name, but I already had everything I would need: a full box of oil paints, other art supplies, and a few small paintings on wood of Florentine landscapes.

On a gloomy, freezing night in November 1967, I embarked on the trip that would change my life. Waiting in Luxemburg to depart aboard a propeller-powered plane on Icelandic Airlines was rather terrifying—this would be my first time flying. The sights and sounds of Florence were still with me, the vivid memories, the voices colored with affection calling me back home. But the sudden roar of the engines brought me back to reality. The plane was off the ground, and eleven hours later an entire new world was unveiled before my eyes.

I had arrived in New York. Next stop: California.

6

THE BEGINNING IN AMERICA

1967 – 1971

The plane from New York was about to land in Los Angeles. It was nighttime, and we were flying over an immense carpet of lights for about forty-five minutes. I had never seen such a spectacle. My heart was beating wildly.

Jill had been anxious to reunite with her family, and they all came to the airport to greet us—Elaine, Jennifer, and Chandra. In the face of this exquisite effusion of emotions, I truly felt included. The next morning, waking up in my new home in America, I saw the palm trees from my bedroom window and was struck by the abundance of light that filtered through these unfamiliar surroundings. I was impatient to get out into the sunshine, so Jill walked with me to the shore. The Pacific Ocean was just a few steps from the house. It was a balmy day for November, and the water was warm to the touch. I could not wait and plunged right in for a swim. When I was done, we set out together to explore the neighborhood. It was all so new and exciting. We were in Belmont Shore, a neighborhood of Long Beach, and the house was located in a splendid area called the Alamitos Bay Peninsula, a seaside community stretching along a blue and gold coast, accented by white sails out on the ocean and the multicolored roofs of houses on the shore.

So boats, water, and reflections became the new subjects of my paintings for the next few years. All of them were painted *en plein air*, under the surprised looks of local passersby. What a contrast from the gloomy coloration of the flood in Florence of just a year before. I made these pictures directly on plywood panels with intense excitement, applying the paint in a frenzy, with a multitude of short brushstrokes that allowed the wood beneath to show through the surface. I loved to capture the moment. I worked with a mad intensity from morning till evening with only one break, when Jill would usually arrive with a basket lunch. After a brief respite, it was back to painting. I began to sell work immediately at the Marina Pacifica next to the Hyatt Regency, where I was invited to exhibit with a local art group. It was Jill who remembered these outdoor Sunday exhibits by local artists, and when I showed the brochure from my Florence gallery to the director of the Pacific Coast Art League, she was delighted to have a Tuscan painter join their ranks.

I remember the first time I set up a display of paintings on easels, waiting with the apprehensive expectations of any artist amidst this most unfamiliar setting of Sunday brunch foot traffic. Eggs Benedict and Bloody Marys were far more on the minds of the people strolling by than a comparative analysis of the composition, color, and technique of contemporary Tuscan painting and contemporary American painting. My works were so new that the paint was still wet. The spontaneity of their animated motion presented an entirely fresh perspective, along with a whole new sense of color. Just to be there seemed unreal.

A couple arrived and started asking about prices, but soon they left for brunch with a promise that they'd be back. Well, at the Uffizi Market I'd learned that "I'll be back" meant I'd never see them again, and "too much," was the first English I had learned. I needed badly to make my first sale in America. I had arrived only a week before, but if I could make a sale… that would be a good sign of things to come. And sure enough, the same couple walked up to me an hour later. "Hello Marco, let's take another look at what you've got here." They bought two paintings for $135. I gladly gave them a discount. I still remember their names: Mr. and Mrs. Kay from Huntington Beach. So that was the beginning.

I set up a studio in a small room off the garage at Jill's home. Her mom, Elaine, had suggested I use that room for painting. The space was far from adequate. The windows were high on the walls and too small to allow for adequate light, but that did not matter, because most of my work was done on location. Best of all, it was a work space.

I had been making great strides in the three months since arriving in Southern California. It was now February of 1968. It was a warm evening in my studio, and I was working on a piece that I had not quite finished on location. Jim Morrison's voice filled the air as Jill ran into the studio with a newspaper in her hands. "This is really cool! Look at this, it's the *Long Beach Press Telegram* with a feature article on you," she said excitedly. I had forgotten the interview with a reporter named Elise Emery from a week before while I was painting on Bayshore Walk. But this was incredible! An entire article and a photo—my first in the U.S.—and only two months after I'd arrived. And as a result of this feature, art buyers from Southern California were now knocking on my door to view my work, clamoring to buy my "creatures," as I called them. This subterranean room, which I called my studio, was soon providing answers to all the speculation, spoken and unspoken, of what would come from this crazy life committed to painting. I felt inspired in that moment, in that unlikely setting, in that distant world.

At the same time, I knew my American journey would not be possible without the hospitality of my new family. They were simply the kind of people you rarely encountered. Elaine Stucker, as I grew to know her, was a beautiful woman of substance. She was the owner of Four J Motors in Huntington Park, near Los Angeles, a dealership named after her four daughters—Jane, Judy, Jennifer, and Jill—that sold Porsches and Volkswagens. Every day she would drive back and forth in her Porsche, fighting traffic forty-five minutes each way, while taking care of her family. I greatly admired and respected Elaine. She loved my artwork and wanted to see every new painting whenever I returned home from location. I took great pleasure in giving her a few of my paintings during the time I spent at her house. Effortlessly generous and willing to please in all aspects of life, we enjoyed trips to the Los Angeles County museums, Knotts Berry Farm, the San Diego Zoo, the Playboy Club, and the Orange County Fair Grounds for the

Newport Pop Festival where, for the first time, I saw Jefferson Airplane, Jimi Hendrix, Ike and Tina Turner, Iron Butterfly, and many more California bands perform live. This was the late '60s, in the middle of the hippie days. I truly loved it . . . but no marijuana for me! I could not inhale, even though on a few occasions the brownies did their job. The girls, Jill and Jennifer, actually smoked in the house at the request of their mom. She told them, "If you have to smoke pot, you do it right here where I can keep an eye on you, not out there!"

I did make a trip on my own to San Francisco on a Continental Trailways bus. I had to see Haight-Ashbury, the epicenter of the hippie hangout. That was something! There, on a Sunday afternoon, I was handed more joints than I can remember. I kept saying "Thanks, but I can't inhale the stuff." No one believed me, and the joints kept coming. I guess I blended well enough into their world with my long hair and Italian looks, though I'd thought of myself more as a bohemian than a hippie since my student days in Florence. I loved the unconventional life, with my black turtleneck sweaters and a sketchbook glued to my right arm. I felt the unconventional life and hippiedom were closely related, despite the stigma of drug abuse that was attached to the hippies, specifically marijuana and hallucinogens. But I had no particular desire for them. My drug addiction was more likely my weakness for the opposite sex. I have always been attracted to women. I admire their appearance, their figure, their innocence, and their strength. Speaking of which, Jill, with whom I was in contact every day, was worried about me and kept asking me to come home. Eventually I did, but first I traveled north to Oregon and Washington, painting watercolors as I went along. Right around Eugene, Oregon, some curious passengers asked me to show them the contents of the large folder that I carried everywhere with me. It was something that could have happened only at that time: there, in the back of a bus, a crowd of people who did not know each other were poring over my work and voicing their critical opinions, loud enough to be heard over the racket of the bus. Straight out of a Fellini movie. The driver kept turning around to see what was going on, like someone who'd been left out of a lively party. So this was the power of art! I sold two watercolors right there and then, at twenty dollars apiece.

Back in Southern California, the Sunday outdoor exhibits at the Marina Pacifica continued to be successful, and I soon began to participate in art fairs and art competitions throughout the Southland. When the Dalzell-Hatfield Gallery in Los Angeles took three of my paintings on consignment, I was amazed. How did these paintings find their way into a prominent gallery? I did not send in any resumes or images, nor did I send a cover letter. Young artists fresh out of art school should keep this in mind: all the conventional advice about how to do things, how to do this, how to do that, how to approach a gallery, is a waste of time. Better to stick to painting until someone notices what you do. Here's what happened to me: a neighbor friend who admired my work drove me and the paintings to Los Angeles. His name was Mike Leake, and he had a way with words. He knocked on a few gallery doors while I waited in the car, until one dealer took the paintings on consignment.

This is what my work needed, I thought. Proper representation. A passionate advocate.

Still, was this enough to keep me here? I knew that sooner or later I had to go back to Florence, to my family and my life there. My round-trip ticket was due to expire before the end of the year. And, meanwhile, the Stucker family continued to provide total support for my life in California. Elaine reassured me that I could come back, that I was welcome should I decide to return to Belmont Shore.

And I did return, after a three week visit to Florence. It was a brief parentheses, full of family affection and memories, along with the realization that my crazy life would continue in California. One full year had gone by and now I was back at my studio in Belmont Shore, with renewed energy and eager to resume with passion my plein air work. But, in the midst of all those colorful interpretations of sun, sea, and sails, the vision of Florence surprised me, re-emerging with the force of the Arno River when it swelled above its embankments.

Incredibly, I started painting a dark series of watercolors and oils right there in the sunshine in Southern California, including a piece which I titled *Aftermath,* a six-foot-square canvas that embraced all the heartache of the great flood of Florence. "What are these?" friends would ask. I never really felt liked pursuing the subject and, more often than not, my replies were brief and evasive. One day, Phyllis Barton came by the studio for a visit. She was an art historian who worked for the *Santa Ana Register*. I had met her one Sunday at a Marina Pacifica show where she had purchased a colorful painting of bathers in the water full of reflections. When she saw the current series of work she was startled and felt an urgent need to talk about it. "*Aftermath* is a masterpiece!" she exclaimed. "I am going to publish this piece in the November issue.... I want to time it with the three-year anniversary of the flood of Florence on November 4."

The feature article, "County Artist Relives Florence Disaster," was impressive. The text also announced that all of the pictures in the series were going to be exhibited in a commemorative exhibition at Aquarium Fine Arts in Santa Ana, CA, in two weeks. What a shock for my patrons accustomed to seeing my sunny landscapes. This would not be my last time to shock them. No sales resulted from this show, but friends and patrons old and new, would continue to stop by to see me. My studio next to the garage began to look like a bohemian hangout, a place to allow the images painted on location to dry, to listen to music, and sit on the couch and converse about all of the cultural differences between life here and in Florence.

The patronage of Elaine Stucker, however, would soon come to an end. She sold the house and was planning a move to Sunset Beach. I had always known that one day I would have to leave, but I had never envisioned the feeling of loss that would overwhelm me. Marco, I said to myself, now you are on your own. With great anxiety, I started looking for a place to stay and found a studio apartment a few blocks from the house. It was tiny, with a bed coming down from a closet on the wall, and it would cost me $90. Unbelievably though, I somehow managed to rent the room next to the garage from the new owners for $25 a month. What a turn of events. My family in America were just a short distance away, and yet it seemed like a great distance. My relationship with Jill would soon transform into friendship, as my relationships had often done in previous breakups. No more packed lunches on location. No more security from a family who had provided me with guidance and affection for the past two years in California.

My friend Lenné, who was part of the group at the Marina Pacifica and aware of the circumstances, called me. “Let me take your mind off this,” she suggested. “Let’s go see the Stones.” And we went together to this fabulous concert at the Los Angeles Forum, with opening acts by B. B. King and Ike and Tina Turner. The place was electrifying as it went pitch dark, with the beginning throb of the band still in the dark, and the appearance of Mick Jagger as the lights came on, tuning up for the Midnight Rambler. Fantastic!

* * *

They all came at once to visit. My friend, Bruno, from New York, Rolando from Florence, and Pontello from London. My new tiny home was not adequate to accommodate them all. However, thanks to Stefanina, my next door neighbor, the problem of lodging for my friends was immediately resolved. I am still indebted to her. Her real name was actually Irene Walter, but for some reason Stefanina sounded more appropriate to me from the moment I first met her at the apartment complex mailbox—a typical 1960s Southern California outdoor wooden structure where residents would bump into each other when picking up their mail. With the strange unpredictability that life teaches us, I would meet Stefanina again, fifty years later, in Toronto. What a wonderful chance encounter, allowing us to reconnect and share memories from that time, when my major consideration every morning was to walk along Bay Shore and discover a new spot to paint all day long.

So with all my friends arriving, the music was loud and the activity intense. This quaint neighborhood was not accustomed to such exuberance—and I paid the consequences: I was evicted from my new home as soon as my friends departed. With no place to go, I took up residence in my studio while I waited to relocate to another affordable apartment. A sense of isolation was ever present in this little room that lacked even water or any other amenities. But it was my only shelter. I recall showering at the apartment of my friend, Daniele, several blocks away, and the hospitality of my new friend Jimmie, a beautiful brunette I had recently met at the playground next to the beach and who lived just a short distance away in Seal Beach. I never gave it too much thought, but the truth was that I was without a home. To make matters worse, my visitor visa was about to expire and needed renewal, something I had already done more times than was allowed. To assure myself yet one more extension, I used to invent all these great stories for the immigration officers about traveling across the U.S., painting on location while learning English.

So I drove to Los Angeles to try one more time. After waiting for a few hours in the large reception room, my number was called, and I made my way to the window I was assigned to. The officer looked exhausted. I decided to start talking.

"I'd like to stay another six months," I told him," so that I can visit San Francisco and do some painting in the Bay area."

He requested the papers and shuffled through them. "We already renewed you several times," he said. "I find it hard to believe that you are here just painting .... Give me your wallet." He motioned for it and looked me straight in the eye.

"I'm not giving you my wallet!" I replied indignantly.

The INS agent didn't even bother to look at me now: "I am giving you 48 hours to leave the country," he said.

Well, this is it, I thought, as I continued to stare at him through the window. A crowd of other applicants were waiting their turn behind me. No home in this country. I'm no longer welcome. I'd better go back where I belong.

With nothing left to lose, I almost decided to give this guy a piece of my mind. But I found myself doing the opposite. The wallet came out and I gently placed it on the counter.

"OK, now we are talking," the agent said while removing the contents from my wallet. He made two piles right in front of me. One pile of the business cards I'd collected along the way and all the rest he placed in the other pile: cash, driver's license, etc., all of which he replaced neatly in the wallet and handed it back to me.

I still didn't get it. But when he started reading aloud the names on the business cards, I understood where he was going. He read out the names of galleries. I remember there was one in Laguna Beach and another in Los Angeles. He read out the business name used by my friend Phyllis: "Artistique."

"Are you selling paintings?" he asked.

"How do you think I'm surviving?" I exclaimed. "Yes, I am selling paintings."

And from that moment, he became my friend. I couldn't believe it. He said, "OK, now I am beginning to like you." Then he walked into the back room and returned to the window with a stack of forms. He handed me an entire application package to become a permanent resident in California on a Preference Status, which is limited to scientists, artists, and clergy! "I'm giving you six months from today to file your application," he said, adding, "good luck with your painting!"

As I left through the big brass doors of the INS building, I did not know whether to cry or laugh. I believe I did both, unnoticed by the crowd around me.

* * *

My work continued under the studio lights, which also provided me with warmth during some cold winter nights. I began to feel that to become fluent in my new language was not insurmountable. I was making progress, even with my limited command of English nuances which had become a frustrating impediment between me and the cultural norm.

Around this time, a brochure advertising the First International Artist Show at the Coliseum in New York arrived in the mail. My instincts told me to participate. I had no idea if I'd be able to swing it financially, but the thought of New York and the possibility of making it there one day were enough incentives for me to go for it. I'd go for broke, despite the fact that my friend Mike Campbell, a watercolor painter, decided not to pursue this one. Mike had been a painter and a partner in many trips to art fairs that we participated in together. "Too scary," he warned me. "You can't possibly cover the costs. And what if you don't make any sales?"

"So I'll be stuck in New York," I replied.

I built a huge crate to accommodate as many paintings as I could, and I immediately contacted my friend Fabrizio in New York, who had moved there shortly after my arrival in California. He assured me I could stay at his tiny apartment that was not too far from Columbus Circle. I was set to go, and Mike and my new girlfriend, Jimmie, drove me to the Los Angeles airport and wished me luck.

The show was a mess from the start and promised to end in disaster. It was one of those shows well-advertised to artists—and poorly to the public. It was staged in the enormous Coliseum building, with hundreds of artists' booths—and no attendance for a week. The fear mounted. How could I get back to California?

And then came Sunday, the last day of the show. That afternoon alone I sold most of my paintings and returned to Belmont Shore with an almost empty crate. Incredible!

I immediately found a new place to live, and life turned around for the better. The rental was a little house only one block from my studio, right on the bay, for $150 per month. I could not have asked for more. Two bedrooms, a green yard, and a view of the bay. And things began to happen for me here. On the heels of the New York show, the *Independent Press Telegram* published an article in the summer of 1970 and followed up with another one shortly thereafter.

That wonderful year culminated in a solo show at Town and Country Gallery in the City of Orange, an exhibition organized by Phyllis Barton, my agent and good friend. I still remember the colorful essay she wrote for the exhibition brochure. She loved my work and always managed to express her feelings with such exuberance. The opening was a great success. Was this to be the end of my struggles, I wondered. I knew I was doing much better. I could actually make a living with my art, something that has often surprised me throughout the years.

One sunny afternoon while I was out drawing on my patio, two Labrador puppies appeared on the green lawn. "Which one do you want?" said a familiar voice.

"Jill, how are you?" We hugged and kissed.

"I'm looking for a home for these two puppies," she told me. "So please choose one."

Both creatures were playing together on the grass. One was beautiful and golden with short hair, the other black and chunky. He could hardly stand up.

"I think I am taking Ciccio," I said, pointing to the black one. "He looks more Italian—dark and fat!"

Which seemed to be the concept of Italians in America at the time, as portrayed in movies about the mafia. It was an image that seemed strange to me, since where I came from people were not fat. But in any event, Ciccio was my first family addition. As he grew up, it was clear that he never thought he was a dog. He ate pasta and understood only Italian. He would chase anything that passed by, from a fly to an elephant. He did not understand the mail carrier knocking on the door and was quick to show his disapproval every time. And that was when I was at home. In my absence, Ciccio would chase the mailman down the lawn, mail dropping along the way. The racket was always lively and entertaining for the neighbors, who were happy to re-enact each encounter for my benefit. Ciccio also did not like those individuals who used metal detectors to find coins at the beach. Given the chance, he'd happily chase them too. But other than that, he loved everyone, especially children.

* * *

The Festival of Arts in Laguna Beach had just opened and 1971 was my first year as an exhibitor, something I continued to do for the next ten years. My work had been juried in and I was excited to be there. This was Southern California's most prestigious art festival at the time. I knew that competition was keen to become an exhibitor, since the number of new artists admitted each year was dependent upon former exhibitors dropping out. The festival included a maze of artists' booths, plus the Pageant of the Masters, known for its *tableaux vivants* or "living pictures," in which works of art are recreated by people who are made to look identical to the original artwork with the help of makeup, lighting, and backdrops. Leonardo da Vinci's *Last Supper* closed the ninety-minute show every evening. And each night crowds flooded into the festival grounds, filling all the artist's booths for an hour or so afterwards.

What a crazy summer. My friend, Pedro, was helping me during the daily trips from Belmont Shore to Laguna and back. He was staying at my home until the end of summer, where there were people coming and going all the time, girls everywhere, and late night spaghetti dinners at the house. I kept reminding myself: it is the balance that counts. I never lost sight of my mission and knew just when I had to go to the studio and paint. The sales at the booth were incredible and keeping up the pace was a challenge: to earn an entire year's income in six weeks takes planning—or you have to paint fast. I was painting fast.

Perhaps I also sensed the need for some stability in my personal relationships. And one day, as I walked into the Bank of America in Belmont Shore, I found just what I was looking for. Her name was Diane. She was introduced to me by one of her colleagues, Sadie, who told me "There is a young woman who would like to meet you."

As soon as I laid eyes on her behind the counter, I knew that I'd certainly like to meet her too: she had blond hair, a slim figure, and a subtly elegant look. She asked me about the festival in Laguna Beach. We spoke for just a few minutes, and I invited her to visit my booth during the last few days of the show. I could not have known then just how much her visit would change my life.

7

THE WEDDING IN FLORENCE

1971–1972

She came with a girlfriend on the last day of the festival. I recall cooking dinner for my many friends at the upstairs restaurant that night. Pedro and I were having a great time and were pleased to accommodate two more girls. Diane and I exchanged telephone numbers and began dating immediately. Actually, these were not dates. I never particularly cared for that word, which reminded me, for some reason, of sitting at a bar and trying to make conversation over the noise. When we met, it was always very special. She looked beautiful and she was always dressed perfectly, with a refined presence about her. I was enchanted by her natural attractiveness, and we shared a feeling of genuine compatibility and trust from the earliest days of our relationship. We felt totally comfortable with each other. She lived with her parents in Huntington Harbor, about twenty minutes south of Belmont Shore, a residential area known for its intricate web of canals where boats, large and small, were docked at the rear of each residence. One day I drove to her home to meet her family. Her mom, Harriet, her sister, Nancy, and her brother, Stuart, both younger than Diane, and Doctor Woody Nelson, her father, who had much pleasure when he led me to the back of the house to show me his most prized possession: a fifty-foot motorboat.

My relationship with Diane evolved quickly into a steady commitment, and at the same time I was preparing for the arrival of "la mamma" from Florence. That was something in and of itself. This was a woman who was usually reluctant to even leave her own house most days. A woman who could always find a multitude of reasons not to go anywhere. Yet, she surprised everyone, not least of all my father, when she boarded a plane for the first time in her life and took off for Los Angeles. For me, to see me, to find out what I'd been doing so far away from Florence. The anticipation mounted by the day.

And Diane? She was wonderful: she put no pressure on me. And made no demands. I introduced her to la mamma and that was it. We went everywhere together. Two women, one blond Californian and one dark-haired Italian. La mamma did not look her age at all. She was lean, with a beautiful figure and skin as smooth as porcelain. She was fifty. The first time she came with me to the Bank of America branch where Diane worked, I got into trouble. Diane was not there at the time, and her co-workers later reported back to her that Marco had arrived at the bank with another girlfriend! We all had a good laugh at home that night. What a special time that was! Although I did not get much painting done, I did receive valuable cooking lessons—including instructions on how to make the perfect cup of espresso. In the '60s and early '70s you could not find coffee shops on every street corner in Southern California as you do today, nor for that matter Italian restaurants.

"Mamma, do you want to take the boat to Catalina Island?" I asked one morning, adding, "I won the Catalina Award in their local art competition."

Ma si, io vengo con te in qualsiasi posto. "But yes, of course, I'm coming with you wherever you go!" she replied. "Which painting did you enter?"

Good question. In fact, it was not one of my popular landscapes that won the prize but rather a composition called *Summer*, featuring a bather on the beach.

Mamma was triumphant. "See, didn't I say you should paint more figurative works!" she scolded me.

The trip to Catalina Island takes about forty minutes by boat from Long Beach. I have painted views of Avalon on several occasions on my visits there. I love the Mediterranean feel of the local color, and my mother truly enjoyed the experience.

But time sped by, and one day in mid-December la mamma took off on her return trip to Italy. She left me with her beautiful smile, her sense of the reality of life, her wonderful, positive attitude, and her free spirit. I had the feeling I was going to see her again soon—and, in fact, a few days after her departure Diane and I decided over dinner at my home to fly to Italy for the holidays. I had no idea at the time what would unfold in Florence as a result of this decision, and Ciccio, of course, didn't like this hasty decision at all! He knew he was going to have to take up temporary residence in a kennel in Long

Beach. The poor guy seemed to hate the idea as he had many times before. Still, we packed our bags and left, stopping over in London for a few days before surprising la mamma and the rest of the family for Christmas and the New Year.

The winter landscape surrounding Florence is one of dramatic beauty. The city's historical center, where my father still lives to this day, was decorated with lights of all shapes and colors, and the downtown streets and piazzas were filled with the aroma of roasting chestnuts. My head was assailed by a rush of sudden thoughts. It seemed to me that I had never left this city and could not make sense of the fact that I no longer lived there. How had that happened? How was it possible that I lived elsewhere? This was my home—the entire city an open air museum, a shrine to the Renaissance with churches everywhere, sculptures and frescos, palaces, and its wealth of monuments from the richest moment of cultural flowering the world has ever known. Even from where we stood, in that moment, a single glance swept us up in the breathtaking elegance of the Renaissance, awed by the facade of the cathedral of Santa Maria del Fiore and Giotto's magnificent tower.

"These were the streets where Michelangelo played as a child!" I told Diane as we strolled through the Piazza della Repubblica and Via dei Calzaiuoli on our way to Rivoire for a cup of hot chocolate. She smiled her acknowledgment, overwhelmed by these extraordinary surroundings as we settled down comfortably into the atmosphere of a splendid holiday season.

* * *

"Il Fagiano" is located in the historic center of Florence, a half block from my family home. I used to go to this restaurant every Saturday evening before I set out on my American journey in 1967. It is still a place where you can enjoy dinner, live music, and song—the classical Neapolitan arias and opera vignettes—all performed by local singers. These included my friend Bibi, whose pièce de résistance every Saturday night was "Granada." He would hit that high note at the end of the song with such an incredible crescendo that his audience would gasp in disbelief. They would rush to their feet and clap their hearts out for the longest time.

But this particular evening was not a Saturday, and I was having dinner with Diane. The place was still lively but quiet enough to talk. In the middle of the dinner Diane set down her knife and fork and said something I had never expected.

"What would you think," she said with uncertainty. "I'm not sure how to put this, but . . . "

"It's OK, really," I assured her. "Go on. Tell me what you are thinking."

She paused for a while, encouraged by my response. She continued, "I've no idea what's ahead of us when we get back to California. I'm still living at home . . . but I am just thinking . . . I think we should do something, shouldn't we? We should get married!"

I had known we were headed in that direction. I was well aware that my love and affection for Diane ran deep, and I always felt totally comfortable in her presence. Still, I was stunned by the initial impact. "You mean . . . when?" I stuttered.

"Now, in Florence!" she told me. "We can do it in January. I'll have my parents fly over from California."

It seemed impossible. But it happened. We were married on January 25, 1972, in the splendid church of San Leonardo, on the street of the same name—a street filled with vivid memories of my early days painting outdoors.

I was at once excited and exhausted. Friends and family converged from Italy and the U.S., and my sisters, Milly and Patrizia, organized a reception at the Villa Arrighetti. My professor, Silvio Loffredo, and his wife were present as well. It all happened so fast, there was no time to think, and it was the hurried pace to meet the deadline that led me, I believe, into a post-nuptial depression. I had a bad case of the blues the day following the ceremony, and for several days thereafter.

On the return flight from Italy, snuggled close to my sleeping wife, I began to reflect on the summer romance that had so suddenly become a marriage. Life, I thought, is so often strangely unpredictable. If you allow it to, it leads you, not the other way around. Now, on our way back to America, it seemed to me that the recent events had led me naturally to where I wanted to be.

I can never sleep on airplanes. At that moment I felt comfortable with my life, and eager to move forward on the heels of my success at the Festival of Arts in Laguna Beach the previous summer. The festival had a rule that requires exhibiting artists to be a resident in the city, but I had previously participated by using a friend's local address—even though I was still living in Belmont Shore. The ruse had worked before, but now there was too much negative publicity about festival participants not being residents, that I felt I could not continue to exhibit without moving to Laguna Beach. So, on our return from Florence, the plan was for me to get back to the studio as soon as possible while Diane would begin looking for houses in Laguna Beach.

"I need a room with plenty of light and, if possible, high ceilings," I insisted.

"We'll find something," she promised me as she climbed into her blue Volkswagen Beetle. And eventually her trips up and down the Pacific Coast Highway were soon rewarded: she found a house on Bluebird Canyon Drive, a winding road that led up a hill framed by eucalyptus trees. Typical of the area, the house was of wood construction. The driveway to the garage sloped uphill as well, leading to a house perched high above the road. There was a patio with flowerpots and a large wooden table. It was perfect. The master bedroom became my studio, with its pitched ceiling and large louvered windows through which an abundance of light filtered gently into the interior. Indeed, there were windows everywhere, including the kitchen, which was located right above the canyon with a lovely view of the hills below. Arriving for the first time, Ciccio was soon engrossed in a frenzied exploration of the entire neighborhood, dashing to and fro between the canyon and the house, as if to make sure we would still be there!

So, this was the great move, only forty-five minutes south but with a completely different ambiance. Closer in spirit to a sunny Mediterranean resort, Laguna's spectacular scenery had been enticing artists since the turn of the century. For me, I felt as though I had finally arrived at exactly the right place.

8

LAGUNA BEACH: LAUNCHING MY ART CAREER

1972 - 1978

That summer of 1972, Laguna's population swelled as usual by some three hundred thousand or so visitors who descended on the community between July and August to attend its internationally famous Festival of Arts. I was ready. The booth I was assigned looked even better than the previous year. We printed up a brochure for the show and distributed a small poster downtown. Diane was supervising the booth, and her presence was a wonderful addition. It certainly made a difference. Almost every evening we could count on sales. Two feature articles appeared in August, one in the *Orange County Register*—"Italian painter finds home, wife, reputation as an artist in Laguna," and the other in the *Daily Pilot*—"First impressions lasting," written by the editor. Both pieces were accompanied by numerous photographs of my paintings as well as of Diane and myself. In one of the pieces, Diane was quoted: "Our whole life is ruled by emotions," she said. "The house is often in a mess because we decide other things are more important. Dinner may be at seven or at eleven." We were thrilled my art career was moving in the right direction. I felt overwhelmed. How did all this happen? It was the result of being focused, taking chances, and persevering, I thought. The quality of my painting was responsible for my being an exhibitor at the fair, but to reach that point, I had to make up my mind and set my goals; I had to make the time to get the work done . . . and then I had to get myself into the studio and do it!

There were other plans already underway. My father wrote from Italy to confirm a solo exhibition at Galleria d' Arte Internazionale in Florence, now scheduled for November of 1973. He had taken the initiative to pursue the dialogue with the gallery director and firmed up tentative plans the previous January. Prior to that, I had booked a show with a gallery in Newport Beach for the month of April. Diane was delighted. "With all this on top of the Laguna festival in the summer, you're set for the whole of next year!" she exclaimed. By now, she herself was working two days a week at a local gallery on Pacific Coast Highway.

And there was more. The *Orange County Illustrated* chose one of my paintings for a cover piece. It was published in June of 1973, with a feature article announcing my upcoming show in Italy: "Marco Sassone Is Taking California Back to Florence This Fall." The cover was a great success and resulted in further commissions for years to come. It was the same with *Air California* magazine, which used to provide generous spreads

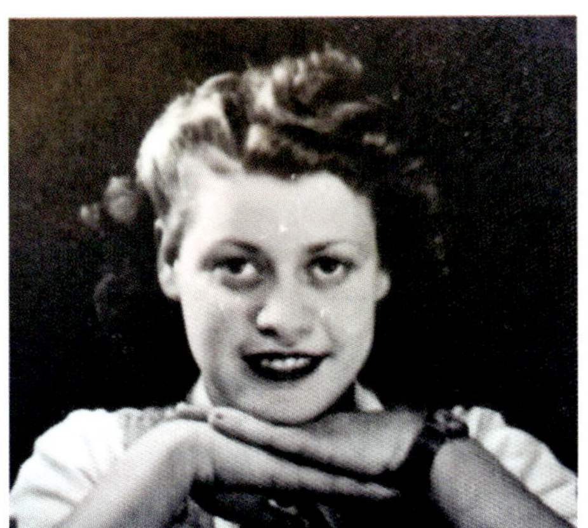

My mother at age 20 in Campi Bisenzio (Florence), 1941. *Author's Collection*

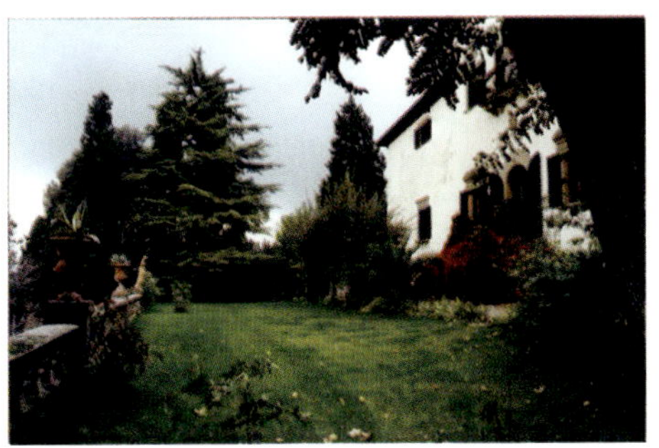

Villa Schneiderf, our first residence on the hills of Florence when the family moved from Campi Bisenzio, circa 1952. *Author's Collection*

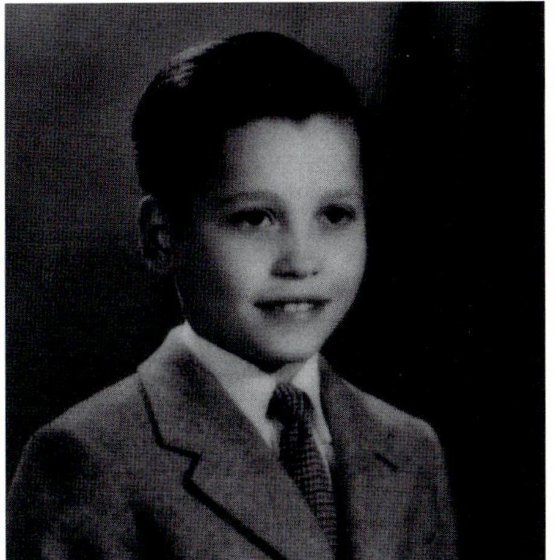

Me at 8 years old, 1950. *Author's Collection*

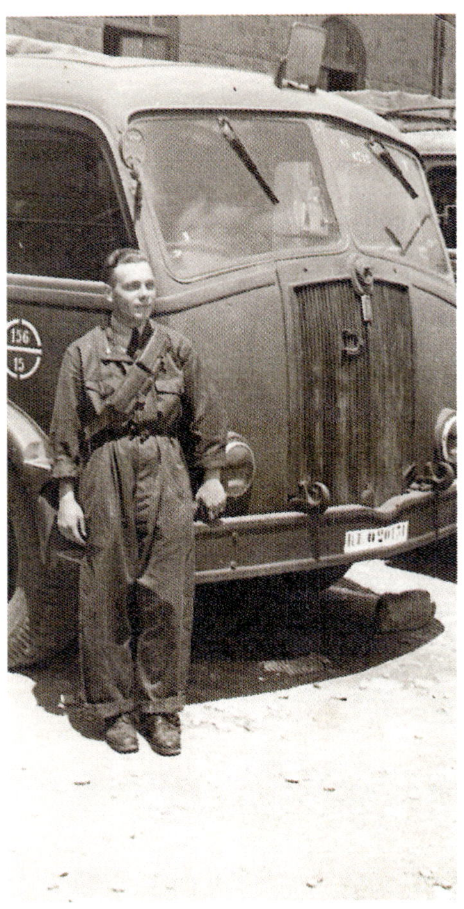

My father at age 22 during the war, Florence, 1941. *Author's Collection*

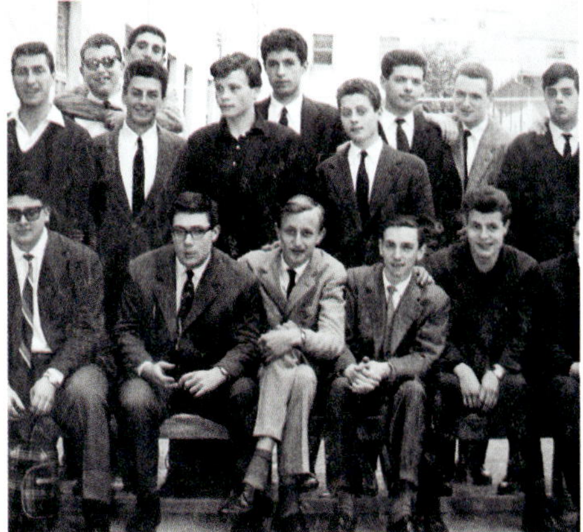

My school photo, (center row, third from left), 1958. *Author's Collection*

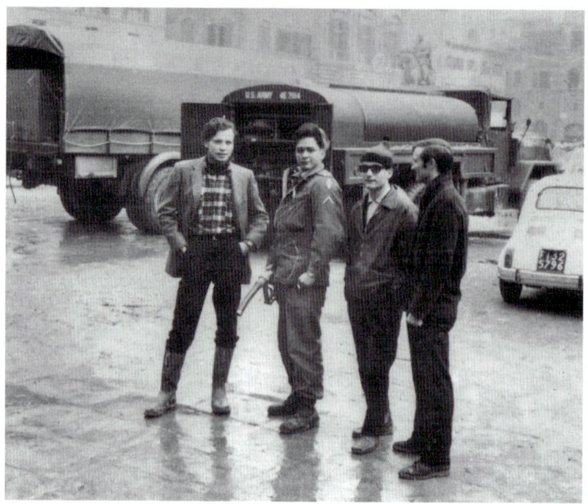

Me (left) during the flood of Florence with an American soldier and friends, November 1966.

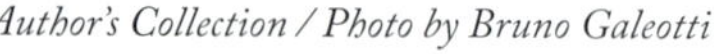

Author's Collection / Photo by Bruno Galeotti

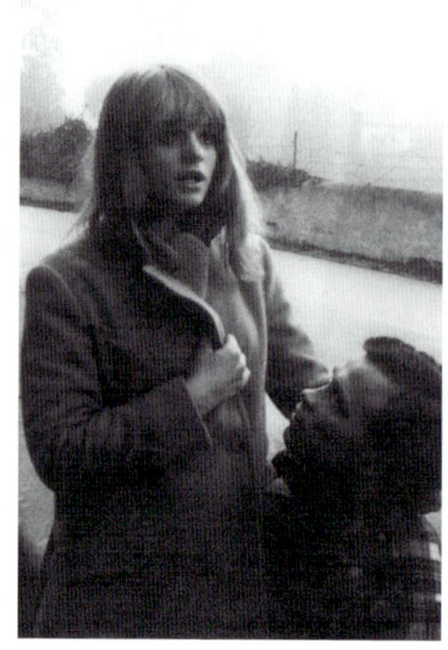

With Charlotte during the flood of Florence, November 1966. *Author's Collection / Photo by Bruno Galeotti*

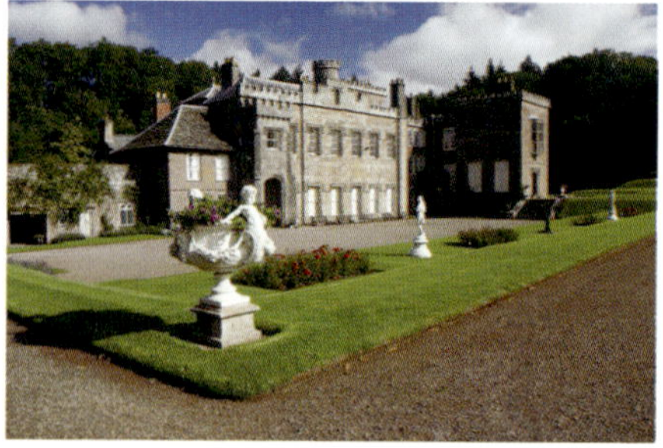

Charlotte's home in Hereford, England. *Author's Collection*

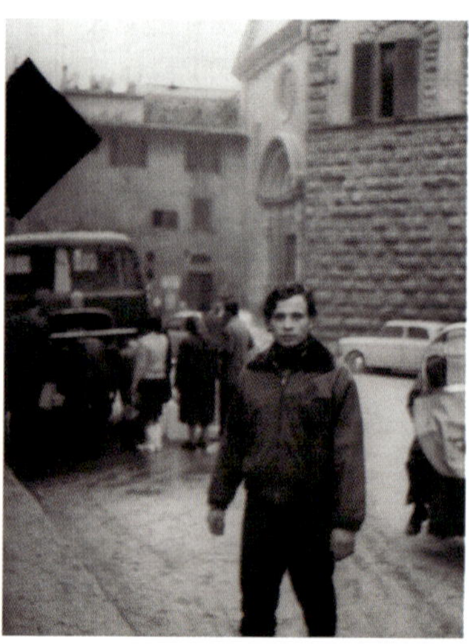

Me during the flood, November 1966. *Author's Collection / Photo by Bruno Galeotti*

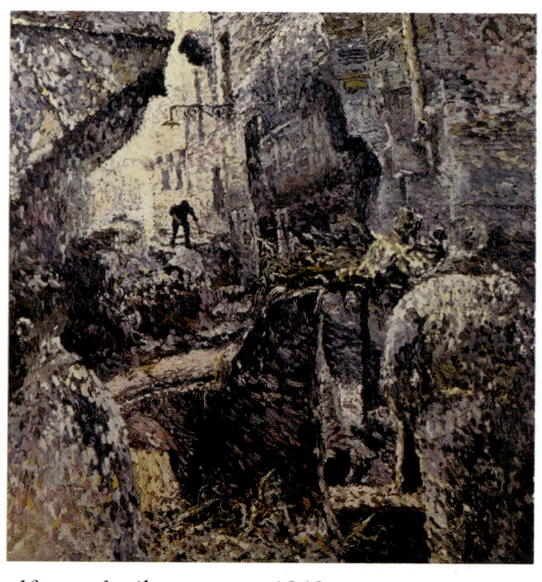

Aftermath, oil on canvas, 1968. *Author's Collection*

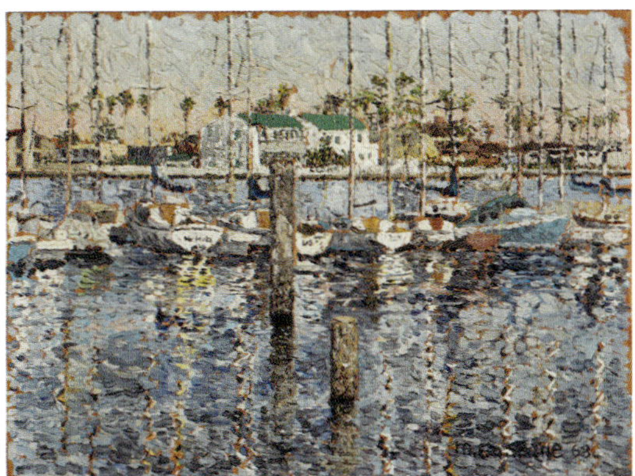

Belmont Shore, oil on plywood, 1968—one of my first paintings on location in California.

Author's collection

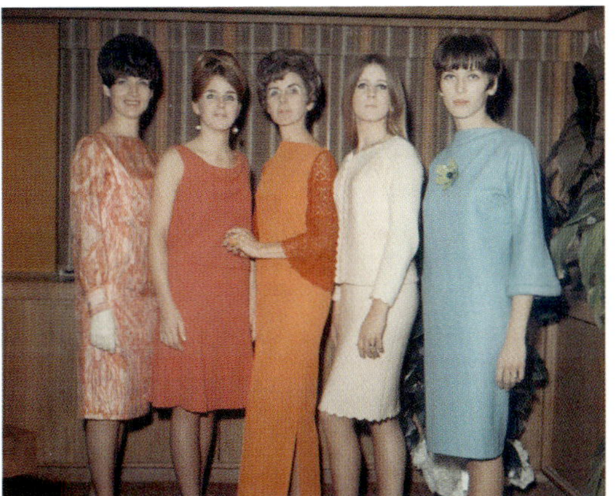

The Stucker family—Judy, Jennifer, Elaine, Jill and Jane, 1967. *Author's collection*

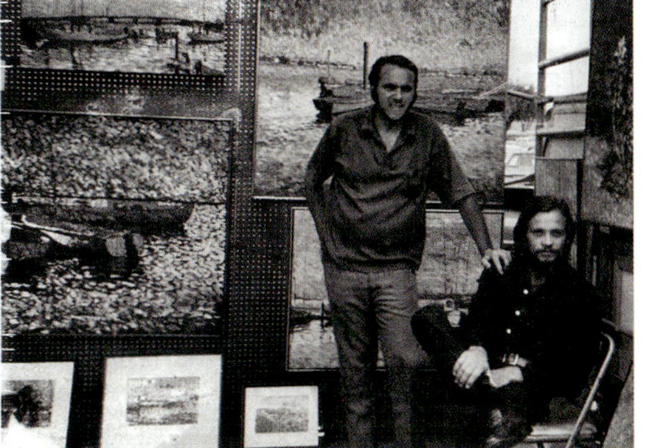

With Mike Campbell (left) and my artwork at a Southern California Art Fair, 1969.

Author's collection

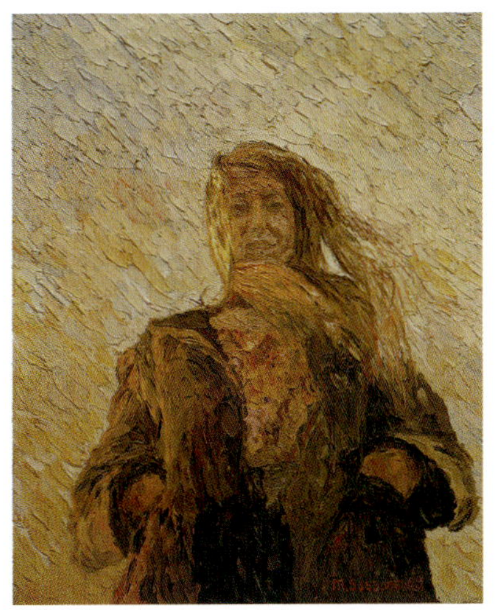

Jill, oil on canvas, 1968.

Private collection, USA. ©Marco Sassone

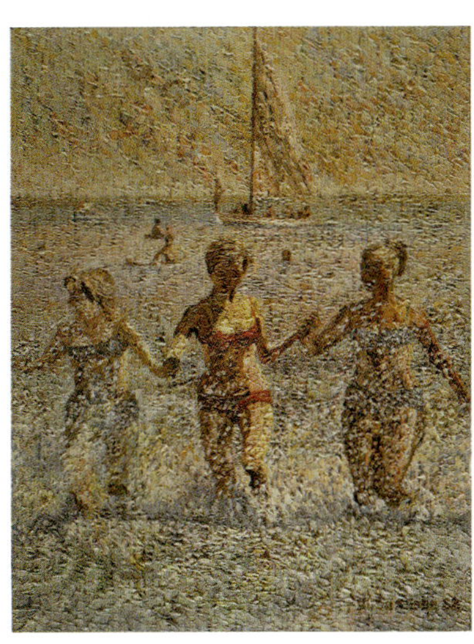

Ragazze alla Spiaggia, oil on canvas, 1968. *Private collection, USA. ©Marco Sassone*

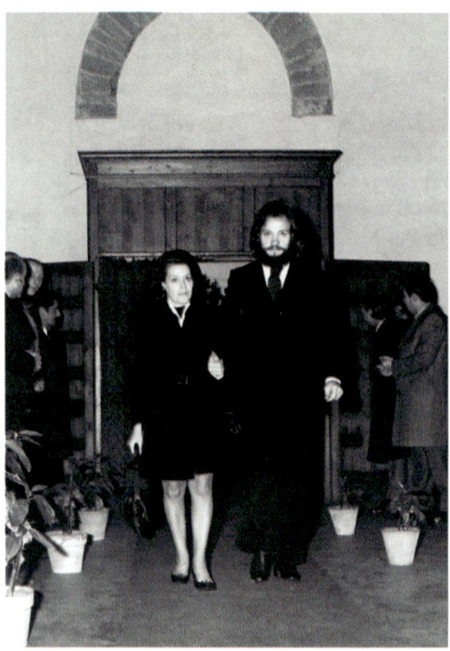

With la mamma in Florence, 1972.
Author collection / Photo by Fabrizio Fioretti

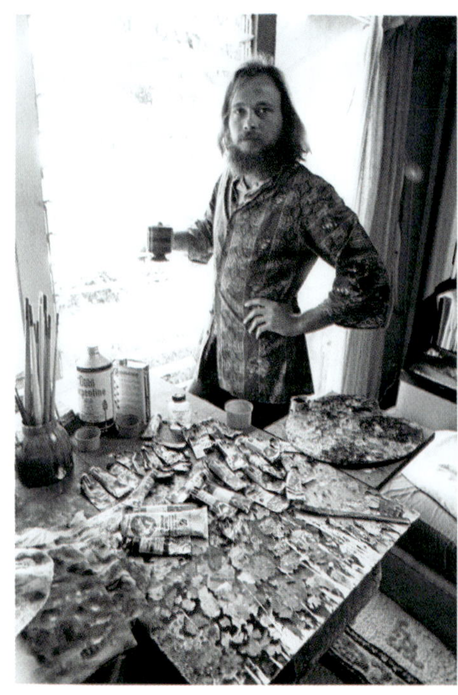

In my Bluebird Canyon studio, Laguna Beach, 1972.
Author collection / Photo by Robert Ratkowski

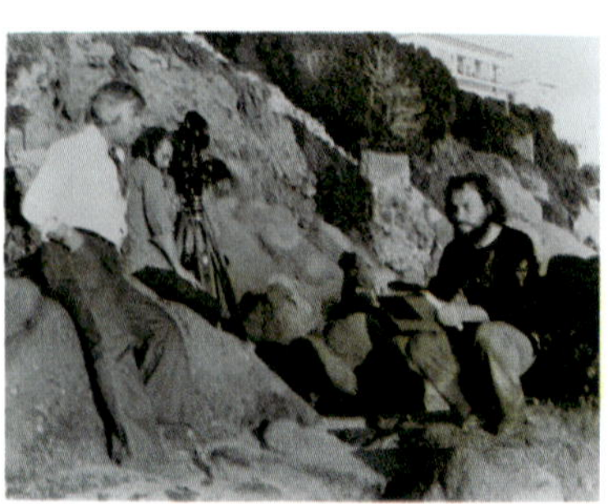

On location with John Wilson during the filming of my documentary, Laguna Beach, 1976. *Author's collection / Photo by Robert Ratkowski*

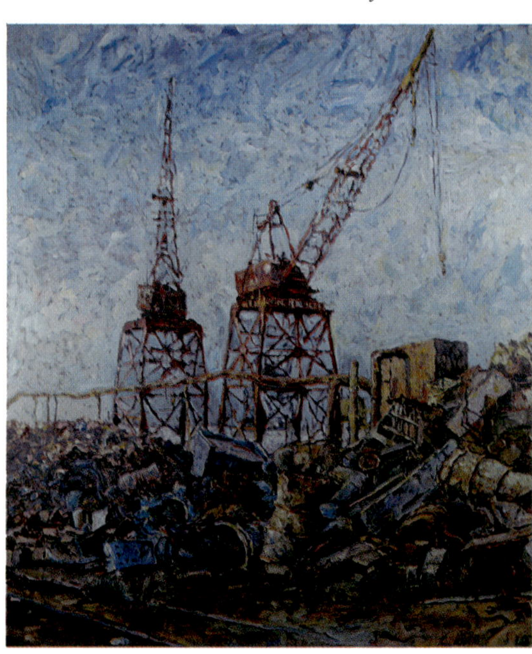

Junk Yard, oil on canvas, 1975. *Author's collection*

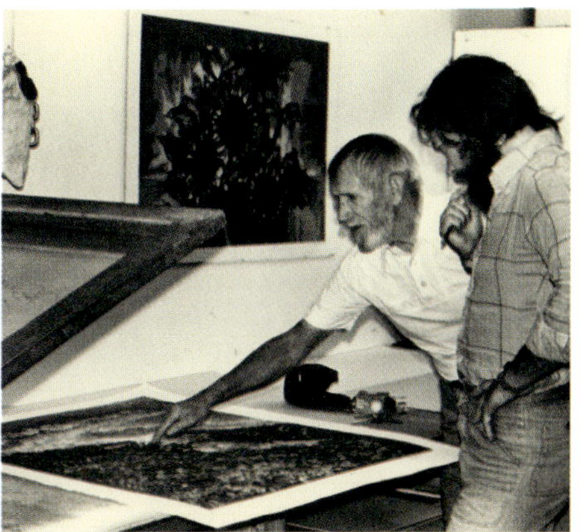

With master printer Guy Maccoy, 1977.

Author collection

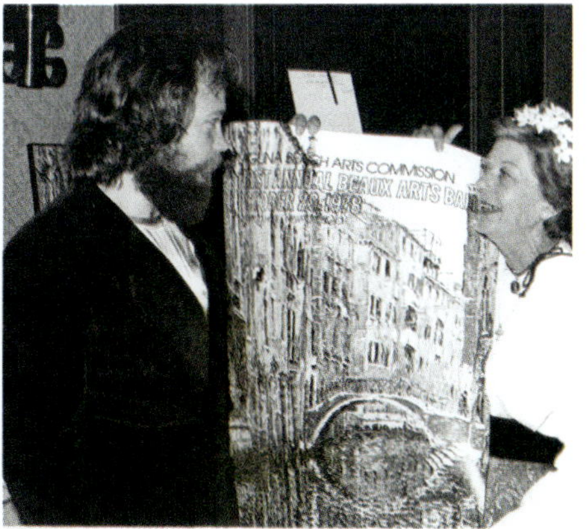

With Harriet Nelson, 1978.

Photo by Rick Lang

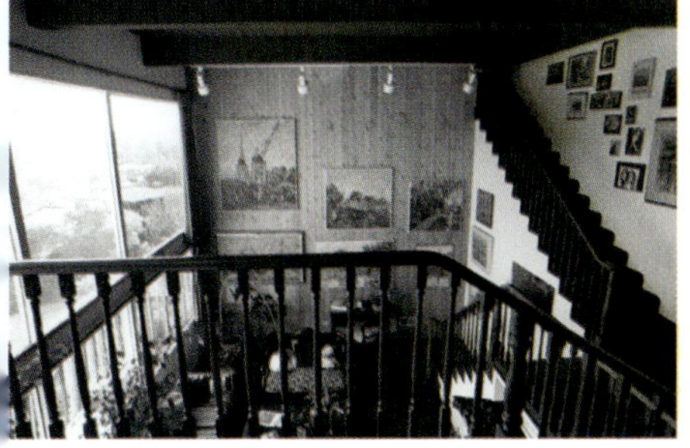

My Mar Vista studio, Laguna Beach, 1978. *Author's collection / Photo by Rick Lang*

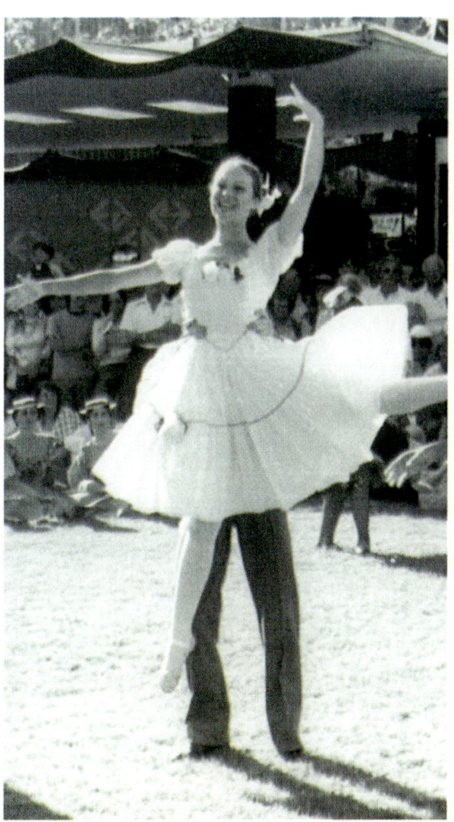

Caroline with Ballet Pacifica, Laguna Beach Festival ground, 1978.

Author's collection

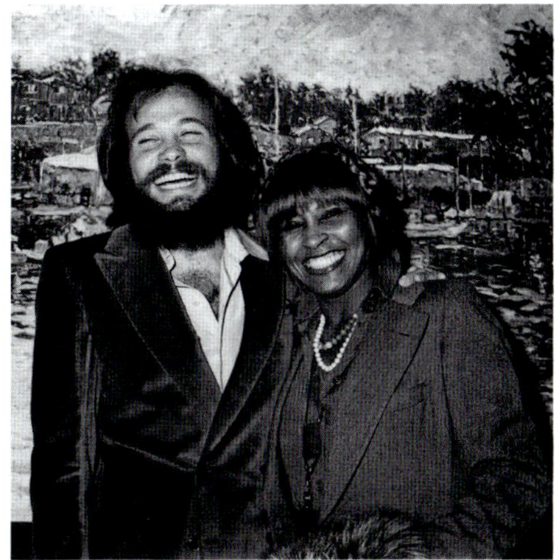

With Tina Turner at my opening at Wally Findlay Galleries, Beverly Hills, 1978. *Author's collection / Photo by Rick Lang*

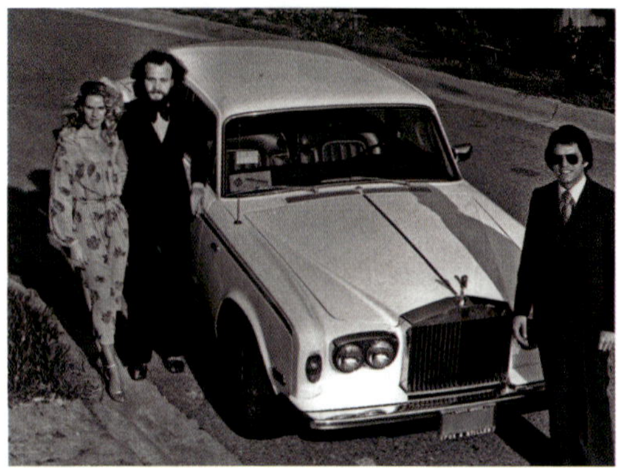

With Diane, departing for the Academy Awards, 1978. *Author's collection / Photo by Rick Lang*

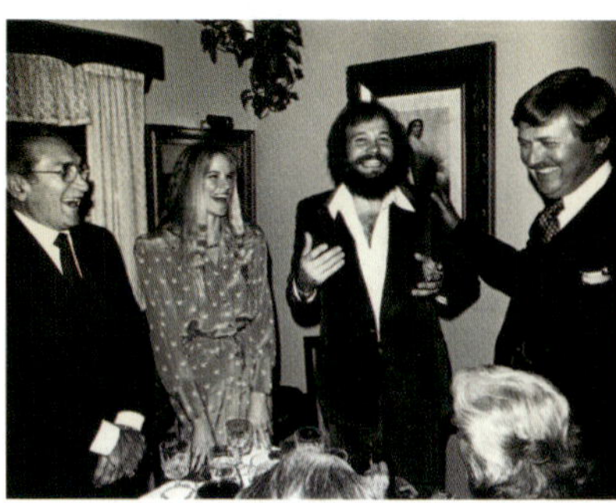

(from left) Consul General of Italy Amedeo Cerchione, Diane, me and author Donelson Hoopes, 1979. *Author's collection*

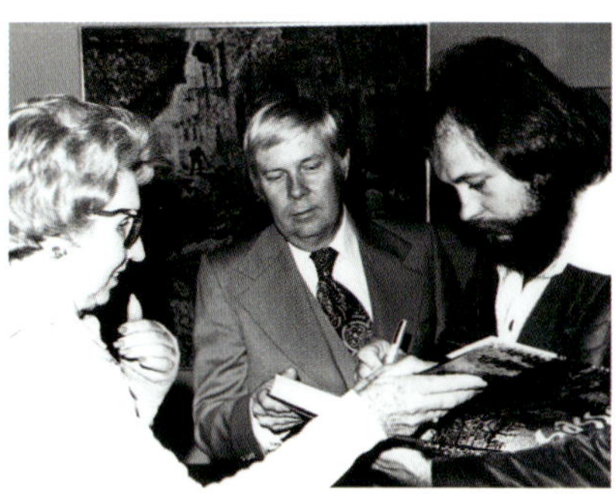

With director Tom Enman autographing my monograph at Laguna Art Museum, 1979. *Author collection / Photo by Rick Lang*

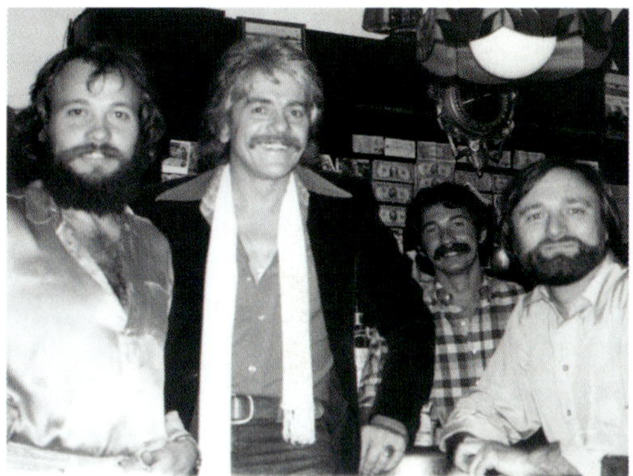

With Bruno (center) and Franco (far right) in New York, 1979. *Photo by Kay Galeotti*

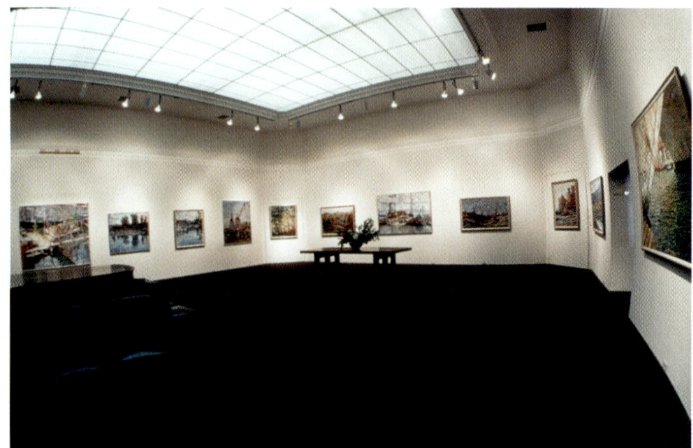

Installation at Laguna Art Museum, November 1979. *Author's collection / Photo by Rick Lang*

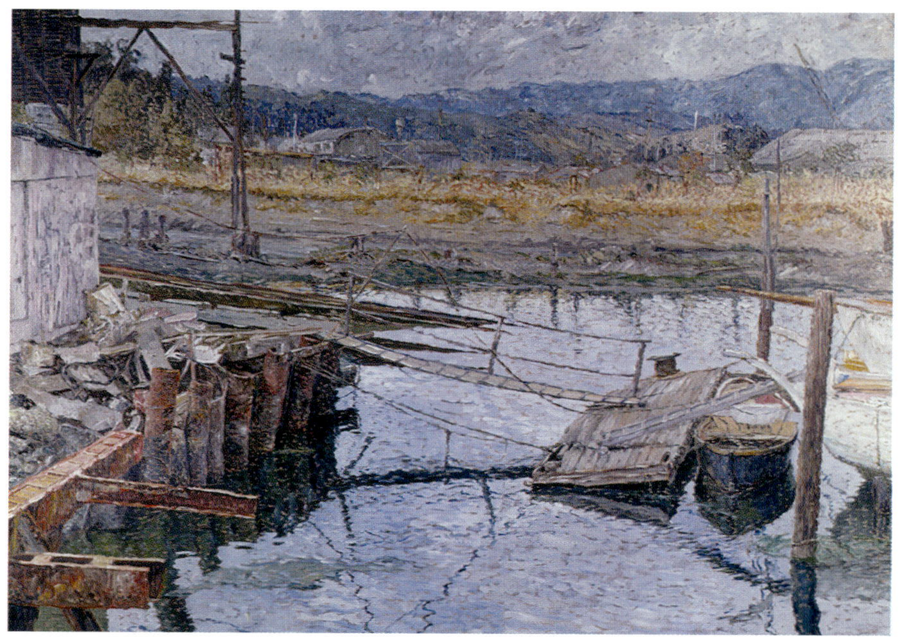

Houseboat III, oil on canvas, 1980.

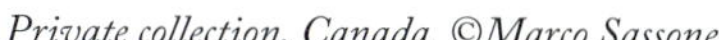

Private collection, Canada. ©Marco Sassone

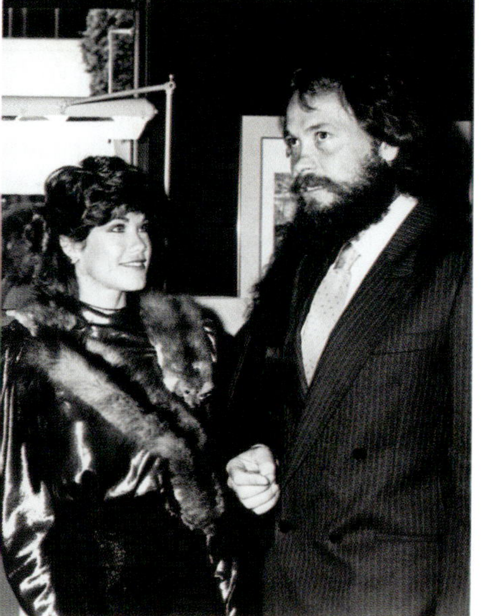

With Barbie Benton at my opening in Beverly Hills, 1982.

Author's collection / Photo by Rick Lang

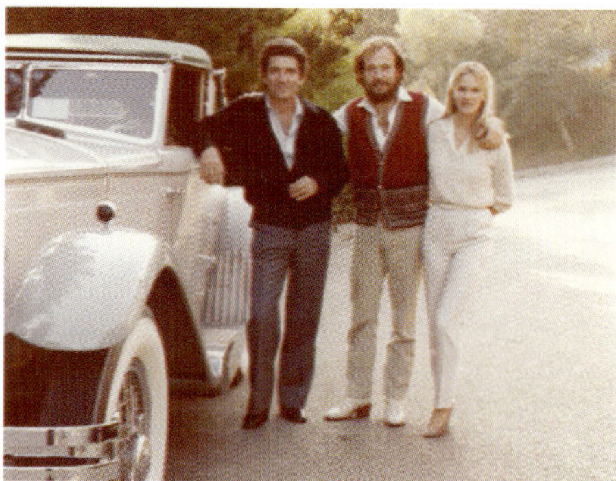

With Diane, Sergio Franchi and his 1950 Bugatti, 1980.

Author's collection / Photo by Eva Franchi

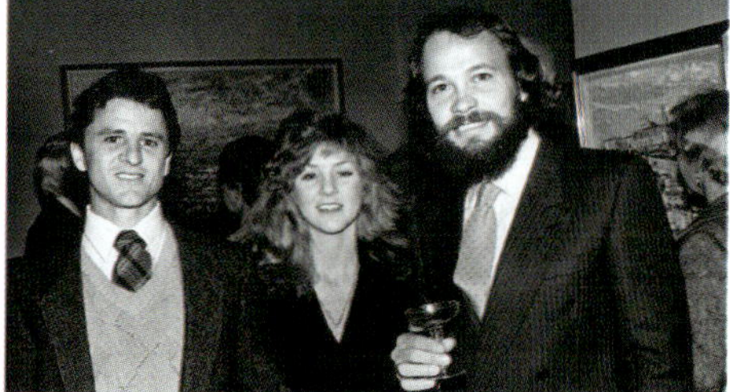

With Sheila and her brother Randy Woodworth, Beverly Hills, 1982.

Author's collection / Photo by Rick Lang

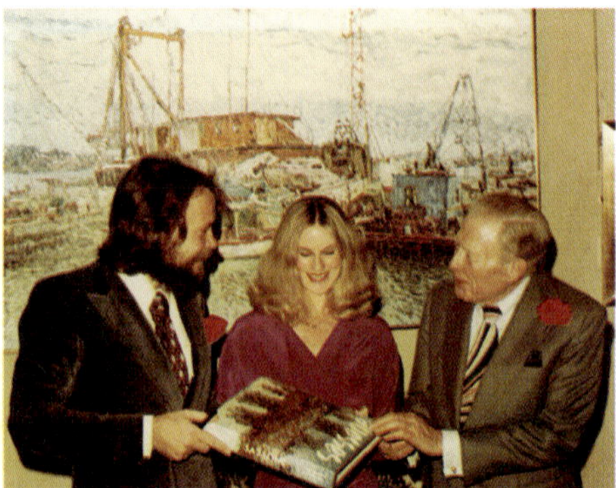

Diane and me with Wally Findlay at my opening in Beverly Hills, 1982.

Author's collection / Photo by Rick Lang

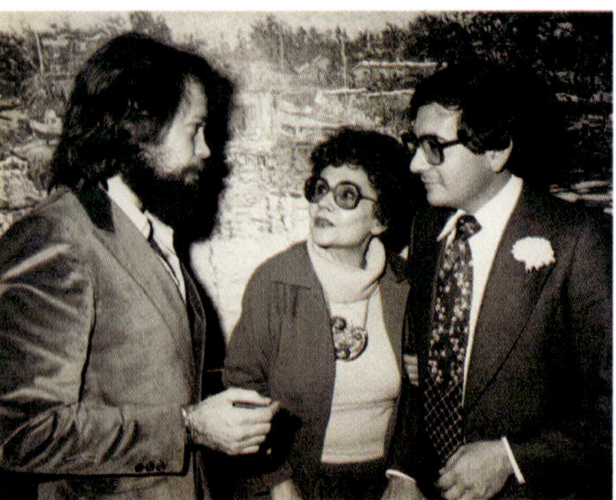

With Carlotta Monti (W.C. Fields companion) and Director Louis Stern at the opening of my exhibition at Wally Findlay Galleries, Beverly Hills, 1982.

Author's collection / Photo by Rick Lang.

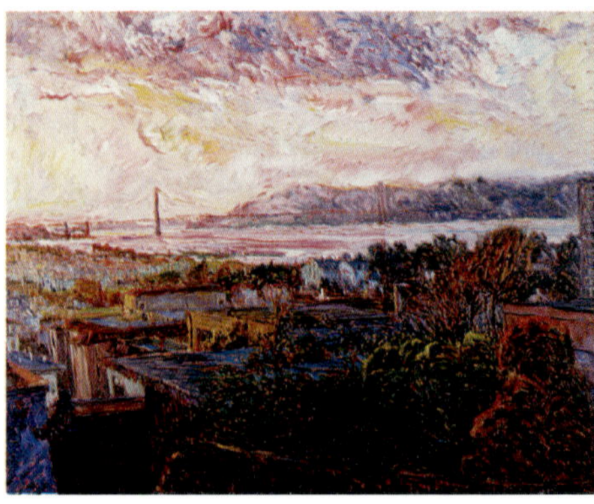

San Francisco Marina Dusk, oil on canvas, 1984.

Private collection, USA. ©Marco Sassone

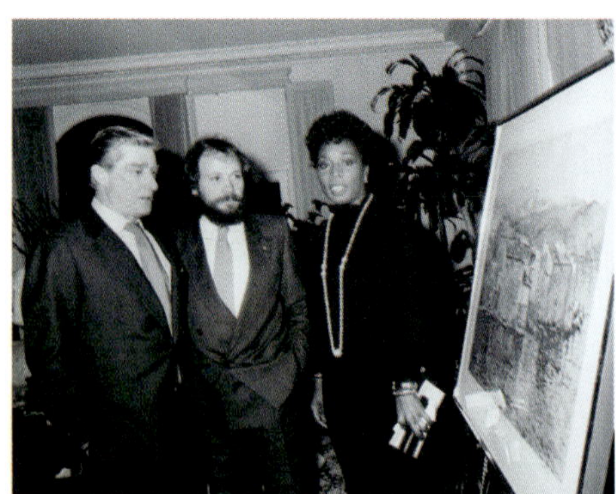

With Richard Molligan and Madge Sinclair at the Inter Aid benefit auction of my work, Beverly Hills, 1982.

Author's collection / Photo by Rick Lang

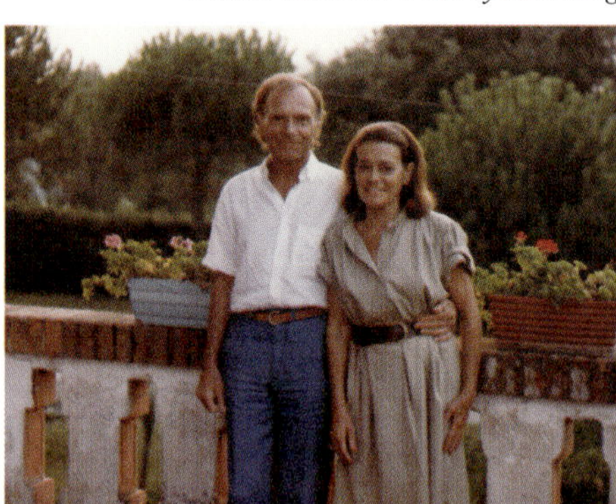

My parents at Villa Oliviero, 1985.

Author's collection

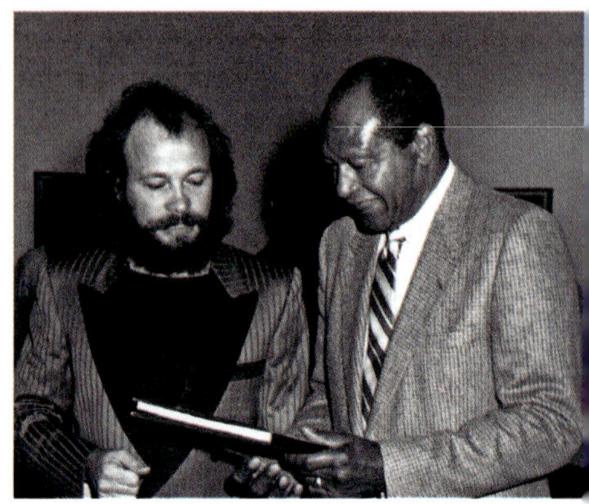

With Mayor Tom Bradley at the opening of my exhibition at the Los Angeles Municipal Art Gallery, 1988.

Author's collection / Photo by Lee Salem

with numerous illustrations. I officially announced my exhibition plans at a weekend reception at my studio on Bluebird Canyon in December of that year, and again this was covered by the newspapers. The studio was packed with friends, collectors and visitors, and news of the exhibition in Italy made quite an impression on the guests. I was convinced that this little city of Laguna Beach, unlike others in Southern California, was driven by an unlikely industry: creative thought.

I met a number of workers in this industry at the Challis Galleries on Pacific Coast Highway, such as the painters Rex Brandt and Millard Sheets, along with Sergei Bongart, whose work I admired at the time for his emotionally expressive landscapes. At the festival, I was introduced to Marjorie Darling, an elderly artist who still exhibits; she became a good friend with whom I frequently discussed "real painting," along with her late husband William Darling, an artist who was also the art director on numerous films and who won an Academy Award for *Cavalcade*. I met the painter Roger Kuntz one day in my booth; he stared intently at one of my small canvases that he found more intriguing than the other ones on display. He commented thoughtfully on the "gray" that pervaded this particular work, which gave it a translucent glow. I thought his series of freeway paintings were fascinating—a sort of contemporary realism that transcended fashionable labels, more visually compelling than any of the artworks by some of the big New York names at the time. And then there was Armen Gasparian, another real painter, who was certainly as good as Richard Diebenkorn. His work was characterized by his admirable chromatic sense. We became good friends and exhibited together in 1991 in a two-person show in Laguna Beach.

* * *

Via de Tornabuoni in Florence is the equivalent of Fifth Avenue or Madison Avenue in New York City. Some art galleries could still afford to occupy ground floor space at the time. Among these was the Galleria d'Arte Internazionale, whose November 1973 exhibition was accompanied by the publication of a monograph called, *California*, written by my agent and art historian Phyllis Barton. She was present at the *vernissage*—an event opened by Piero Bargellini, the mayor of Florence during the Great Flood of 1966. I was excited to have my wife by my side, and to see old friends from Italy and the U.S. My family and my mentor Silvio Loffredo were also on hand to view the progress of my work. Narciso Parigi, a famous Florentine singer, arrived with an entourage and chatted happily with la mamma. Two paintings and several small drawings were sold, and a splendid review by the critic Aurelio Ragionieri appeared in *La Nazione* a few days later. "A rare power of construction," he wrote. "A terse sense of color.... And often, a melting beauty of past memories." All in all, the exhibition was a tremendous success, and one that left me with a new sense of accomplishment.

Diane and I made it back to Laguna Beach in February, leaving behind the sights and sounds of Florence and the echoes of those familiar voices calling me back. But by this time, I was well aware that my journey had to continue in America, and after the usual period of adjustment, both physically and culturally, I went back to work with renewed energy.

But what about Ciccio?

It was a quiet afternoon on Bluebird Canyon. I was painting in the studio behind the house when suddenly I heard a loud noise coming from the garage. It was some sort of racket involving Ciccio, for sure, but I had no idea what else. I rushed to the scene and could not believe my eyes: There was a chicken in Ciccio's mouth and feathers all over the floor. Apparently, the chicken had found its way into the garage and had died—possibly from fright—in the course of the ensuing scuffle. I had no idea of what to do. Ciccio came bounding into the house, proud of his hunting trophy. Not wanting to make a mess in the house, I hung the chicken on a string from the ceiling and cleaned up the garage, sweeping up the feathers in order to remove all evidence of the crime.

"What happened here?" exclaimed Diane, arriving home from work.

"Well," I joked, "Ciccio caught this chicken, so maybe we can have it for dinner."

"Are you crazy?" she exclaimed. "Can't you see how big it is? It's probably somebody's pet."

"A pet chicken? I never heard of such a thing," I told her.

"We need to get rid of it . . . but where?" she asked.

At that very moment, through the kitchen window, I saw a lady walking up the canyon from below calling, "Betsy, where are you . . . ? Betsy, where are you?" She caught me looking at her. "Have you seen a chicken?" she asked.

"No," I lied, without the slightest hesitation. How could I possibly have told her the truth? I felt too guilty. That evening we waited until dark, wrapped up the dead body, and drove up and down the hills of Laguna for quite a while before finding a suitable place to hide the corpse.

Married life seemed perfect. Diane instinctively knew how to provide assistance and support right when it was needed the most. By the mid 1970s, after five years' participation in the festival, I'd become a prominent member of the art community, included in the inner circle of significant painters. Still, I was increasingly aware that the Laguna Beach art scene was held mostly in derision by the Los Angeles critics. The need to expand my horizons had been on my mind for a while when a phone call from the Haggenmaker Gallery provided the answer to my dilemma: "Marco, we're opening a gallery in Beverly Hills … and yes, of course, we are keeping the one in Laguna.… I'd like to confirm your show this November. Why don't you stop by the Laguna gallery and we'll talk over the details."

Replacing the receiver, I was delighted. This was short notice, I thought, but it has finally happened! A while back, I had visited the gallery's location in North Laguna, across from the museum, because I'd heard they might be moving or expanding to Beverly Hills. We had agreed that I would not be able to exhibit with them in Laguna, but I would be very interested in their new location. Mr. And Mrs. Haggemaker, the owners and directors of the gallery, knew my work well and proposed an exhibition for November of 1975, in Beverly Hills.

"We have a show this November—and it's not in Laguna," I told Diane excitedly as she came back home, the car keys still in her hands.

"Let me guess" she said. "Oh, this is good … your visit to the Haggenmaker Gallery was … what can I say, a brilliant move!" Diane remembered my visit there. "It paid off!"

"So," I said, "There's work to be done now. . . . We can't just leave it in their hands, we need to contribute, we need to help them with the planning."

We arranged a follow-up meeting and arrived well prepared. I brought along a mock-up of an 8 x 10 inch folded invitation. The front side read: "A première Beverly Hills exhibition," and underneath "Sassone." Inside, on the upper panel, I pasted the color image of a new oil painting, *Sausalito Bay*, measuring 40 x 56 inches, and indicated that a monograph by the artist would be available, with all the pertinent details. On the bottom panel, I included a sample text—inviting Vittorio Farinelli, consul general of Italy, as an honored guest.

The Haggenmakers were impressed. They studied the image and asked, "So would this painting be available at the show?"

"Of course, I'll save it for the exhibition," I replied. "And by the way, the consul has already confirmed his intention to attend."

I told the Haggenmakers that the monograph had already been printed in 1973, in Italy, in a limited edition of one thousand. And now that I was sure my presentation had passed their approval with flying colors, I showed them a layout for a full page ad in *Art News,* featuring the same painting and asked them to consider the ad to promote both the gallery and the artist to an international audience. With barely a moment's hesitation, they accepted all my plans, thanking me effusively for all the work I had put into the presentation.

Things were moving along exactly as I'd hoped and planned. I felt amply rewarded for the energy I spent painting in the studio—and for keeping my brain focused on what I loved doing the most. Everything seemed to be flowing in a natural way.

By way of additional promotion, the *Orange County Illustrated* published a cover with one of my paintings just one month before the exhibition, along with an article announcing my "upcoming show at the Haggenmaker Gallery in Beverly Hills."

Diane and I arrived at the Saturday night opening fifteen minutes late, and the space was already packed. The consul general was there with his wife, and my agent Phyllis Barton was already being interviewed for a TV program called *Italia'75*, which would air on their Sunday broadcast. The TV crew kept me busy for a while. I could not see the guests clearly, nor anything else for that matter, beyond the glare of their lights. But no matter, about half of the thirty-seven works on display were sold on opening night. The success of the event was evident. The press was soon covering the exhibition, and on the following Friday a review by William Wilson appeared in the *Los Angeles Times*. "Sassone is impressively gifted as a colorist," the noted art critic wrote, "and skilled in rendering reflections and color in light."

"This is what we needed," I told Diane as we drove back to the show the following Saturday.

She concurred. "The review came out at exactly the right moment," she said.

I couldn't have agreed with her more.

Mrs. Haggenmaker greeted us with a smile when we arrived at the gallery. "I think we caused quite a commotion," she said happily. "We had two hundred people here on opening night. And now this review is bringing in a whole new crowd of interested visitors."

"Yes, we're thrilled," I replied. I showed her the November issue of *Southwest Art,* with a feature entitled "Sassone's Personal Renaissance." It had just arrived at the house.

Mrs. Haggenmaker was duly impressed. She noticed immediately that *Sausalito Bay* was featured in the article. "That was the first red dot on opening night!" she exclaimed.

We spent some time looking back through my exhibition before leaving the gallery. "Let's walk around a bit before we drive back to Laguna," I said to Diane.

We went for lunch and then continued window shopping, hand in hand, down Rodeo Drive. "Let's take a look at the competition," I said as Diane scanned the display window of the Wally Findlay Gallery.

Soft music floated through the climate-controlled air as we entered and wandered through the gallery. We were met after just a couple of minutes by an impeccably dressed gentleman. "Excuse me," he said, "aren't you Marco Sassone?"

"Yes," I acknowledged.

"I'm Louis Stern, the director of the gallery."

"This is my wife, Diane," I told him. He took her hand politely. He liked the pieces on display at the "new" Haggenmaker Gallery on Canon Drive, he told us. In the course of the ensuing pleasant conversation, we learned more about the history of the Wally Findlay Galleries. It was established in 1870, apparently the same year the Metropolitan Museum opened its doors. While they specialized in French Impressionist and Post-Impressionist masters, the gallery also had exclusive representation of a group of contemporary artists in Beverly Hills, New York, Chicago, Palm Beach, and Paris. I was impressed. And when Louis asked me if I'd like to meet Mr. Findlay, the owner, I told him I'd be delighted. We traded business cards, and Diane and I headed back to Laguna Beach.

I received a phone call from Louis Stern just a few days later with a proposed date for a meeting and a request to bring three recent paintings. So this was not just a courtesy meeting, I thought; they were actually considering my work for their galleries.

We drove up to Beverly Hills in near silence. I was satisfied that the three pieces we had loaded in the van would represent me well. They were recent, strong, and mature paintings. The years at the festival, the numerous exhibitions, and the press coverage had established my reputation and provided me with the confidence that I had, by now, developed in my work. The income from sales had afforded us many trips to Italy over the past few years. But beneath the surface of our silent ride to Beverly Hills, we both knew this was the big one.

"Diane, Marco, thanks for coming. Mr. Findlay is looking forward to meeting you," said Louis, as he greeted us and led the way to the back of the office area. As we walked through, I took note of a collection of paintings by Monet, Renoir, Pissarro, and Sisley—and also by Childe Hassam, one of the primary exponents of American Impressionism. Louis pointed to a room where he had set up easels for the pieces we had brought. "Make yourselves comfortable," he said. "Mr. Findlay will be with you in a moment."

Louis left us and returned to the front of the gallery. We waited a good ten minutes, and I started to wonder if the dealer would ever show up but he finally did, walking in behind Louis, who made the introductions. Wally Findlay was a man of about seventy-five, I guessed, and impeccably tailored. He extended his hand to Diane. "Nice meeting you, Mrs. Sassone," he said. "Marco, I'm Wally Findlay. Good to meet you. You brought us some of your paintings, I see.... Nice." He walked over to them for a closer look. "This is good... but I think this canvas needs more sky, it's too short from the horizon up." He delivered this critique, his eyes on this one piece, without so much as a glance at the other canvases.

I steamed for a few moments in silence. Then I said firmly, "Diane, come on, it's time to go." I was already collecting my canvases and heading for the door. Louis Stern stood frozen, in obvious embarrassment off his boss. But Findlay walked towards me and urged me gently. "Marco," he said, "wait a moment."

"Mr. Findlay," I told him without hesitation. "I came here because I was told that you liked my work. But now I hear you criticizing the sky for being too contracted.... Either you like them, or you don't. Otherwise, I know where to find the door!"

"Oh, no, no, we like your work," he said calmly, with what I took to be sincerity. He led Diane back to her chair and signaled Louis to help me replace the canvases on the easels. "Your work is some of the best contemporary painting I've seen in the European mode," he assured me. "Louis will send you a contract. I think you'll find it satisfactory although perhaps different from what you are used to." He looked me steadily in the eye, then turned back to look at the paintings. "All I want from you is to paint," he said. "We will take care of everything else. I look forward to our fruitful relationship, Marco."

"That was quite a meeting," I told my friend Guy at his studio in Los Angeles as we were working on a serigraph later that week.

"Marco," he told me kindly, "making art and business are two different things. When they send you the contract you're going to have to deal with that." We were mixing a color for the next screen. Guy Maccoy was reputed to be "the father of the serigraphic process" in the U.S. He brought this form of printing to the west in 1947 from the Work Projects Administration, and with his wife, Geno Pettit, developed it into a fine art form. I had met Guy the previous year and studied printmaking with him, producing my first serigraph at his studio. It was a once in a lifetime opportunity to be under the guidance of this extraordinary man. He was a wonderful person, dynamic yet gentle. When I first stepped into his space in Canoga Park, near Los Angeles, I was taken by the warmth of the studio's ambience and the simplicity of his basic equipment. The process was fascinating. These were not photo-stencil screens made with the mechanical squeegees that many artists use these days for their editions. In Maccoy's process, every action was by hand and each printed color required a screen painted with tusche, a greasy substance soluble to solvent. The remaining area of the screen was then blocked with glue. After the tusche was washed off with solvent, the screen was ready to print the first color. Paper was placed under the screen and a squeegee was used to force ink through the screen and onto the paper. The process had to be repeated for the total number of prints in the edition. Each sheet was then hung to dry on a line with clothes pins. I remember repeating this process for each and every color. My prints required anywhere from fifty to a hundred colors, some of which were solid and others transparent, in order to create additional subtle effects. Other artists who worked at the Guy Maccoy Studio included Peter

Hurd, Frederic Whitaker, and Millard Sheets. Guy taught me the "ingenious gems" of resourcefulness and technique during an eight-year relationship of mutual affection and respect.

I had decided to include a few of my silk screens in an upcoming exhibit at the Bernard Gallery, which had offered to publish my prints. I had met Felix Bernard at the festival, and he was genuinely excited by my work, which appealed to his European taste. He was born in Vienna and was gifted with a great sense of humor. He told me right then and there, "Marco let's book a show before this contract arrives!" I recall going over our agreement one evening at my studio in Bluebird Canyon with his wife, Kay. He told us a bit of his history as vice president of the Kaiser Corporation and eventually his early retirement to follow his passion, art. I thought the computer above his shoulders was so sharp, I could hardly resist a spontaneous comment: "Felix," I told him, "you are the smartest retarded man I know!" He laughed so hard I thought he'd never stop, and we all joined in the contagious laughter. Even by the mid 1970s, I still couldn't tell the difference between "retired" and "retarded." Anyway, that spontaneous burst of laughter sealed our agreement.

"Guess who I met at the gallery?" Diane told me with great excitement one evening as she came into the living room: "A Hollywood filmmaker!" I gave her a curious look. "He loves your work," she continued. "His name is John Wilson of Fine Art Films, and he wants to make a documentary about you . . . he's coming back next weekend." And, indeed, John came back many times with his crew, driving up and down the canyon, where I posed and sketched for the camera. I recall we went to San Pedro to film large piles of metal scraps where I was working on a series of junkyard images. Then he did a studio shoot showing me painting simultaneously on a canvas and a glass panel of the same dimensions. The effect was fascinating, to see the painting in progress at once on the canvas and through the glass. John also arranged to film at Sotheby's, in Los Angeles, where one of my paintings was up for auction.

As it turned out, the documentary proved a useful addition at every lecture and guest appearance I made throughout Southern California. It became the opening part of my program and solved the logistics of painting a picture in front of the audience, something I had done up to this time with a certain level of dissatisfaction. The artwork produced under such circumstances could never compare favorably with my studio painting.

* * *

The Wally Findlay contract arrived from Chicago, the gallery's headquarters since 1931. Diane and I read through it a few times to make sure we were not missing any of the small print. Actually, it was typed in large print and all of the points were clear. This was to be an exclusive representation and, as Mr. Findlay had indicated, the gallery would take care of everything, from the printing of catalogs to invitations, shipping, advertisement, and promotion. The contract then stated that the commission was to be 60/40. So where was the catch, we wondered? We soon discovered it: the 60/40 was reversed! The 60 percent was for the gallery. Still, I didn't linger over it too long before signing. My first solo exhibition would be scheduled for the following May in Beverly Hills. The offer was too good to turn down.

The next thing to do was to notify those galleries that had supported me in the past—particularly, of course, the Haggenmakers, who had given me the Beverly Hills exhibition that first attracted Louis Stern. I contacted them, along with the others, to express my gratitude for their support, and to let them know that I'd been offered an exclusive contract with a reputable gallery of national standing. This was something that no one else was able to offer and that I felt obliged to accept. I was met with gracious, if reluctant, understanding.

Did I question this decision? No. But I could not possibly have known at the time how my life would change with this exclusive representation. "I just sold my soul to the devil," I told Diane jokingly. "But these are the Findlay Galleries," she reassured me. "You're dealing with one gallery... while being represented internationally by five galleries. And the checks will be coming in from Chicago every month," she added. It sounded good. And then again, it was already a done deal.

News from the National Academy of Design in New York also came early that year: one of my works had been selected for their 152nd annual exhibition in February. I could not have been more pleased as I had been working on an intense schedule for the near future. *The Los Angeles Times* wrote about me again and the studio was part of a benefit tour for the Laguna Art Museum. The month of May came quickly.

* * *

Diane and I arrived at the opening in Beverly Hills. This was Rodeo Drive. One of my paintings was prominently displayed in the large storefront window, along with the dates of the show. Photographers were at the entrance and inside a multitude of collectors, friends, and gallery patrons, to whom I was introduced by Louis Stern, mingled throughout the evening. Diane was busy as well, engaged in conversation with John Wilson and his wife regarding the success of his documentary film. New collectors were purchasing the paintings as I noticed numerous red dots appearing next to the artworks. Wally Findlay came up to me toward the end of the opening and asked, with a look of satisfaction: "How did we do?" Then he took us out to dinner in his white Rolls Royce, driven by his girlfriend, Florence Horn.

Back in Laguna Beach, we resumed a dialogue with a real estate broker regarding a property right across from Bluebird Canyon. The price was fair, so we bought the house immediately. It became the Mar Vista Studio: four floors, with large-paneled windows that looked out over the Pacific from a hill less than a mile away. We remodeled the interior and painted the outside stucco red, causing something of a commotion with the neighbors. One lady passing by, I recall, asked the painters up on their tall ladders, "Is this the primer?" "Yes ma'am," replied one of the painters. "But the final coat is exactly the same color," he added. The lady left in disbelief. My studio occupied the large master bedroom on the fourth floor, which I reinforced throughout with an additional layer of plywood. There was a terrace that offered an unobstructed view of the hills below and the blue water of the Pacific beyond. A Laguna Beach paradise. Diane placed several pots of flowers on all three terraces and on the small patio entrance to the back of the house. It was time to get ready for summer and the Festival of Arts, which I had been able to exonerate from the exclusivity of the Findlay contract. Life was beautiful.

* * *

Ballet Pacifica, Laguna's own ballet company, performed every Sunday afternoon on the green lawn of the festival grounds. I had watched it on numerous occasions in previous years but could not have imagined what was going to unfold this time around.

It was a sunny afternoon and the crowd had already circled around the lawn, awaiting the arrival of the dancers. There were many spectators. When the ballet started my eyes kept picking out one of the dancers as normally happens in such moments; then I would lose her in the group as they performed, and then, again, her face would reappear. I must admit that her face had affected me, and I decided to retreat to my booth, just a few steps away from the performance. Later, as the sun was setting on the grounds, I saw that same face approaching to view the art in my booth. I was frozen, at first. But soon we fell naturally into a lively conversation as she kept asking questions about the paintings, some of which had aroused unusual sensations in her. Her manner was kind and gentle, and her stance projected a delicate, sensual allure. She seemed in no hurry to leave and see the work of other artists. So we kept talking, until it occurred to me that we both wanted to continue this dialogue without the constant interruption of questions from casual passersby.

We left the booth and went for a coffee. Her name was Caroline.

Her image stayed with me. In the studio, or wherever I went. I was unable to dismiss it. I called her. We met briefly on a street near Moss Point, talking about nothing. I just needed to see her, to catch another glimpse of her face. Our meetings continued through anxious gazes, trembling kisses, and languid caresses. I told her I was married, but Caroline expressed no wish to call off our encounters, nor did I. But I had the gut feeling that this friendship was sure to end in trouble. Trouble in Paradise.

And it did. It made me think of Dante's passage from the "Inferno": *Nel mezzo del cammin di nostra vita mi ritrovai per una selva oscura che la diritta via era smarrita.* "In the middle of the journey of our life I found myself in a dark forest where the straight road was lost." Which was precisely where I was. But who could I talk to? Who would listen to me? This was not something I felt comfortable about, to say the least. There was no one I could think of, except for the one person who deserved to know: my wife. And so one evening, as we left the festival grounds, I told Diane that I needed to talk with her over dinner. She smiled in agreement, though she could not possibly imagine what I needed to talk to her about. I was still not completely sure I could share it with her either. But half-way through dinner the words came tumbling out of my mouth. The mood changed immediately, of course, but Diane remained perfectly pleasant and composed.

What to do? This was the question.

I felt somewhat relieved after my confession. My attraction to Caroline was ever-present. I felt helpless in the face of it. Knowing that Diane's intuition would not have failed to sense it, I was sure I had done the right thing. And in actual fact, a few days later, in what I thought at the time was an unbelievable decision on her part, she came upstairs to my studio to tell me she was willing to help, that she was moving out of our house. "Use the time to your advantage," she said. "And don't come looking for me. I will be at a friend's house." I was overwhelmed with gratitude and respect for her understanding, beyond all reason, of the situation at hand.

So I pursued a relationship with Caroline, basically with my wife's approval, in order to achieve more clarity before arriving at a possible decision. I was confused, I must admit. It did not feel right to me, especially when Caroline would come to the house. I far preferred to stay with her in Corona Del Mar, as guests in the apartment of my friend Romano. I had known him since the early '70s. We had met in Florence, at Il Fagiano restaurant, and he had told me at the time that he was living in California, so we made an immediate connection. He really liked Caroline but never offered an opinion about the crisis I was going through. We often went out to dinner together with a girlfriend of his, and I recall one time we went to see that beautiful film, *Romeo and Juliet,* by Franco Zeffirelli.

But most of my time was spent with Caroline. It was wonderful, especially when I could rid myself of other thoughts. We seemed to be living in a dream world, as in our trip to La Jolla and our stay at the La Valencia Hotel. Such moments were not always easy. I was facing a critical choice—a decision that would affect my entire life. What would make me happiest? I had no answer to this question. I felt simply that there would always be more to achieve, and that being happy with who I am seemed the only real goal to strive for. But I was not there yet. I remember the good things. I remember going to see Rudolf Nureyev with Caroline and Emma, her younger sister, at the Greek Theater in Los Angeles. I remember many other things.... But I saw no decision looming on the horizon, and after a couple of months Diane returned to the house.

My scheduled exhibition in Chicago in May of 1978 was only a few months away and at Diane's suggestion I agreed not to see Caroline in order to prepare for the show. It felt like a self-imposed decision. Quite honestly, it was painful. But I stuck with the program. It was the least I could do to move my life along and face the numerous commitments ahead.

In the midst of everything else that year, I was invited to attend the Oscars. I was looking forward to it, as Bob Hope was hosting the event for the nineteenth and last time. Diane and I arrived at the Dorothy Chandler Pavilion in a splendid white Rolls Royce. It was the year of *Saturday Night Fever* with John Travolta, and the star was chatting with Diane as we walked the famed red carpet. I met Marcello Mastroianni. I introduced my wife, and we had a pleasant conversation in Italian as I wished him good luck with his film, *A Special Day*. It was a fabulous evening, culminating in a lively conversation with Richard Burton as we were waiting for our respective cars and drivers. As our Rolls Royce approached, he looked at us and remarked in his distinguished British accent: "I call that traveling with class."

"We'd be happy to give you a ride," I told him. But he declined.

* * *

Diane came with me to Chicago for the opening. The Wally Findlay Gallery was located on North Michigan Avenue at the Water Tower, where we encountered a good number of traditional patrons and found an impeccable presentation of my work. The usual limousine service—compliments of the gallery—offered us a tour of the sights of this gorgeous city.

Prominently displayed at the gallery was my new series of junkyard paintings, which drew much attention but no sales. The paintings that sold at the show reflected the mood and style that were typical of my earlier work, and this, unfortunately, presaged a pattern many patrons would follow throughout my career.

I could not wait to see Caroline on my return to Laguna. She was a wonderful vision as always, but I felt I was looking at her through frosted glass. Time had taken its toll on our relationship. It was evident that I could not allow the current stalemate to continue for much longer, but no easy answer was going to appear in the sky any time soon. Shortly thereafter, Diane became pregnant, and life resumed its status quo, as it tends to do. My next exhibition was looming up ahead, scheduled for December of 1978 in Beverly Hills. I managed to paint and to continue numerous other activities. I presented a few lectures, including one at Orange Coast College, where I was delighted to see Elaine Stucker in the audience from my time at Belmont Shore. We exchanged kisses and hugs. It seemed so long for both of us—ten years—since those early days. Otherwise, I kept playing football—soccer that is—every Sunday afternoon. This was an activity I had started years before, and one that kept me in shape playing against much younger teams in the Southern California area. The Laguna Beach team reflected our multicultural village. It was made up of English, German, Italian, Swedish, and Belgian players, as well as Mexican and American. To this day, I stay in touch with some of my old soccer friends. (Incidentally, we won the championship that year, which added to the fun.) And, finally, I continued to serve on the local Arts Commission at City

Hall, organizing the First Annual Beaux Arts Ball that year with Harriet Nelson of *Ozzie and Harriet*, who was a longtime resident of Laguna. I designed the poster for the event, for which Harriet was extremely appreciative.

Still, those internal questions continued uninterrupted. This was not a good time to be in love with someone else because I also loved another woman, my wife. Human beings are weak in the face of love, and history shows us that the timing has often been far less than perfect! Love doesn't wait to choose the right time. It just happens. It's an illness with no cure. Reduced to a hopeless inability to act, we keep procrastinating until the inevitable happens.

I continued to see Caroline. By now, she had moved to Los Angeles and was living in an apartment near Beverly Hills, where she would work out at a local ballet school. Sometimes I would surprise her, arriving to watch her on the dance floor. Our encounters were wonderful and surreal. I'd drive up from Laguna Beach to Los Angeles on the San Diego freeway, then back to Laguna, never knowing with any certainty if and when we would meet again. But we did, both of us aware that we were living on the edge of reality, but still willing to continue for those brief and elusive moments of happiness.

* * *

December arrived, and Diane was showing her pregnancy with a wonderful glow at the time of the opening in Beverly Hills. This was my third exhibition with Wally Findlay, who was already there when we arrived, greeting guests at the door with Florence Horn. The installation of the paintings had been beautifully handled by Louis Stern, who had told me a few days earlier to leave it in his hands. I was wise to have done so: his professional touch was evident in the continuity of his selection between the paintings' subject matter and their coloration. My first impression was that the show accurately reflected the progress of the work itself. As the evening progressed the crowd spilled out through the door and onto the sidewalk of Rodeo Drive. Crowds of people were deep in conversation, right there on the street in front of the gallery's huge storefront window. There was electricity in the air. Then Louis Stern, who by now had become a good friend, was beckoning to me from across the room. Elbowing my way toward him through the crowd I felt a sudden rush of excitement. "Marco," Louis was saying, "I'd like you to meet Tina Turner … she has been admiring your work."

"Delighted, thank you, Louis," I replied. And disappeared quickly with Tina to a quiet corner upstairs, where we talked about painting and singing. I found her both perceptive and charming, and I was curious enough to comment on her transformation on stage. Speaking of electricity, she can generate enough wattage to leave anyone else on the stage in a shadow.

"I saw you in L.A.," I told her. "You were opening for the Rolling Stones with your husband Ike."

She stiffened at my comment. "Let's not talk about Ike," she retorted. Still, she felt comfortable enough to start telling me something of the abuse she had experienced in her life with her husband. I changed the subject as soon as a photographer arrived, setting up to take pictures of the two of us. "Let's see whose smile is wider," he said. We both burst out laughing, and the photos I saw later captured the moment perfectly.

And it was truly a special moment. Later, at dinner, I was trying to describe it to Wally, but all the dealer could do, with his one track mind, was to keep asking Florence: "So how many paintings did we sell?"

"Most of the show," Florence assured him, "most of the show."

9

NEW YORK: NATIONAL FAME AND SUCCESS

1978–1980

On our way back to Laguna that evening, Diane commented on the success of the opening and the excitement she'd felt on the floor of the gallery. She was in a fine mood and did not look at all tired, despite her pregnancy. "Your paintings deliver beauty in each brush stroke," she said. "Someone told me that tonight—so congratulations—and next stop New York!"

* * *

My friend Fabrizio came to visit us in Laguna Beach that January, providing some distraction from the constant pulsating emotions that consumed my mind. I could not stop thinking about Caroline, and my desire to be near her was overwhelming. I kept wondering what was happening to me. I knew that physical passion could exist without real love. However, this was much more than passion. I had already experienced an array of physical symptoms: walking on air, lack of concentration, feeling sick, loss of appetite. But now I had returned to Earth, and what I felt was much deeper than a mixture of these strange feelings. This was no romantic fantasy. I was in love with Caroline. I loved her both for who she was and how I felt when I was with her. My inability to be next to her only intensified the crisis.

Still, I managed to play tennis with my friend, and we talked incessantly, catching up on the past and the present. This Fabrizio was not the one who had been living in New York. This one still lived in Florence. He was a generation younger than I and the boyfriend of my sister, Patrizia, with whom he'd attended my wedding in 1972. Their relationship had not worked out, but we remained friends. Fabrizio was traveling through the U.S. on his own and I was happy to see him. Diane introduced him to her girlfriend, Patricia, who seemed to enjoy Fabrizio's company a great deal more than we had expected. One day, as we were driving home from tennis, my mind was on the approaching due date for the baby. Diane met us at the door and asked me if we could go to the market together. As I was driving down the hill, she suddenly began to feel queasy and seemed to be going into labor. In a panic, we laid her down in the back of the van and I changed directions immediately, driving up Laguna Canyon Road toward the 405 freeway, just in case; the hospital was in Long Beach, about forty minutes north. Fabrizio was sitting in the front seat looking helpless. He and I were still in our tennis clothes.

Diane was now quite sure that the time had come. I sped down the freeway onramp, into lines of traffic that were already unbelievable at four o'clock in the afternoon. No problem, I thought; I had learned to drive in Italy where people treat one lane as three. I merged quickly over to the emergency lane on the left and sped ahead past a police car. Slowing down, I lowered the window and yelled out to let him know what was happening. I turned down his offer to escort us and accelerated off again toward Long Beach. Amazingly, Diane was able to direct us to the hospital from the floor of the van, and we arrived with seconds to spare.

It was January 17th, and Nicola was born.

His birth required a completely new set of arrangements in the house. Nothing was the same. Diane's maternal instinct kicked in. Waking up in the middle of the night to feed him, she'd change his diapers and did all those things that mothers have to do. I was surprised to find that I was quite good at helping with these tasks, too. I loved to hold little Nicola in my arms, and I recall taking breaks from painting periodically, to go and check up on him in his crib while he was sleeping. Ciccio didn't like the new arrival at first and did not appreciate all the attention that was diverted to this little being, but as time went on he became Nicola's best friend and protector. It amazed me how he would circle around the stroller when we went out for a walk, a big black thing breaking into a frenzy of barking to keep strangers at bay. It was a scene that I watched often from the windows of my fourth floor studio while painting for my upcoming exhibition in New York.

I was quietly excited about the show. Hands and knees on the studio floor, I sorted through hundreds of charcoal sketches that I had made on location in Venice and around the Mediterranean. I decided this time to do an exhibition with predominantly Italian themes, and canvases with titles like *Tyrrhenian Sea, Porto Santo Stefano,* and *Rio Belvedere* had already been picked out for shipment to New York. I was still greatly enjoying my own process—custom-stretching each canvas, applying gesso and additional layers of color to simulate the hard surface of the wood panels on which I had grown used to painting during my en plein air period several years earlier. And then, as I painted, allowing small parts of the background coloration to show through at random, to produce a more textured effect on the surface. It was this process that characterized my work, and I was by now pretty much aware that my pictures looked nothing like other people's paintings. In Venice, I had always been entranced by the visual surprises you encounter at every turn. I loved to paint the experience of emerging from a narrow canal with its encroaching walls, and then suddenly breaking out into brilliant sunlight. I could recreate the sensation of that startling moment in a dramatic chord of color. But I also loved to show Venice in the winter, when the city endures months of a damp chill and the mood shifts to a wintery stillness. As I painted, I was always aware of the thrill of watching the painting in progress and eventually completed, bringing something into existence for the very first time. It's a visual pleasure that I have carried with me throughout my career.

One day I had this crazy idea: I wanted to take Nicola with us to New York. "But how can you do that?" Diane protested. "He's barely five months old."

"We'll visit Carlo and Melissa in Connecticut, and Melissa can babysit Nicola while we're at the opening," I replied. "She has already volunteered, remember?"

Carlo was my friend in Florence from the early days. He was not part of the Pappagalli group because he had moved to America long before, but I had introduced him to Melissa right before I left for my military service in Naples. When I returned to Florence a year later, I heard that they had married and moved to Fairfield, Connecticut. Diane was still doubtful until she spoke with Melissa on the phone again, and Melissa reassured her she had plenty of experience, having raised three kids of her own. So we were set to go.

We were greeted with great excitement on our arrival. I had not seen my friends in years, but we felt completely comfortable in their large home, enjoying lunches and dinners prepared outdoors by Carlo, whose elaborate cooking equipment included a real wood barbeque. Friends were often invited over for martinis to meet us and the little one in a typical East Coast ambience.

Diane and I went to New York a couple of days before the opening to meet Wally and his new girlfriend, Simone Karoff, for lunch. Actually, I was told she was a former girlfriend who had reappeared in Wally's life and taken over as director of operations for all the galleries. The staff was intimidated by her presence and her imperious attitude, but I admired her direct approach and we always seemed to enjoy each other's company. This time was no exception. We arrived in a black Rolls Royce for lunch at the Pierre and had a fabulous time. This was not a particularly lively restaurant, rather too stiff and proper for my taste, but we stirred things up, with the waiter rushing back and forth as Simone kept changing her mind. She ordered her favorite white wine from France, Pouilly-Fuissé.

I was wondering what we were celebrating. The opening was only two days away, and I was already feeling a bit tense inside.

On Thursday, May 3, 1979, we said goodbye to Nicola and our friends Carlo and Melissa, and boarded the train for New York. I was thinking about that first meeting in Beverly Hills and the reversed 60/40 commission, but Wally Findlay had been as good as his word. Everything had been taken care of in the past four years, from invitations and catalogs to framing, promotion, and advertising. Every detail had been attended to with professionalism and care. The openings had been society page events, from the guest lists to the catering. My 40 percent was amounting to much more than the 50 percent that I'd expect from any other gallery. And, I supposed that Wally Findlay also had not been disappointed.

That evening, a limo picked us up at Grand Central and dropped us off on the sidewalk in front of the Findlay building on 57th and Madison, forty-five minutes early. A poster in the storefront window announced "SASSONE" with the dates of the show: May 3–June 2. An exhibition catalog was also on display. Diane and I paused for a moment and looked at each other before stepping inside.

Simone greeted us as we walked in. "Marco, Diane, good to see you . . . how was your ride into town?" She introduced us to the gallery director, Jimmy Borynack, who escorted us up to the third floor where my exhibition was installed.

"Everything looks great," I said, acknowledging the staff's good work in organizing the exhibition. I walked over to where Wally stood by the windows, remarking on the fact that, unlike previous openings, no guests had yet arrived. I cast a curious glance through the window overlooking 57th, where a line was forming in front of the building. "What's happening down there?" I asked. "There's a line about a quarter of a block long."

"Oh, those are the people who are coming to your show," Wally told me.

"They're coming to my show?" I asked. "Why don't you let them in?"

"Oh, no, Marco. The gallery is still closed. On opening nights, we open at seven prompt. It doesn't matter who's there."

I looked at him in disbelief. *Jesus Christ*, I thought, this is unbelievable.

"It's about time," Simone said. "Let's head downstairs and let those people in." She set down her wine glass and headed for the door. By the time they got down to the foyer and Simone unlocked the door, the line stretched halfway down the block.

As the guests entered the third floor gallery from the balmy evening outside, Wally had me stand by his side to personally greet all one hundred and fifty guests. The show occupied the gallery's entire third floor space. It included twenty-eight canvases, including two large paintings, *Rialto Bridge-Dusk* and *Ponte di Rialto,* with an inscription of Nicola's name and birth date on a marble plaque painted on the side of the bridge.

The muscles of my face were soon sore from the obligatory smiles, from repeating thank you, thank you, to a non-stop stream of well-wishers. But this was a classic New York art crowd, dressed in the formal attire of the late 1970s. Openings are not normally the time or place to talk about art, and even in the most intimate settings, collectors rarely asked me about my paintings. At most, they would tell me what they owned and their plans for their collection. However, I was surprised that here, in the middle of this packed house, I was cornered on a couple of occasions with serious questions that led to meaningful dialogues. Meanwhile, new guests kept pouring into the gallery, and Wally himself came to rescue me a few times, wanting me to be available to converse with all the patrons. Then Diane tried calling me over and eventually made it through the crowd to introduce me to Italian Consul Alessandro de Bosis. He was a perfect gentleman, very excited about the show and generous with his compliments. He was captivated, he told me, by the mood of the Venetian canvases and their deep perspective. As the stream of guests continued to flow into the gallery, I could not help but feel grateful that New York was responding so exceptionally well to my work.

As the last of the guests were leaving, Wally walked up to me as usual and asked his signature question: "So, Marco, how did we do?"

But Jimmy Borynack joined us before I could answer. "We sold every piece, gentlemen," he announced, "an hour and a half into the opening."

Wally took us to dinner to celebrate, and for the occasion he regaled us with his story about selling paintings to a blind person. Louis Stern had warned me that I would have to hear this story eventually, and now, with what he felt to be a receptive audience, Wally gave it his all. To make a long story short, the name of the gentleman who was visually impaired was Thomas Gilcrease, an American Indian who had made a fortune in the oil business in Oklahoma, and apparently Wally's description of the paintings in question was so persuasive in detailing the imagery, coloration, and style, that Thomas felt compelled to purchase them immediately.

After dinner that night Wally's Rolls Royce dropped us off at the Pierre Hotel for an overnight stay, but by early next morning I sensed Diane's growing impatience. We had not seen Nicola for two days. So we boarded a train for Fairfield right after breakfast, both of us still exhausted and stunned by the opening. As the train approached the station we could see Melissa on the platform holding little Nicola in her arms, but when we tried to get off the train the doors refused to open! Diane panicked. We rushed to try another set of doors, but by the time we got there the train was already moving again. Melissa caught on immediately to what had happened and reassured Diane with a smile, gesturing with her free hand that she'd pick us up at the next station down the line. I believe it was Bridgeport where we finally got off, and Melissa was there with Nicola, which put a look of contentment and relief on Diane's face.

On the plane back to California, our little one did not make a peep for the entire flight. I could not stop thinking about New York. I kept flashing back to a quotation on the wall, right next to the large sign at the gallery's door. It was an excerpt from *Southwest Art* magazine: "What strikes the eye at first in Sassone's art is a sensuous presentation. His works are pervaded by the joy of painting what truly pleases and fascinates him. This elegant idiosyncrasy is expressed in full light, fragrant with tonal harmony and luxurious from the sweep of his thick brush work." Well written, I thought, and a good selection of text for the paintings in the show. At the same time, I could hardly help wondering if my work deserved that kind of exuberance. I recalled the writer. She was definitely seduced by my painting process. And apparently these patrons in New York agreed with her judgment, since they felt compelled to acquire each and every piece in the show.

I was still overwhelmed by this crescendo of events in my career. It had been only ten years, after all, since my arrival in America. It all seemed so unreal. I could hardly believe that this kind of success was possible. I found myself back in the real world the moment I set foot in my studio, recognizing the full extent of my commitments for the year ahead. A large monograph of my work was already in production, and my retrospective for the Laguna Art Museum was scheduled for November–December at the invitation of the director, Tom Enman. These projects in themselves were huge, and I still wanted to keep my commitment to show my silkscreen prints at the Festival of Arts that summer, and to give a lecture to the Bakersfield Art Association members at my studio in June.

Unfortunately, some terrible news also arrived that year: my friend Jill had passed away. Her sister, Jennifer, delivered the news in a dramatic phone call. I was shocked. This was my first girlfriend in California, the one who made my journey possible. It was she who brought me here. I was appalled by the unpredictability of life. Jill had been hit by a car in Indianapolis, Indiana, under suspicious circumstances. She had been driving by herself from California to visit a friend in Cleveland, her ultimate destination. The family never received the full details about her death; they knew only that she was struck by a car on a street below an overpass. Her purse was later found in a nearby park and her car was discovered at a gas station. Diane and I attended her memorial on June 5th, and I was struck again by the unreality of it all, reflecting on the fragility of our lives—and on the sad truth that this sort of despicable violence is also very much a part of reality in America.

* * *

Collaborating on the design of my book and the selection of the artworks, I realized it was now time to locate a writer for the text of the monograph. We drafted a few inquiry letters to prospective writers, and after a few hits and misses I found precisely the writer I wanted. His name was Donelson (Don) F. Hoops. I researched his background, as it could not be just any writer. I needed someone with knowledge of art history and who understood my paintings. I contacted him, and when Don called me back, he expressed precisely those points. I was truly pleased when he agreed to take the job.

Don had already published numerous books on American art, including a study of Winslow Homer's watercolors and monographs on John S. Sargent and Thomas Eakins. In 1973, he published the first modern study of Impressionism in the U.S. called *The American Impressionists* and, in 1979, a monograph on Childe Hassam. I felt I was in good hands. During several visits over espresso at my studio we became good friends. Don studied at the University of Florence and had written a catalog for another Florentine artist, Pietro Annigoni, for his 1969 exhibitions at the Brooklyn Museum and the Legion of Honor in San Francisco. Don and I discovered that we had much in common. In fact, I had exhibited with Annigoni in 1967 at Lo Sprone Centro di Cultura in Florence and had remained in touch with him since my departure for California. Just the previous year, I had received an affectionate note from him, in which, among other things, he complimented me on "my fresh and bright landscape impressions, rich in local character." I had always thought his figurative work was exceptional, and he was widely known for his 1955 portrait of Queen Elizabeth. Annigoni was a painter who never abandoned his faith in humanistic traditions, directly inspired by the Renaissance. His detractors tended to view him with dismay, seeing his career as misguided for using his talent in pursuit of discredited ambitions. But I remember that he seemed to care very little about any of these hostile comments. I told Don that I had already been the recipient of similar jabs: I remembered the critic who wrote in the *Los Angeles Times* in 1975 that I was "impressively gifted as a colorist," but at the same time that I squandered my talent on ordinary subjects.

I squandered my talent? What do these people know about talent, I wondered. Talent is a word we use for lack of a better one. Talent is an inherited and inborn quality that is part of the artist. There can be no art without it. The ability to transmit one's own sense of life through color, form, and line is the most precious gift an artist has; this is what establishes an artist's creative identity. Everything else about art can be learned, but not that. And thanks to that creative identity, the artist is talented as much in his choice of subjects as in how he paints those subjects. It's this inner sense of security that enables an artist to freely conceive and express form with pictorial emotion that even an "ordinary subject" arouses in him or her, thus stimulating the unique capacity to see that object merely as a matter of color and light.

* * *

The Sassone monograph was officially published in 1980 and a few dozen copies arrived early, just in time for the opening at the Laguna Art Museum on November 6, 1979. It certainly made an impact on all the guests. Don was there, along with Louis Stern and his wife, the Italian consul general of Los Angeles, the mayor of Laguna Beach, Harriet Nelson, Marjory Darling, and many other artist friends, and what seemed like the entire city of Laguna Beach. Tom Enman, the Laguna Art Museum's director, was kept busy all evening, handing me copy after copy of the book to sign for museum patrons. And later that night, Louis Stern took us all out to dinner at Rothschild's Restaurant in Corona del Mar, compliments of Wally Findlay Galleries.

* * *

My work continued at the studio with an ongoing series of paintings featuring the house boats moored in Sausalito, across the bay from San Francisco. I was interested in the same man-made clutter and chaos that had captured my attention earlier in my paintings of the San Pedro oil refinery, where that immense wasteland, devoid of organic nature, inspired me. Yet, I found it rich in color and texture, a subject worthy of pictorial study. My intention was not so much to comment on the state of a society that produced such waste, though the nature of the paintings certainly prompted this kind of association. The random accumulation of floating habitations in the Sausalito harbor seemed like a natural continuation of my interest in living on the edge, which in this case was evident in the residents' rejection of normal social values. In the process of creating this new series, my trips to the San Francisco Bay

Area became more frequent, and I began to feel my time there would uncover new and unforeseen possibilities.

In 1980, my parents arrived for a five-month visit, thanks to my mother who convinced Papa to travel with her. He had to conquer his fear of flying for the eleven hour flight to Los Angeles, during which he kept whispering in her ear that he did not wish to die so far away from Florence and from everything he held dear. I took them with me on one of my trips to San Francisco with Diane and Nicola, and we also visited Los Angeles and the Orange County area. But most of all, they simply enjoyed staying at the house in Laguna, cooking and taking Nicola for walks. I had announced their arrival to all of my friends, so many of them were eager to come over for a visit. Sylvia, a singer with a most beautiful voice whom I had met in Florence long before my arrival in the U.S., came down from Palos Verdes and performed a duet, singing a couple of classic tunes with Papa. One day Sergio Franchi came for dinner as well. Diane and I had met him in the early '70s in Los Angeles. I told Papa that he was a big star who had performed in Las Vegas since the late '60s; his venues included the MGM Grand, where Joan Rivers was his opening act. A dramatic tenor like Mario Del Monaco, Sergio possessed a powerful voice, and his Las Vegas show included several operatic arias and a medley of Neapolitan songs, all choreographed using his big showman personality. He arrived in a vintage 1950s Bugatti with Eva, his wife, and his personal mechanic who followed him in a second car. Despite several requests from Papa, however, he could not be persuaded to perform for us, having only recently recovered from a throat infection. But the conversation at the dinner table reached a high plateau when Papa and Sergio reconstructed the history of lyrical performances by a multitude of tenors and sopranos, all of whom had left their indelible mark on the world of opera.

Still, what provided the most pleasure for me that year was the exhibition I had arranged for Papa and me to show our artwork together—his oil paintings and my watercolors—at Bernard Galleries in Laguna Beach. He was touched at the opening when Mayor Wayne Baglin and his wife purchased one of his landscapes. That night, seeing Papa surrounded by his canvases, I found myself reflecting upon his life. This was the man who taught me the value of education, and, above all respect, and who placed a brush in my hand as soon as he felt that I could hold it. Even having reached a certain age, he still looked great, and no matter my regret for what I saw to be the missed opportunities of his life, he appeared content with himself. Like his paintings, he projected a distinct and natural charm. I felt proud to be his son.

10

A NEW LIFE IN SAN FRANCISCO

1980–1982

My parents' departure left an insurmountable void in the house. They had been with us for five short months and their presence was still tangible. Diane and I had a chance to talk about them as we drove to Los Angeles one day to visit Mayor Tom Bradley. The meeting had been organized by the Italian consul, who was sponsoring an auction of my paintings at his residence. In fact, my parents had wished to be part of the event, but the auction had been postponed already on a couple of occasions, so Papa and Mamma had to return to Florence.

We were received enthusiastically by the mayor and members of the Los Angeles City Council, to whom I presented a commemorative poster in aid of the three hundred thousand victims of Italy's great earthquake on November 23, 1980. The *Sassone Earthquake Benefit Auction* was conducted by Sotheby's and took place on March 14, 1981. The response was overwhelming and all eighteen paintings I had donated sold that night. I was extremely pleased that the funds, as I learned later, were enough to cover construction costs for a new house for one of the homeless families. This event also marked the beginning of a treasured and friendly relationship with Tom Bradley that would last throughout the years. I know he made a difference in the city during his record five-term tenure, but I was particularly grateful to know him on a personal basis, and I was always grateful for his friendship and support. He was a gentle and genuinely kind human being, who often made time from his busy schedule to attend my art openings.

With Laguna's Festival of Arts approaching again that year, I received a call from a contributing editor of *American Artist* magazine regarding an interview about the status of my career. Her name was Diane Casella Hines. She had selected an image of one of my well-known silk screens, *Laguna*, to be featured on the front page of her article. Her questions seemed to gravitate around my need to operate in this town, while critics continued to label the place "commercial." In essence—as I had heard before and which was now implied in this dialogue—she wondered why I would find inspiration for my work in the physical beauty of Laguna Beach. I insisted as kindly as I could that I had very little interest in what the critics thought and why they sneered at representational art in general. What I neglected to mention was that my days in Laguna Beach were already numbered.

I had in fact recently arrived at a threshold that needed to be crossed, and soon for the sake of my own sanity. Confronted with the urgent need to make a choice, I had been feeling torn and impotent. For quite some time, I had been feeling somewhat misunderstood not only by friends, but by the entire world it seemed—and not least by myself. At times love catapults us into unexpected situations and involvements that we would not wish upon ourselves, that we have criticized in others, and that leave us lost and confused by the irrational demands of our hearts.

How did I get involved with two people at the same time? Certainly not because I nourished a fascination about the conquest and engagement of collecting seduction trophies. My mind was always far removed from the narcissistic need to feel attractive and sexually appealing. But here I was, involved in two relationships simultaneously, something that certainly did not work to my advantage. We are not all the same, of course, and what's perfect for one person is not so for others. Love is a state of being that results from our ideas and our intentions. Love happens. We can deny it, but we cannot eliminate it or avoid it. A man who finds himself in love with more than one person can't prevent himself from experiencing those feelings. He can try to manage them in such a way that those closest to him are not hurt, but he can't simply expunge those feelings from his heart. A subtle prejudice can sometimes rage against the emotions, denying them the right to exist, and labeling them as pathological when they exceed the reassuring bounds of common sense. A man who is seriously involved with more than one person is often branded a womanizer and is excluded from the privilege of love with a capital "L." There is no hearing, nor understanding, for such people whose accepted morality usually condemns, religion chastises, and society misunderstands. They are seen only for their abuse of sexual attraction as an end in itself. I felt as helpless as one of the sinners tossed and whirled by the wind in Dante's Canto V of the "Inferno."

Intolerance is the illness of our world, and whoever separates himself from the behavioral norms of society often becomes the target of that intolerance. It's already difficult enough to love one person; loving two, according to all logic and common sense, seems utterly impossible. But then, when it happens, when the heart takes its dive into the murky depths of passion, we are suddenly confronted with the recognition that logic and common sense never did understand much about human feelings. Our certitudes can do nothing but deal with the reality in which we are living, even when that reality was not programmed, expected, wished for, wanted, or sought after. Love is an inexplicable event. It cannot be locked up in the familiar and reassuring cage of our convictions. We can only know its depths by living it. Once I came to a full understanding of myself, this paradox—sad as it was—came into focus: impossible to be with one while knowing there was another, and vice versa.

* * *

I had not been in touch with Caroline for a while now and I began to feel that she had disappeared, since her phone in Los Angeles kept ringing unanswered in my ear. I drove up to her apartment one day and to the ballet school nearby. But she was not there to welcome me with her delicate smile and languid embraces. I returned to Laguna. Driving back up the hill, I could already see my house in the distance and a great sadness reached deep into my soul. I turned around, not knowing where I was going, unable to shake Caroline's image from my mind. And then, suddenly, as I approached the center of town on Glenneyre Street, there she was, walking down the sidewalk. I could not believe it. We hugged each other without saying a word; there was no need for us to talk. We both knew that our story was coming to an end, and yet I could not find closure for she was still embedded in my heart. And now she shared with me that, given how things stood between us, she would soon be moving to New York City. She had found a place to stay at a boarding house for women on 13th Street. I told her my friend, Franco, owned a restaurant called Zinno on 13th Street, and another friend, Bruno, was running the large bar at the entrance to the restaurant. She knew of Bruno, and I reminded her that my friendship with Franco also dated back to Florence, where we all went through the 1966 flood together. "Go visit them in New York," I suggested. "They'll take good care of you." Then we kissed and hugged . . . and that was the last time I saw Caroline in California.

Diane and I had already talked about the need to separate, which seemed to be the best solution for both of us. I had located a space in San Francisco and had moved my entire studio there by September of 1981. When you love a city and have explored it frequently on foot, your body and soul get to know the streets so well that, after a while, your legs begin to carry you with a certain melancholy toward unplanned destinations, which is precisely how I discovered my studio. One afternoon, buffeted by a chilly bay breeze, I found myself on a narrow road leading up the hill to a semi-detached building with a long wall of large paneled windows. In the excitement of the moment, I noticed on the front door steps an imprint of the letter "S" etched on one of the red clay bricks. I entered through a small iron gate in the back and could not help knocking on the door. It was soon answered by a woman who welcomed me inside to see the space. "I am visiting my son from New York," she told me, adding that her son was moving to Oakland, across the Bay Bridge, and therefore, unbelievably, the apartment was available. There were two bedrooms on the ground floor and upstairs a large space with soaring ceilings and a wall of glass with northern exposure and light suffusing everywhere. From there, a spiral staircase led to a large terrace on the roof overlooking Alcatraz Island and the entire San Francisco Bay!

I made a deal on the spot, without a moment's hesitation. My assistant, Jeff, helped with the move and the organization of my studio. Jeff had worked with me over the past several years. He was the best assistant—loyal, responsible, and always curious about life, but he was also well aware that he and I had arrived at the end of a cycle. We drove back to Laguna Beach with an empty truck, and the following day I was ready for the final trip to San Francisco in my own car, in my faithful yellow Jaguar, filled with my personal items. Even though I knew I'd be back to visit soon, I was dreading that moment of departure. Diane stood in front of the antique double doors at the entrance of our home, holding our two-and-a-half-year-old Nicola in her arms. She took a few steps forward, looking at once contemplative and concerned. Her hands spoke volumes, touching Nicola's little feet in an intimate gesture that reminded me of an iconic image of the Madonna and Child.

I will remember that drive to San Francisco for the rest of my life: eight hours in complete silence with tears often coursing down my cheeks. I kept telling myself: don't cry because the story ended, but rather smile because there was a story. But as I was crossing the Bay Bridge at dusk that September night, with the immense San Francisco skyline enveloped in a spectacular golden red glow, my eyes filled with tears again.

The moment I set foot in my new studio, though tired from that emotional drive, I felt both restless and excited. I went out for a while just to calm my spirits, and before I knew it I found myself roaming through the night. As I walked and walked through the darkened streets surrounding my new neighborhood, my footsteps echoed off the walls of houses, schools, and churches, and my fears and heartache gently subsided.

The next day I woke up early and could not wait to go out again. I took a long walk, with a sketchbook under my arm and a few black markers, a habit I acquired in those early days in Florence. It felt like the morning had freed the city of its crowds. All was quiet and slow. From the waterfront near Pier 39 and all the way to the middle of the Golden Gate Bridge, I gazed with reverence at San Francisco. The dome of the Palace of Fine Arts shone brightly in the sunlight that broke abruptly through the clouds. I felt right at home from the first. It seemed as ideal as any city could be for an artist or writer, perhaps like London or Paris—a city small enough for human congeniality, yet large enough for ardent creative ferment and with a cosmopolitan sensibility. The clean, sharp shadows of the high-rises projected patterns that resembled early morning shadows, though it was already afternoon. The city appeared majestic, its hills rising and the air itself flushed with crisp sunlight, so different from the hot glow of Southern California.

During those late September mornings I found myself nervously touching some of the objects on top of my large painting table, holding and rearranging tubes of oil colors, brushes, pencils, cans, mixing sticks, charcoals, and pastels. I found myself pacing the floor with a cappuccino still in my hand, gazing out through the large windows, almost as to acquire familiarity with my resplendent new space. Then I was out again, retracing my footsteps to the house boats in Sausalito, to see if anything had changed from my previous visit and to discover any new subtle coloration within this disorderly arrangement of floating habitations. I was passionately attracted to the entire range of this exquisite mess.

Back in the studio, the madness eventually sorted itself out into the ritual that takes place before reapproaching the easel following a long period of inactivity, opening and closing tubes and jars at random, smelling the pigments while gazing down on the floor at the piles of sketches and drawings I had produced on location. And unconsciously my attention would then shift, as it did now, to the work of stretching canvases and preparing the surfaces for the multiple images that had already taken up residence in my mind—images I could now visualize as paintings, along with the urgent sense of compulsion to create.

I have often been asked how an artist chooses his subjects, and the answer this time was the same as ever: the subject actually chooses me. As I immerse myself in the complexity of that vision, it becomes a part of me. Painting is often autobiographical. We are simply responding to impulses, to our predilections, to what resides within ourselves. Making art is a process that helps me to rediscover my formative emotions—emotions that later on, in the age of maturity, have emerged on the surface of my own pictorial language.

As I was engaged in the construction and preparation of several large canvases already assigned to the subject of houseboats, I tiptoed toward the easel early one afternoon and began to open up my paint jars. The colors had partially dried, but the seductive smell of paint was ever-present. With a knife, I proceeded to remove the thin layer of skin that had formed on top of the paint. I gently stirred the pigment in each jar. The paints looked beautiful, colors previously mixed and now ready to use. I added a few small dabs on a palette, cerulean blues of slightly different tones. And dropping the last mixing stick onto the tabletop, I swept up a few small round brushes and began to sketch out an image in alizarin red on the small square canvas that awaited me on the easel. Silence ensued, except for the brush making contact with the surface of the linen, previously primed with washes of light-reddish ocher tints. Glancing back and forth from a drawing I had made on the wharf, I sketched in rows of fishing boats with color indications for the hulls, a part of the sky, and the water in the foreground. I felt myself loosening up as I progressed, conquering the residual fear that is often present when I begin a painting. A few slightly larger strokes of peach and mustard yellow began to appear, applied with a couple of flat brushes I must have picked up as I went along. The shape of the boats began to emerge in a muted coloration, ranging from gray-greens to red oxide tones. The sky was rendered above the horizon in pale violet, breaking through at the top center with a glow of Naples yellow and peach highlights.

Without any conscious awareness, I quietly dropped all the brushes on the table, staring at the painting in progress while I cleaned my hands with a rag. I retreated backwards to the open kitchen, gazing nervously at the easel. Two hours had elapsed in a moment. Was it a good idea to take a break—or should I have continued? This is often the question on my mind. Sometimes, with small canvases, I would not stop painting until the work had been completed in order to keep the flow of delivery intact. On this occasion, I unconsciously opted to take a break for a plate of spaghetti, a glass of red Chianti, and the customary espresso after lunch. I wanted to resume work immediately but managed to control the impulse in order to get back to the easel with renewed energy.

As soon as I tied the strings of my black painting smock again, the pace picked up. I rendered the reflections in the foreground, at the very bottom of the canvas, in a crescendo of larger strokes that added a reddish glow in a muted dance of chromatic effects. I found myself pacing back and forth in front of the easel, mixing colors, cleaning brushes with turpentine, adding a couple of smaller clean brushes in my left hand. All in the same breath I proceeded to paint in a small leftover area of the canvas in light cerulean tones, in an effort to capture the reflection of the sky as it merged with the tiny shapes of a few fishing vessels in the distance.

Two more hours passed, yet it seemed only minutes. I worked on, touching up a few of the masts that were reflected in broken patterns in the water below, to simulate an overall sense of undulating motion. I was pleased with this new creature. To the casually observant eye, the piece offered some delightful, purely descriptive qualities, but I found in it a deep range of personal emotions. I inscribed on the verso of the canvas "Painted in San Francisco," and kept this work as a reminder of a time often imbued with melancholy.

A solitary rhythm had been established and the painting continued. From this city of maritime blue skies etched into a lavender twilight skyline, a new passion emerged with a new palette and a stronger, more expressive, brushwork. The patterns of my Laguna Beach life had vanished. The sound of fog horns, the cool sunlight of San Francisco, and the crowded streets beneath a constantly shifting gray sky composed the fabric of a new life—a life observed from a table and jukebox music at Caffe Puccini or through the large windows of Caffe Roma on Columbus Street. This was North Beach, the Italian and bohemian center of the city with its historical coffee shops, each no more than a block from another, tucked between innumerable storefronts—delicatessens, patisseries, flower shops, bakeries, restaurants, and of course the City Lights Book store of Lawrence Ferlinghetti, the distinguished poet who resided next door to my studio.

Conversations with Ferlinghetti were inspiring, while also often repetitive. He would usually begin his rhetoric insisting that North Beach had to be protected and then he would continue with his own lengthy list of complaints: automobiles that would destroy more of the poetry in the city; the Blue Angels attacking the sky every year in their frightening militaristic displays; and the "chain stores" he referred to as "chain gangs." The poet had a particular dislike for these businesses that were killing off long-established independent stores, wiping out local color and tradition and, in the case of bookstores, literary history. There was nothing that I particularly disagreed with in what he had to say, including his suggestion of closing part of the original inner city to cars similar to the historic centers of some European cities. I wonder what his thoughts would be, now that San Francisco has exploded and has almost completely been taken over by the clever brood of workers from the Silicon Valley. But at the time, my eyes could see only a city that appeared beautiful, somewhat mysterious, perhaps provincial, strangely magnetic, and endlessly enigmatic.

* * *

Nicola arrived for the first time in San Francisco with Diane, though he was soon to travel on his own in the care of the Air California flight attendants. I drove to Oakland to pick them up at the airport, anxious to spend time with both of them. As soon as he saw me, Nicola ran toward me, arms wide: "Papa! Papa!" Diane looked on, smiling. Back at the studio he started running in circles, scurrying around the canvases, easels, tables full of paint, and brushes. "I am going to get you," I said, crouching down, taking big, long ogre steps. "Got you!" I said, hoisting him up in the air. Diane turned around to watch us, our laughter roared back at us from the ceiling. Those were precious moments, full of joy and excitement, with trips everywhere, rides on the cable cars, and dinners at North Beach Restaurant. By now, this place had become my home away from home, where I found refuge and warmth late at night after painting. Lorenzo, the owner, became my friend. He would personally deliver Nicola's favorite dish to the table, Veal Milanese, accompanied by their famous hand cut fried potatoes seasoned with fresh sage. This was a remarkable establishment—the epicenter for San Franciscans of all social standings—that specialised in authentic Tuscan cuisine. I would eventually meet them all—judges and mayors, doctors, teachers, artists, musicians, real estate agents, and tourists from all parts of the globe. One of them I met nearby, in the middle of Stockton Street, as he came out from the Cavalli Bookstore with a copy of my large monograph in his hands. "Maestro, would you please autograph your book..." he asked, "for me and my wife Clare?" His name was Cliff Abbey. They both became part of my life in this marvelous city. Most of my new friends would meet here for lunch as well, enjoying the Halibut alla Livornese or grilled swordfish with Swiss chard. I usually sat at a favorite window table overlooking Stockton Street, which was alive with bustling sounds and rhythms that offered a stimulating contrast to my private sanctuary at the studio.

Following the completion of three large paintings in the houseboat series, I sensed my attention was shifting to the city itself because my attraction to this urban landscape had increased dramatically. I found myself perched up high on Telegraph Hill, gazing at the marina below and the piers laid down across the deep blue water while in the distance I could catch a glimpse of the outline of the Golden Gate Bridge through constantly shifting fog banks. Russian Hill offered a spectacular view as well in the late afternoon, gradually descending from the top of Green Street—one of my preferred vantage points—to the houses below, flooded with warm sunlight that merged with the bay and the sky above, and colored with intense shapes of cobalt blue. I found in these views a strangely beautiful panorama, a chaotic field of images of random accumulations of houses, tenements, and architectural structures—all of which attracted me. Painting pictures from these visions was like trying to find the hidden truth behind them, in a naturally intricate process that involved a good deal of fear and posturing.

Working in oil with a dark crimson red in the middle of a canvas, I began to sketch the numerous shapes of buildings and other smaller constructions where they merged with the water below. It suggested the outline of a body of land from a distance, protruding from the right side, under a sky I was planning to paint in various tones of dark and light blue. On the left side of the canvas large tree branches sketched in black began to take shape, going from the bottom to three quarters of the way up the canvas against the blues of the sky. The foreground had no definition other than the outlines of a few large structures. Then I found myself going back to the middle of the canvas, applying a frenzy of small strokes to evoke some of the chaos seen through the branches of the tree; and then on to the right side, where with a few strokes I outlined the church of Saints Peter and Paul that came into view from Washington Square. I paused for a moment and stepped back to see what I had done so far. I liked the dramatic balance of the scene. Not wanting to lose the gestural sketch marks currently present on the surface, I was not sure how to hold the work together as a whole, but I had been here before and I proceeded to attack the surface energetically, working from left to right. The tree trunk and branches began to take a clearer shape in dark tones of muted greens and rusty reds. Some of the strokes I had previously made on the very left appeared almost black, breaking through the tree at intervals and allowing a glimpse of the housing structures, now painted in a deep golden variation of ocher and mustard-orange. On the right, the church appeared in shades of muted blue-gray tones, all the way up to the spires.

I took a break. Was this work OK? Gazing at the surface of the picture, I was still not able to answer the question one way or another. As I continued examining the canvas from different angles, paint dripping all over, I arrived at a decisive moment. I came back to the scene and instinctively started sketching the foreground in black paint over the previous outline, a concrete stone terrace with columns from which to see through to the mass of landscape below. The creative process eradicates shallow assumptions in favor of deeper truths. But this time the act of painting was yielding an unexpected outcome. The terrace railing was solid, anchoring the composition from side to side. I was applying the brush strokes in rapid succession, in a multitude of tones of deep ultramarine gray-blues, with slightly lighter highlights on the left of each column to suggest the roundness of their spiral stone elements. I dropped everything I was holding onto the worktable and stood there for a few moments, utterly exhausted. Then I began cleaning brushes and reconditioning paint in the open jars. I always enjoy this part of the process, in the course of which I am constantly gazing at the work on the easel, often nervously taking mental notes for the following painting session. At this stage, there is no way you can resolve the picture or quell your unsettled feelings. There comes a moment in the creation of a painting when the work is what it is, whether or not you are ready to live with it; it would be dishonest to force it to be anything other than what it is.

The following day the unfinished blue terrace, as I had begun to call it, was anxiously awaiting me. The smell of fresh paint pervaded the studio. I felt that I was actually breathing through the canvas as the activity around the easel began again while I slowly and quietly began touching and selecting brushes, opening tubes and cans, moving them around on the table, and mixing paint without even looking into the bowls. A few moments later I found myself approaching the canvas, touching up certain parts already painted, as if to re-establish the rhythm of the previous day. And pretty soon the strokes seemed to pick up their own pace as I applied numerous shades of blue in the water to create the right tone in juxtaposition with the hot coloration of the residential construction merging with the bay. I could hear the music playing in the studio for the first time now as I moved back and forth to the canvas with a sheaf of brushes in my hand, dipping into jars of paint and linseed oil to keep the right consistency; moving and sweeping in and gazing at the painting's surface to catch the moment, to catch that elusive spot where I could drop in the exact right tone and highlight to make the canvas sing. Continuing this dance led me back into the furthermost part of the painting, the background—in this case, the large overhanging sky. The background, for me, is always the last area to be painted, the area that makes or breaks it. But no fear now. The rhythm was pressing, the urgency unstoppable. The large, flat brushes swept across the upper part of the canvas, close-up now, with a mixture of gray Prussian blue, gray cobalt—and gray ultramarine to register the darkest hue, from which to descend chromatically through the sky with hundreds of strokes and subtle shapes. Lighter tints of light gray-greens and pale cerulean, all were applied with additional rapid brushstrokes, adding dimension to the stretch of sky that now pushed further and further back into the distance. The horizon was now defined in light lavender and blue-violets merging with the water, partly visible through the tree branches on the left side of the canvas.

The phone rang. I did not pick up. I listened to the message later. It was Louis Stern, reminding me that the deadline for my next show was approaching. It was scheduled to open in May, and we would need transparencies of the new pieces for the catalog. My exhibition, he told me, would mark his last show as director of the Wally Findlay Gallery in Beverly Hills. It was time for him to move on, and he was opening his own venue. He asked me to consider allowing him to represent me at the new Louis Stern Gallery. By this time we had become good friends, and I knew him to be knowledgeable and trustworthy, so I had to seriously consider his offer.

Once finished with the canvas, I titled it *San Francisco Terrace*. I recall it as a solid painting, rich with expressive coloration and emotional tone. The work I produced at the end of 1981 and the beginning of 1982 had a special meaning to me, in that the act of discovery and the act of execution had become simultaneous. That restless, persistent quest for an aesthetic point of view became a key element in the process of my work. A slight distortion of the image also began to appear at that time, achieved through the overlay of chromatic elements. Paintings like *Filbert Downgrade* and *Telegraph Hill* reflected the essence of this evolution, while still maintaining the underlying characteristics that had become my recognizable style. I began to sign all of the new paintings with a small round brush, using a tint or a shade that complimented the color of each work. Then on the verso—a practice started in the early seventies—I inscribed the title, my name, and the catalog number which included the date of the completion of the piece. I have always enjoyed this ritual, which feels like issuing a birth certificate for each of the new creatures I have brought into existence.

And then, one splendid morning in February of 1982, a few months before my upcoming exhibition in Beverly Hills, I received astonishing news from the Italian consul in Los Angeles: I had been honored with a knighthood in the Order of Merit of the Italian Republic by President Sandro Pertini. I was stunned and did not know how to take it all in. My immediate reaction was total silence, with the feeling that I could not talk to anyone about it. So I just continued painting for a while, before reaching for the phone to share the news with the only person whom I knew would understand what I was feeling: my father. There was silence for a moment when I told him; I could sense through the telephone wire that Papa was deeply moved. In his own gentle, loving, eloquent way he managed to convey a sense of the immense personal pleasure I had given him. Hanging up, I went back to my painting. At peace with myself and surrounded by my work, I felt embraced by my father's love. All around me, the news—exciting as it was—seemed to resonate silently in the studio and reach through to the core of my existence. Who was I to have earned the highest honor of my homeland? I had no answer, and as I picked up the rhythm again and the strokes resumed their flow, my question seemed slowly to dissolve into the paint.

With the opening of the Beverly Hills show approaching, I was already anxious to get back to the studio, but at the same time I was feeling a good deal of anticipation and excitement about my return to Southern California. Unlike other artists I know who dislike openings and rely on other people to take care of such things for them, I have always been comfortable participating in these events and never thought of them as "something to get through" or an "ordeal to be endured." Even though nothing creative takes place at openings and the important work happens long before the exhibition, I also enjoy spending time with the people who make the journey to the gallery for the simple pleasure of seeing my artwork. As part of the plan discussed with Louis Stern, I attended the show with Diane, despite our separation, in order to avoid sending negative signals to our loyal collectors. I had moved to San Francisco less than a year before, but it seemed much longer. Now the relocation and my new life up north contributed greatly to my state of mind as we walked down Rodeo Drive towards the Wally Findlay Galleries. Diane looked striking, as usual, and the photographer met us right outside in front of the gallery's large window display. I'll admit that I enjoyed being in the Beverly Hills crowd again, with numerous figures from the entertainment industry, as well as a contingency of new collectors from San Francisco. Among them was my new friend Oliviero, who surprised me at the opening with his contagious smile. He was an elegant elderly gentleman from Florence who spent six months of the year in Carmel and was a famous retired restaurateur (*Oliviero* in Florence, *Club 84* in Rome). His humor, his stories, and our birthplace were our wonderful common ground in the course of many late dinners together in San Francisco. I loved his tale about the gift he was once offered of a Lucio Fontana painting. He declined the gift, stating that he was able to slice canvases on his own.

Once in the gallery, I began to recall how I had made the paintings. I went through the entire process of their creation from conception to birth. Unlike other pleasures in life, where feelings fade quickly as the memory of details becomes cloudy, I find that with paintings I frequently remember everything—whether the creative instinct flowed naturally, or I was distracted in the process, or trying too hard. It's all there on the surface of the canvas. The painting *San Francisco Terrace* generated a good deal of comment at the opening, along with *Houseboats III* and *Telegraph Hill*—the cover illustration for the catalog. These paintings laid the groundwork for themes I would develop further, and they were the first pieces to be acquired by collectors that night. During a time when painting had been declared dead by the elite American art critic, I was convinced of the opposite and would work even harder to capture the authenticity of my experiences by painting rich images of what captivated my imagination. I was conscious of the fact that my paintings were far from anything that could be considered avant-garde, that I was working precisely in a tradition that many critics dismissed out of hand as outdated. But I was painting the only way I knew how or cared to. No matter how often I continued to question my natural instincts, I was well aware that I had no choice. No critical theory has the power to uproot us from the ground that has nourished us.

Louis Stern had once again proved his expertise with the installation of the show and a catalog that included an exquisitely written introduction bearing his own signature. He did not miss a detail, including reservations for dinner, prepared for us all that night by Wolfgang Puck at his newly opened restaurant Spago on Sunset Boulevard. At the end of the opening, right before we left the gallery, a man who had purchased my large monograph asked me if I could please autograph the book and inscribe it to his aunt. "Of course, it would be my pleasure," I said. "What is her name and what may I write to her?"

His polite reply: "Just write, To Audrey Hepburn."

11

THE INNER STRUGGLE

1982–1988

My new life was transformed by my decision to work with Louis Stern as both my agent and dealer. Louis had never followed trends. He had the unique ability to recognize talent when he saw it and possessed an intuitive sense for authenticity. Relations between an artist and his representative can be tense when their interests diverge, but in this instance, we were leaving the Wally Findlay Galleries together, because the arrangement had become stagnant and conventional for both of us. I knew I was taking a big risk in leaving a well-established gallery, but I was attracted to my friend's offer because of his integrity as a dealer. Louis wanted to open a contemporary venue in his own name, reflecting his personal taste in art, and I was grateful to be included in his project. I had the feeling that he was capable of carrying me further as an artist, but could not yet imagine, at the time, the implications of my decision. While searching for a suitable space, Louis was already operating under the name of Louis Stern Galleries from his office in Beverly Hills. I had no problem with the wait, since I knew that we would work well together.

So once again my journey had taken an unexpected turn. At the beginning of the 1980s, the art world was starting to explode in new directions. European artists had begun to make their presence known in America, gaining access to the once locked-up New York art establishment. Curators and historians who claimed to predict future directions had been proven wrong, failing to understand that the primacy of abstract painting was over. It became apparent that no one style would dominate the art world in the near future, as artists pursued their quest for an individual identity. Traditional standards of quality disappeared in favor of the illusory and ephemeral significance of discovering something new. This allowed new and effervescent art forms to bubble up to the surface—art that often incorporated strategies of appropriation and exploited pop imagery as a substitute for craft. It was, as I saw it, a decadent art—clever but eventually meaningless. The justification for this mockery was even more pathetic with artists claiming their paintings were not meaningless but were rather paintings about meaninglessness. It was fascinating to watch it all unfold. Art writers, professionals whose careers depended on being on the right side of the fence, had to be extraordinarily vigilant. It would have been disastrous for them to promote a new talent or theory, only to have the critical consensus decide otherwise; and yet, if they waited too long, someone else might steal the credit for being the first to spot it. Their thought process was almost palpable as they watched and waited for an artist's next move. When it happened, they would pounce, hungry to be the first critic—along with dealers, curators, or collectors—to hype the latest product of the day, or to purchase it, or include it in a museum exhibition. Others, who were smart enough to be aware of what was going on, would wait just long enough before adapting their own model to bring it more in line with the latest trend.

Critics rushed to be the first in print with their reviews—though very little of what was published in art journals made the slightest sense. It would take a while for the dust to settle, for reason and judgment to regain the upper hand, and for the pitfalls of misjudgement to subside. Pronouncements about the death of painting had been around since the late 1960s, and it has already taken some time for a significant reassessment to take place. Even today, the issue remains unresolved in the minds of some art "experts," thanks largely to the posturing and hype that have camouflaged the real issues, not to mention the large sums of money that have been invested in new media.

For better or worse, the commercial world in which the artist is constrained to live within today is dominated by fads and fashion. Anything outside the accepted norms, no matter how good or interesting in its own right, is considered a peripheral interest at best. There are subtle, generally unspoken guidelines as to what is to be taken seriously and what is not. The fact that these guidelines are nowhere explicitly spelled out makes very little difference. Anyone who visits museums regularly, talks to curators, or reads art magazines knows well what is accepted and what is barely tolerated. Even as the language of contemporary art becomes more and more incomprehensible, there is a thriving market in which dollars flow in multiples of millions, and where the public is overpowered by a mere handful of collectors who "invest" in those works the market deems important and valuable. From time to time, I've had the dubious pleasure of talking with some of these dealers, curators, critics, and collectors—those reputed to be knowledgeable of the current art world, the ones who make the decisions. They love to banter with me after returning from their travels in Italy with their spouses—especially Florence, since I was born and raised there—and spout idiocies like: "It was in Florence that I discovered Michelangelo and Donatello." Discovered? Thus do these people reveal the naked truth about themselves. Or else, "We saw that other famous Florentine artist, Titian, in the Santa Maria cathedral in Florence . . . " Titian, of course, was from Venice, not Florence, and the work they're referring to is the *Assumption of the Virgin,* also in Venice but in the church of Santa Maria Gloriosa dei Frari. At least the "Santa Maria" was correct!

In the quest for originality in creating a work of art, it's true that something new must occur: the artist in some way must break from the values of the past. Real artists, in painting as well as in every other art form, will have taken the time to study and digest the great lessons of the past *before* presuming to interpret and revolutionize them in their own work. Today, unfortunately, the majority of so-called avant-garde artists think they can trash these values without knowing anything about them in the first place, without owning them; they destroy what they don't even know, and the effect becomes simply mechanical. And this misapprehension is passed on too readily to the viewer, who mistakes what is, in fact, no more than basic ignorance masquerading as complexity of thought. The study and understanding of prior art was an essential part of the aesthetic experience as Giotto showed us in his own revolution of 1305 when he painted the frescoes in the Scrovegni Chapel in Padua. Up until that moment, the relationship between art and the public was characterized by an act of faith; in other words, religious congregations were privy to art because churches at that time were the galleries and museums. The act of faith was in the representation of Christ, Madonna, and the saints. To get his message across, Giotto instead chose to transform these religious figures into everyday people, which opened up access to his paintings to a much broader audience than the narrow circle of educated clerics.

While some paintings can communicate immediately, others may need an intermediary, such as an art critic. But there are critics who, even looking at a readily accessible artwork, choose to complicate the issue in order to make their own discourse and their own role more interesting. Many of them seem to delight in spinning verbal webs that confuse rather than clarify. One of their more annoying assumptions is that art needs to be classified as either "good" or "bad," and that it is the critic's responsibility to decide which is which. In my view, it's not the technical qualities of the work but the intensity of the artistic process that counts, the pressure under which the creative act takes place. Some people respond to the expression of sincere emotion in art, while others appreciate technical excellence. But there are very few who can recognize when the expression of significant emotion comes from the artwork itself—and not from the personal life story of the artist. Emotion in art is transpersonal, and the artist cannot achieve it without surrendering totally to the artwork.

According to the art historian Vittorio Sgarbi, there are two types of creative art makers: the supreme artists, who are able to represent both reason and passion, instinct and feeling, in a single breath, such as in the works by Rembrandt, Michelangelo, Velazquez—artists who grab your attention by recreating the world as it is, the world that you, the viewer, experience in the living and the feeling of daily life. From tragedy and suffering to love, passion, and death, you sense the entire range of human experience in their works. And then there are others who seem to direct all their energy into passion at the expense of reason. Artists whose work is primarily emotional would include, for instance, Giorgione and Titian, who manage to communicate largely through sensitivity and feeling, whereas the paintings of Vincent Van Gogh reflect passion and intuition. By contrast, Piero della Francesca would belong in the former category; his works represent a greater rationality and project both physical excitement and intellectual engagement.

In my own development, the artists I was most drawn to, and whose painterly sensibilities I was attracted to early on, were Vincent Van Gogh and Oscar Kokoschka. My teacher and mentor Silvio Loffredo was a pupil of Kokoschka in Salzburg at his "School of Seeing," which he founded in 1953. He taught students that careful observation must be filtered through the artist's inner vision to produce an "expression" of feelings in their own work. Silvio Loffredo was born to Italian parents in Paris, where he met Picasso and Modigliani and exhibited there from 1949 to 1954. I consider myself fortunate to have inherited Kokoschka's lyrical expressionism through Loffredo's guidance in his magnificent studio in Florence. Kokoschka, in turn, was one of the numerous artists to be influenced by Van Gogh, whom many consider to be the first expressionist painter. Van Gogh's lesson was passed on to Picasso, Matisse, Munch, Kandinsky, and the German expressionists from Nolde to Kirchner. It included Klimt and Egon Schiele, who painted various versions of Van Gogh's *Sunflowers.* I remember well what it felt like as a young man, still jet-lagged during my stopovers in Amsterdam, to be face to face with his paintings in the Van Gogh museum. His raw delivery is unsurpassed in terms of projecting his emotions through the remarkable efficiency of his brushstrokes. With so much emphasis today placed on the value of an academic education and the perfect resume, it's astonishing to recall that this painter was practically self-taught. I relate to the dark palette of his *Potato Eaters*, which provided me with the inspiration for my painting, *Aftermath,* in 1968, and other works in my series of images of the great flood of Florence. Van Gogh's prodigious canvas is laced with darkness. It depicts a table surrounded by figures whose intensity is emphasized by the brightness that highlights their faces. There is a similar effect—and I am drawn to these darker images—in the magnificent landscape, *Starry Night*, which is painted in cool, dark colors that spark the viewer's memories and imagination; once again, a luminous quality emerges mysteriously from the darkness. An earlier piece that I like equally, *Starry Night Over the Rhone,* shares many similar qualities, except for the addition of two figures, a man and a woman in the right foreground, that give the painting an aura of profound emotion.

The light that manages to shine through darkness has been a theme that I have explored often in my work, most recently in a series of watercolors of urban landscapes for an exhibition titled *Through a Glass Darkly,* at the San Angelo Museum of Fine Art in Texas. Even though I risk getting ahead of myself here, I want to briefly mention Van Gogh's portraits and self-portraits. Best known for his landscapes, he seemed to find in painting portraits the resolution of one of his greatest ambitions, producing more than forty canvases, each one of them of varying intensity and color. These are spectacular works that project his own turbulent emotional experience and allow the viewer to peer more deeply into the artist's mind and his internal life than does the work of any other master of Western civilization.

Kokoschka absorbed Van Gogh's lesson well, producing portraits that remain unique, even among the German expressionists. As the art historian Peter Selz astutely noted, he transformed his sitters into highly individualized figures. The portraits engage the viewer's attention because of their difference and strangeness, not only from the rest of the world but from one another. Each subject has large, shadowed eyes and tensed hands, their skin painted in colors suggestive of decay, yet each of them confront us with their own peculiar characteristics, expressing primarily individuality and personal identity. At the same time, we find in these portraits the projection of the artist's own inner self.

What I learned about Kokoschka from Loffredo included his magnificent urban landscapes of European cities. What Loffredo learned directly from Kokoschka was to embrace the violation of image and the rich tonality of color that typified the extremely personalized expressionism of the Austrian master. From him I learned the use of rapid brushstrokes, full of light and vital color. Kokoschka's London scenes are among my favorite artworks, imbued as they are with his observations of that vibrant metropolis, where he painted numerous panoramas characterized by their high horizon lines. *London Chelsea Reach* is one of his most remarkable canvases. It seems to have been painted through a wide angle lens, and according to his wife's account, entirely on the spot without sketches or preliminary studies. These spectacular views of the Thames, along with his Prague and Dresden cycles, constitute one of Kokoschka's most comprehensive and satisfying series.

Van Gogh and Kokoschka were possessed of a powerful authenticity, each in his own natural theater of operation. Together, they represented a tradition of painting that I absorbed into my own work, a continuity of style that flowed in the same direction. Both of them imparted a compelling psychological necessity through the physical language of the paint. They offered me a natural path to follow.

During the early 1980s I was faced with a crescendo of activities that were coming my way, and I was often struggling to find balance between social commitments and my perennial desire to be locked up in my studio. Painting often guides me through the complexities of life and experiences that are sometimes otherwise hard to understand. It teaches me also to be observant of the passage of time, aware of the paradoxical spontaneity of its own process even as it enables me to summon memories with clarity and resolution.

The image of Caroline came to mind often during this period. Since Laguna, I had seen her only once in New York, where she was staying at a boarding house for women. After the time we had shared together, I had moved to San Francisco, where my new life there assisted me with my own personal recovery process. When I visited her in New York, we spoke at great length and understood each other well in the course of our long walks through Greenwich Village. She had not yet visited my friends as I had suggested, and I encouraged her to do so since their restaurant was located right next to where she was living. A year or more went by after our visit, before my travels brought me back to New York to attend an art fair at the Javits Center. Segal Fine Art was exhibiting my graphic work there, and I thought this would be the perfect occasion to take Ron and Maya Segal to dinner—and visit my friends who now owned two of the most popular restaurants in the city where I never had to make a reservation. Da Silvano, an authentic trattoria, was the place to go at the time. But I opted for Zinno's on 13th Street, equally excellent for rustic Tuscan cuisine, where Franco and Bruno were always ready to take care of me. I had not seen them in a while, and after a warm and lively reception and introductions for my guests, we were seated right away at a quiet table away from all the noise. A few minutes later, as we were chatting together with menus in our hands, Franco returned to the table and asked me to follow him to the front of the house where someone was waiting to meet me. I excused myself with my guests and followed him through two rooms packed with Saturday night diners. Noting the smirk on Franco's face, I was more and more curious. Could this person waiting for me be Caroline, I wondered? After all, she was living on the same street as Zinno's. But surely Franco would have mentioned her name? Approaching the large bar I spotted Bruno waving his arms about, as he always does when he talks with customers at the counter—in this case with a woman seated on the farthest stool, mostly hidden from view by a group of people drinking and socializing. At first, I could catch only a glimpse of fair skin and long blond hair cascading over her shoulders. As I made my way through the crowd, however, the woman's pose and her natural sensual appearance was enough for me to put together the image I knew so well.

It was Caroline! She turned and stood in front of me in her familiar ballerina stance, and I smiled over her shoulder at Franco as I hugged and kissed her. But I could already sense in that moment there was something not yet spoken, a kind of anticipation of something that remained to be said, and yet no one quite dared to say it. And a moment later I heard Franco talking, right there in that noisy bar where it was hard to hear anything other than broken fragments of conversation. He did not care or mind that Caroline and I had a story, I heard him saying. He was just happy that the two of them were now together, just grateful for my having introduced them. He seemed genuinely moved as he broke off into silence.... I was left in a state of utter shock, overwhelmed suddenly by a sense of loss, a feeling complicated by a whole range of other emotions. Still, I managed to convey the happiness I felt for them without a moment's hesitation.

Back in San Francisco I was able to reflect on my love story with Caroline, a story that was finally resolved in a most unexpected way, providing me with closure and a sense of release. Everything passes, like the weather, good or bad—even the present.

Much was happening during those years: shows, lectures, travel, the publication of a book, and a feature article in *Cosmopolitan*. The Louis Stern Gallery had not yet opened its doors, but Louis kept my schedule full, with two sold-out exhibitions in Oklahoma City and two more upcoming, one at the Los Angeles Municipal Art Gallery and the other at the historic Bernheim-Jeune Gallery in Paris. I still recall the fun we had in Oklahoma City. While I was conversing with patrons of the gallery at one of the openings, the owner and director, June Durland, came over and asked if I liked the red dots next to the paintings. She had a definite sense of humor and a thick southern accent, so I could not catch exactly what she meant, but it soon came to me that every one of the paintings had sold. Louis and I had barely recovered from the previous evening's event, for which I had personally prepared dinner for the gallery's VIP guest list, including a first course of spaghetti with artichokes, followed by Tuscan style pork roast with garlic and rosemary scented potatoes, and accompanied by a Ruffino Chianti wine. We were both overwhelmed not only by the warm Oklahoma hospitality, but also by the remarkable response to my work.

In 1984, there was another big event, one that I was pleased to sponsor. It was organized by Barbara Eden and Barbi Benton (Hugh Hefner's ex) in Beverly Hills to benefit children in crisis. I donated twenty-one works to be auctioned off. Throughout the years, I have always felt rewarded by contributing my artwork to support worthy causes. I have always thought it an artist's duty to share as a way of participating in the world in which we live. I'm fortunate that, for me, it has been a world of painting and happiness. In return, I have tried to make generosity the mainspring of my life.

The creative process remains as unpredictable today as it was a half century ago when I began this journey. When I am working and find myself in the flow, when I am lost in the moment, reacting intuitively to what is happening on the canvas, the meaning of my work reveals itself to me in an astonishing way. Each painting is a revelation, a process that unearths emotions buried deep in my unconscious mind.

But the risk in today's world lies in the trap of making things too easy. Anything that burdens our patience, our understanding, our skills, provides us with a fine excuse to opt for a shortcut. Drawing made simple in ten lessons, learn to play the piano in your spare time—these are the kinds of easy options we are offered. The reality that we are living is always challenging our need to understand things for ourselves and assign meaning to them. We delegate too easily, renouncing our own cultural individuality and accepting the definitions placed on us by others. But commitment to the historical moment is the responsibility of each individual and cannot be delegated to others.

What still seems to defy any shortcuts is the art of love. The practice of any art demands more than skills. It's not enough to know how to make love, it's essential to be in love with what one does. In love, the ego is eliminated. Only the beloved counts. One must be whole-heartedly in the relationship, and of it. Before the subject of a painting can be transformed into art, it must be consumed and absorbed.

The long line of my urban portraits that began in San Francisco and bear witness to the pleasure I found there, represents to me the embodiment of the unique characteristics that define this city. My first stay, a few years earlier, was brief and resulted in a single charcoal drawing. But what followed was my cycle of houseboat paintings and subsequently my love affair with the city that inspired the canvases that I exhibited in Beverly Hills. *Telegraph Hill* comes to mind as the last piece in the series, the one whose lasting impression left me with the need to get back to the studio. Coit Tower was the heart of the composition. In the lower left corner, the Saints Peter and Paul Church blended with the background in multiple tones of rose madder and orange. In this painting, I was able to create special, translucent effects that emanated from the solid matter of the cityscape and reflected a new experience of reality. I was attracted to the structural images of San Francisco viewed from numerous vantage points, and the dramatic settings of the magnificent Golden Gate Bridge and the horizon beyond.

My work became more expressive, more dynamic, and more self-referential than descriptive of its subject. I discovered Alcatraz, too, a dot in the middle of the intense blue, always projecting eerie sensations, desolate, and cold. I made hundreds of sketches to capture the presence of that abandoned prison and the aura emanating from the island. Blue was the entire mood of *Alcatraz,* with its overhanging sky above the bay and the architectural structures of the piers in the foreground. This view was intense, and my gestural brushstrokes evoked some deeply felt sensations. The act of painting was in itself an altered state.

Another work that captured a fraught, mysterious moment was *Coit Tower Night,* an emotional work characterized by large shapes of purple and charcoal gray applied quickly with the weight of my brush. Mystery is the beauty of the creative process. Once you manage to reach your true inner nature, an endless assortment of fortuitous incidents and lucky accidents flow through your process.

In contrast to the cool coloration of my earlier work, I remember the excitement I felt when I approached the canvas that would become *San Francisco Marina Dusk.* I had a creative conception of what I wanted to paint. As with the preceding paintings, I chose a view from above to create a new impression of spatial breadth; this time, however, suffused with warm light. The surface was already prepared with various washes of pale yellow-ocher, over which I had sketched the outlines of numerous trees and foliage occupying the right foreground. Merging with the cluster of housing at the center, the sketch moved slowly to the left, suggesting smaller housing structures that vanished toward the water's edge. The thin outline of the Golden Gate Bridge occupied the space just over the middle of the canvas, above which, in a sparse evocation, appeared the overhanging sky. Built to move on wheels, my large palette was prepared with jars and cans of my selected colors, already mixed and customized for what I had in mind. There was a predominance of warm colors, ranging from pale Naples yellow to peach and light orange tones, a variation of rust reds with a few sap greens and gray blues.

I took a breath, calmed myself down, and approached the easel. Tentatively, at first, I touched the canvas with a brush loaded with dark alizarin red, working right smack in the middle of the surface, delineating a few small houses and some larger ones adjacent to them. Next, I began applying flat strokes of paint that suggested the small housing complex and the larger structures to the left. I was soon inside the painting, getting into the rhythm. My brushstrokes retreated from the center of the canvas down towards the foreground. Unconsciously, I had picked up larger brushes, and the trees began to take shape in a variation of greens and rust reds to the right. As the colors hit the mark, my confidence grew. I could feel the beginnings of a silent thrill. Back and forth, the pace picked up in an intense dance as a whole scale of chromatic effects took hold of the piece and suffused the foreground. For the next three days, hours passed like moments, with only quick breaks. Two blue houses in the middle were filled in before I tackled the bridge structure, moving from left to right. Then came the light tones of the water under the bridge, with its multiple, subtle highlights. Addressing the sky now, the pace of the brushstrokes accelerated, working down from the top with hundreds of subtly different shades on the blue spectrum that nonetheless maintained the warm coloration of the canvas as a whole; then, gently descending into a pale glow of colored light that mirrored the broken hues of the water.

A few days later I sneaked up on the canvas in amazement, gazing at it with the veneration of a lover who steals a look at the beloved while she sleeps.

* * *

My annual trips to Italy in the mid-1980s were mostly during the months of July and August. These were not pilgrimages of exploration, but rather simple periods of time spent on the beach—and always the same beach, under the same blue umbrella, a habit that never failed to puzzle my friends who would travel from Rome, Venice, or Portofino, to spend a few days with me. For myself, though, the pleasure was about reuniting with my family both on the Mediterranean and in Florence. Women began to make an appearance in my life again. My first serious relationship, following the personal fiascos of the past few years, was with Sheila. With long, wavy blondish-red hair and green eyes, she was strikingly beautiful. On the surface, she seemed perfectly happy and well-adjusted, a woman with whom I thought I could establish a serious relationship. One summer I brought her with me to Italy, where we were guests of my friend Oliviero at his villa in Forte dei Marmi, on the Tuscan coast of the Mediterranean. My parents took a liking to her immediately. Even though I entered into the relationship with every good intention, I was not ready for it. I seemed to have built an inner resistance to commitments that would last for some years to come. Shortly after we returned to California, in the course of one of those silly lovers' arguments, we decided to break up.

And sometime later that year, I met Karen. She was tall, exuberant, with an imposing presence, and a short blond haircut. She was exciting and excited about life. In Italy, her name became Karina. Extraordinarily attractive, she made a great impression wherever we went. People often mistook her for the actress Brigitte Nielsen. She loved people, and in a crowd she exuded a natural energy and charm. She was a hit on Via Carducci, the main drag of Forte dei Marmi, where the shops and fashion boutiques stay open until 1:00 a.m. One evening, walking with my parents on this fashionable street, we passed the *Ristorante Lorenzo,* one of the finest in Italy. It was dinner time and Karina thought we could "just pop in for a bite"—which was an absurd idea. Lorenzo was always booked up for months in advance. But Karina insisted we should try. Papa and Mamma waited outside, too embarrassed to go in. They underestimated her. Believe me, when Lorenzo's eyes landed on "Brigitte Nielsen," we were escorted to a table without a moment's hesitation!

Forte dei Marmi is a resort town like no other on the Mediterranean coast. The name translates as "marble fortress" because of the quarries in the hills behind it. There are stories of Michelangelo escorting mules laden with huge slabs of marble through the steep, narrow passes of the Apuan Alps, past the fortress in the center of the town. But the place is better known nowadays for its beaches, barely an hour's drive from Florence on the blue-gray Tyrrhenian Sea, and in particular for its *bagni,* or bathing establishments, and the languid life that goes along with summer. It is a predominantly Italian destination, even though these days you also see Germans, Americans, and especially Russians. This is not the South of France—St. Tropez or Cannes—where the beach scene is still somewhat casual. Forte dei Marmi is an unobtrusively elegant resort where the beach is meticulously maintained by the *bagnini* (lifeguards), who rake footprints off the sand and line up the chairs and umbrellas whose color schemes vary according to the different establishments. Most bagni are very exclusive or, rather, they tend to attract people of similar tastes and social class who are also, often, from the same city. My sister Patrizia has reserved the same *bagno* for the family since 1985, and our *ombrellone* was located in the first row by the shore. It was not uncommon, back then, to see Andrea Bocelli with his voice coach, enjoying lunch at the trattoria right there at our bagno, an ideal place to get a taste of the *villeggiatura,* which is different from *vacanza.* On a villeggiatur*a,* you're actually living in a villa or summer home, and leave it only to go to the beach or to town, returning for a siesta or to change for dinner. A vacanza, on the other hand, is an exhausting "*tour de force*" packed into a few days, visiting historic sites, tramping through museums, elbow to elbow with one's traveling companions for twenty-four hours a day. By the time it's over, you're so exhausted that you need a good villeggiatura!

To break up the routine, we would often go to spend an evening in Pietrasanta, my favorite hilltop town, only a few miles away and a mecca for sculptors from all over the world because of its marble workshops, foundries, and skilled artisans. One summer while dining with Karina and Oliviero at a local trattoria, I met Fernando Botero, who told us he had purchased a home here just a couple of years earlier. One of his sculptures, *The Warrior*, stands boldly at the entrance to the town, his gift to a city that has made him an honorary citizen. Pietrasanta is a historical medieval town of Roman origin, a veritable *plein air* museum. Art parades here with all the confidence of a beautiful woman, no guidebook is needed to find her—she is on display as you walk.

I spent the rest of the summer thinking of how I could possibly stay longer, that maybe I didn't need to live full time in the city. And yet, that fall, back in San Francisco, I was happy to return to that environment as real life resumed its hectic pace. A short time later, Karen and I moved into a beautiful Victorian apartment in Pacific Heights and tried to get the hang of living together. I was determined to give it a chance. We furnished the flat with antiques and hung the walls with artwork. We had a guest room for Nicola whenever he came to town from Southern California. No more rolling out of bed in the morning, and strolling over to the easel to examine the work in progress. I had to drive to the studio. This was something new for me, but at least, I thought, I didn't have to share my space, like a couple I knew living in a warehouse in South of Market. The good thing, they tried to explain, about living with a fellow painter, is the unspoken understanding of what it takes to make your work. We give each other space, they'd say, and we support each other with a shared sense of purpose. We paint in the same space, but we put up a wall to keep our work separate. That sounded just fine for them, and I admired their dedication to each other. As I saw it, though, just being a couple was already hard enough, and when both of you are artists with ambitions and egos to match, that kind of arrangement looked particularly challenging. For me, it was out of the question to be in a relationship with someone like myself, with the same demands, the same shifting moods and all the rest of the peculiarities with which I was all too familiar. An artist's life is an interior one, in my view, self-absorbed and often selfish. So, in retrospect, my studio away from home was just fine.

In the beginning, Karen and I went out to dinner almost every night, and I began to observe that a bottle of wine between us was often not enough for her. She seemed convinced that one more bottle was a fine way to celebrate, and it made her even more incredibly social. But in fact the alcohol, I began to think, had the opposite effect: it made her disappear with company. Worse, she disappeared from the people she cared most about. It reached the point where I would often have to tell her: either you stay home and drink, or go out and stay present when you socialize with your friends. She worked hard to downplay what was obviously, by now, a drinking problem. I was convinced she drank to dull her fears and insecurities, to help her put on a show around other people. This situation was soon creating a good deal of tension between us, and affected our relationship. So she agreed to get help and we found a wellness center up in Napa, where I drove her for a two-week stay that included a daily spa and health counseling. It did not work out. Karen called me the very next day, crying into the phone and insisting that she did not have a problem; that she loved me and missed me terribly. I missed her too—and decided to pick her up.

That year, 1987, I was invited to present a lecture at the University of California in San Francisco and then drove south with Karen to attend my retrospective show (1970-1985) at the Diane Nelson Gallery in Laguna Beach. This was my former wife Diane, who welcomed my new girlfriend enthusiastically at the opening; she thought Karen was a genuine person who loved Nicola and embraced him in her life. In the summer we flew to Italy with Nicola, now eight years old and who already had his own friends at our bagno. My whole family, of course, could not wait to see him. That year we also flew from Pisa to Paris to meet with Louis Stern at the Bernheim-Jeune Gallery, where I was scheduled to have a show the following year. I was introduced to the directors, Michel and Guy-Patrice Dauberville, both descendants of the Bernheim-Jeune family. It was a truly special moment for me. I was overwhelmed with profound sensations as I stood inside this authentic temple of the arts, a historic gallery founded in 1795. I was well aware who had exhibited in this space throughout the years. The list was a long one and included such luminaries as Monet, Gauguin, Cezanne, Bonnard, Matisse, and Modigliani. It was here that Van Gogh had his first show in France in 1901.

As I continued to grapple with people and events from the past, my present was taking off in ways I never anticipated. Back in California, I returned to work on the houseboat series, completing a few large canvases that had been left in their preliminary stages before I found myself deeply engaged in the San Francisco urban portraits. My attraction to the Sausalito Harbor and its random floating habitations became as much a commentary on the notion of contemporary life on the edge, as it was an exercise in rendering the elements of air and water—both, closely associated with my work. But the selection of the available scenery was pivotal in rendering a microcosm of a larger experience. Paintings like *Houseboats IV* and *Houseboats VII,* both selected for inclusion in the Bernheim-Jeune catalog, reflected this concept in the way the real-world object was reduced to simple shapes, devoid of associative value, and in the manner in which color was used to realize my creative vision.

* * *

Mayor Tom Bradley was on hand to open the exhibition at the Los Angeles Municipal Art Gallery on Hollywood Boulevard, with more than eight hundred people in attendance. It was a Saturday night, and the local crowd was present in large numbers, but I was also happy to greet and speak with many collectors and friends who converged from all parts of California. There was excitement in the air. As I started signing posters and books, the line that quickly formed spilled out onto the sidewalks outside the museum. The exhibition catalog was published with a full bleed illustration of *San Francisco Marina Dusk* on the cover, and the text, written by the art historian

Janet Dominik, had also been translated into French, to accompany the show that was scheduled to travel to Paris the following month.

The trip to Paris was organized by my studio that included an Air France flight with approximately one hundred friends and collectors aboard. Lodging had been reserved at the Hotel Intercontinental, across from the magnificent Tuileries Gardens. On the spur of the moment, before leaving for France, Karen and I flew to Hawaii with Nicola for his spring break vacation on Kuai, the island I loved best at the time for its unique characteristics, including the stretch of sheer cliffs on the wild Napali Coast. I still hold onto a couple of the watercolors that I painted from the terrace of the Kiahuna Plantation, where we stayed in a splendid condominium above a bright manicured green lawn that merged into the sand on the beach below.

In April of 1988 in Paris, large posters of the exhibition were distributed throughout the city, encased in window boxes atop 10-foot high poles. *Houseboats IV* was the image chosen for the poster, and the one that greeted me first on my way to see the installation at the gallery. Karen and I arrived a few days early, as did my parents and sisters from Florence. Oliviero and his girlfriend, Giulia, were among the friends who traveled with us, and we were all booked at the Intercontinental. Even John, one of my soccer teammates, made the trip from Los Angeles with his wife Sharon. Despite the substantial number of guests arriving from the U.S., this was predominantly a fashionably dressed French crowd, with manners and tastes in an unmistakably European style. The gallery put on a splendid opening, and I was gratified to see guests responding to the artwork. It seemed obvious to me that their intuitive connection with my paintings was rooted in a style that resonated with a long tradition of art history in their country. The attraction, I thought, was also in the surprise they felt in seeing paintings like these in the current art environment, and in the dynamic evolution from the tradition they represented. The press, too, responded favorably in numerous publications. Among them, the critic Jacques Dubois noted in *L'amateur de l'art:*

> There is [...] an essential difference that distinguishes Sassone from the Chatou painters (Maurice de Vlaminck, Andre Derain) who created a pleasing assortment of views that captivate the viewer, while Sassone seems to integrate himself with the landscape, participating in it with the commitment of a performer and projecting himself into it, animated by his own burning enthusiasm.

Following the opening, Louis Stern hosted a special dinner for us at the Rotisserie Rivoli at the Intercontinental Hotel. Most of the paintings were sold to American collectors during the run of the exhibition. *San Francisco Marina Dusk* was purchased by a couple in California, and I later learned with great pleasure that their collection also includes paintings by Monet, Renoir, Chagall and Picasso.

12

THE HOMELESS ERA

1988 – 1994

April in Paris left me with memorable impressions upon my return to San Francisco. My spirit was riding high. I was filled with excitement and eager to catch up with work in the studio and resume my ongoing path of discovery. Painting is autobiographical. It is a process that leads you back through vivid experiences that you could neither describe nor understand at the time. It retrieves memories and feelings, bringing them back into the foreground, often with astonishing clarity. Painting is like a journey through which you reach deep into the emotions that are left buried somewhere in your unconscious mind.

My schedule of exhibitions that year concluded with several openings in both Northern and Southern California and continued through the following year with an exhibition at the Italian Cultural Institute of San Francisco in March of 1989.

The show comprised several new, large canvases that built further on the houseboat series, a theme that by now had preoccupied me for a number of years. These new paintings did little to describe the actual houseboats; all that was visible was the bow, stern, or a railing of the vessel. Rather, in these images, I selected essential elements to capture life as it played out onboard, with the inclusion of such objects as bicycles, dilapidated automobiles, and, in one case, watch dogs. I sensed in these works a loosening of the image as well, and at the same time a deeper exploration of the subject.

Sensing the need to work on a larger scale as my canvases increased in size, I began to look for a new studio. In late spring, I purchased a raw space with 15-foot high ceilings on the top floor of a downtown warehouse. It was perfect, though somewhat dark, with windows only on the north side of the loft that looked out onto an alleyway. The idea of giving up my current studio, so full of light, made me very nervous at first. But the five large skylights projected in the remodeling plans helped to quiet this momentary feeling. The design also included living quarters with a bedroom, a bathroom with a large Jacuzzi tub and bidet, a kitchen with a vented hood system, a fireplace, dark wood cabinets, and large countertops. I told myself I would not move into the new studio until it was completely finished. I would keep my present space for as long as necessary.

When construction began, I traveled to Italy for the summer to see my family, as usual, in Forte dei Marmi, at the same bagno, under the same beautiful umbrella! After two weeks, I interrupted the villeggiatura that year, having promised my son, Nicola, that we would go to the Cinque Terre on the rugged Ligurian coastline, two hours north from our base at the beach. My girlfriend, Karen, flew to Italy and met us just in time for the trip. We stayed for a week in Monterosso at the Hotel Porto Roca, which sits on sheer cliffs high above the blue Mediterranean Sea. I had been here on painting trips several times before when the Cinque Terre had not yet been discovered by tourists. The name translates as "five lands" and it is actually a group of five villages. Part of the beauty exists in the trip itself; the train goes through many tunnels along the coastline, making a stop at each of these tiny villages, carved into the hillsides amongst ancient vineyards clinging to steep terraces and overlooking breathtaking scenery. Their names—Riomaggiore, Manarola, Corniglia, Vernazza, Monterosso—add to the aura of romance about this place, whose origins date back to the eleventh century. Every afternoon we would follow Nicola, eleven years old now, down to his favorite spot, where the beach merged with a natural formation of overhanging rocks, from which we would take turns diving into the crisp, clear, deep blue water.

The trip was over too soon. I was back in San Francisco by early September, and I was not surprised to discover that the new studio was not yet ready by any means. It took another month. In fact, I remember exactly when the space was finally finished—on October 17th, the day a big earthquake struck San Francisco. I was at the easel that late afternoon. The first jolt hit a few minutes after five o'clock in the evening, and the shaking continued as I launched myself down the stairs and out through the front door. I stood in the middle of the street and watched for a few terrifying moments as the buildings swayed back and forth. I feared catastrophe. But as the aftershocks subsided, nothing collapsed, not in this part of town anyway. Apparently, though, I had done a foolish thing in leaving the studio. "Marco, what are you doing?" one of my neighbors exclaimed a few minutes later as he emerged from his house. I knew that in an earthquake you were supposed to dive under a table or stand in a doorway, but in my case that was easier said than done, especially when I saw an entire wall of large paneled windows shift frightfully with the cracking sounds of stress. I learned later that the quake was a big one, measuring 6.9 on the Richter scale, and caused enormous damages in the city and the Bay Area. That night, without electricity anywhere in town, I went to inspect the brand new studio. I knew the workers had just finished with the last coat of paint that afternoon. I entered with great anxiety, flashlight in hand, but much to my surprise there was no damage, not so much as a crack in any of the walls.

I had decided anyway to postpone the move into the new space for a while and to keep working without interrupting the present flow of painting. On the home front, my relationship with Karen was degenerating, causing another earthquake—only this one was internal. I felt like the enchantment was irreparably broken and arguments prevailed over our sense of reality. It became apparent to me that I could talk with her only in the morning. And so it was that on one of those November mornings, at the breakfast table, I told her that I had had enough and moved out of the apartment. When a certain time arrives, when you are numb, even with all the love and affection you may feel towards a person, there is no turning back. I kept painting even longer hours, perhaps as a kind of therapy to heal the effects of the breakup.

My painting schedule remained intense through the end of the year. I felt somewhat unsettled during this period, not only for the abrupt changes in my personal life, but also for the persistent state of limbo in which I found myself while I waited for the Louis Stern Gallery to open. Just recently he had been in touch to tell me that he had not yet landed on a suitable space, despite an active and ongoing search. Still, seven years had passed since I had accepted the offer to be represented by his gallery in Los Angeles—a representation which I thought was far beyond the technicality of gallery-artist relationships. He was my friend, a dealer who embraced my work, and a man I believed in, a partnership with unlimited possibility. For this reason, I continued to wait.

* * *

One late afternoon day in December of 1989, the light in my old studio was glorious as crisp air flowed in, scented by the eucalyptus tree that grew below the balcony door. I had just taken a break from painting when an unusual sight appeared suddenly before my eyes: through the large windows, opening to the street below, I saw a shopping cart so stuffed with countless layers of colorful belongings, they hardly fit into this bizarre container on wheels. A figure dressed to match, in the same motley mixture of outrageous colors, was pushing the cart along at a brisk pace. The sight was irresistible. I quickly grabbed a sketchbook and a camera and chased this character down the street without knowing exactly why. I could never have imagined the impact this encounter would have on my life. I caught up with him at the Embarcadero. We started talking and didn't stop until we reached an abandoned railroad track. The man was happy—and articulate. He loved to be out and about. The shelter was only for sleeping, he insisted. When I asked him if I could do a sketch right there and offered him some money in exchange for his time, he replied: "For sure, yeah, man." He posed for me right there on the tracks and watched me draw. He appeared to be as fascinated as I was by our encounter, but I'm sure he had no idea that I was equally taken by the imagery of his presence. I also shot a roll of film, thanked him, and made my way back to the studio. The next afternoon he walked by my studio again, perhaps hoping to pose. But that was the last time I ever saw him. His name was Willie.

A few days after this encounter, I made a watercolor sketch of railroad tracks in a blue-gray coloration. I was puzzled at first. Why, if I was so fascinated with the colorful appearance of this man who was homeless, did I paint an image of railroad tracks? As I continued to gaze at this watercolor, with pictures of Willie pasted up all around it, I had a dramatic epiphany: In a flash, I conceived an entire exhibition of artwork devoted to the homeless. I still have goosebumps as I tell the story. In 1989, the astonishing perception took me completely by surprise, and I immediately began to research the whereabouts of people like Willie. I collected daily newspaper articles on the subject and soon embarked on frequent pilgrimages to areas of the city populated by this underground society of men and women without homes.

In the midst of these activities, I finally moved into my new studio space—a move that only added to the current sense of displacement in my life. And from the new studio, I would continue with my research every day. I prepared for each outing with a pocketful of $10 bills, a camera, a sketchbook, and a stash of different pencils and charcoals in my black leather jacket. My hair was long, and I'd had a beard since 1969. Back then, I had grown the beard because I thought I looked too young. Now, I took care not to trim it, so that I'd look the part as I mingled with the people who lived on the streets. I was still not quite sure exactly what was happening. I only knew that I was irresistibly attracted to this whole new mission, to this new, surprising subject matter for my painting, to this way of living on the edge. This was the connection, I thought, with my houseboat series and the life that I had observed on board these vessels. It was life on the edge there, too, although in a different way. But there must have been some deeper connection with the homeless. Was it perhaps my friendly encounter as a child with that street bum in the 1950s? Or my experiences during the 1966 flood of Florence? Most likely both of these experiences were subconsciously affecting my current state of mind. At the time, I didn't give it too much thought; I was simply captivated by seeing these people, by talking to them, as no one else would do, by passionately drawing their faces and expressions right there on the streets of San Francisco. I had several conversations about it with my friend Tom Bradley, long-time mayor of Los Angeles, who was a great advocate of the homeless in that city. I flew down to see him once and he took me on a tour of skid row, where everyone we passed on the sidewalk said hello to the great mayor. I learned a great deal from Tom about the plague of the homeless, a crisis that was then affecting—and continues sadly to increasingly affect—all major cities in the U.S.

But my source of inspiration and personal journey of discovery continued in San Francisco. I approached my subjects one-on-one, in the same manner I had done with Willie, by offering them a $10 bill in exchange for their time. Their names were as real to me as their painful stories—diverse narratives and tragedies, but with one common denominator: a vicious downward spiral that had brought each one of them to the streets. I collected newspaper articles on the homeless, and my on-site sketches began to pile up on the floor, offering glimpses of faces and studies for possible full portraits and paintings. Some of the articles from 1989 recounted disturbing facts of the alarming numbers of unhoused people in a city whose shelters were ill equipped to handle the volume. As a result, deaths increased. An article in the *San Francisco Chronicle* in late December headlined: "110 homeless died on San Francisco streets in 1989," while an earlier article, also in the *Chronicle* was titled: "Plans to end homelessness," which proved later to be a total delusion in more ways than one. My own pictorial research was mounting too. In 1990, I made hundreds of drawings and several paintings, including a canvas, *Untitled,* measuring 72 x 81 inches, that captured a universal image of homelessness: a desolate figure sitting on a bench at night under the cold streetlights, with the dome of City Hall looming from behind. The palette was reduced to various tones of charcoal gray and brown melting in with yellow-white highlights. As I completed the painting, one of the earliest in this series, I stood for a long while in front of it to get a sense of its overall effect and its meaning to me, and then I decided to write in the lower left corner the names of cities in the U.S. with their corresponding homeless populations. The numbers were staggering: 80,000 for New York, 55,000 for Los Angeles, and 10,000 for San Francisco. While the inscription lent a narrative aspect to the canvas, it also provided extra substance to the painting itself.

Another early canvas, *Granny*, measuring 90 x 120 inches, addressed a similar theme—this time from inside a shelter. It told the story of an elderly woman seated, holding a newspaper, with her dog beside her, dejected and alone, and reflecting on the misfortune of her life. The painting's coloration was reduced to blacks and grays, with a cold yellow light to further signal her discomfort and distress.

I began to exhibit some of these works at the Chicago International Art Exhibition in 1990 and at the Basel Art Fair in Switzerland. I was also invited to show a few of them at the Jan Baum Gallery in Los Angeles, where Tom Bradley made it a point to attend the opening in order to see the progress of this new series of paintings.

Although my involvement with this new theme was my primary focus at the time, I also continued producing work consistent with my previous series. My first show in Canada reflected just that, with the inclusion of paintings and watercolors of houseboats, mostly produced the previous year, along with a number of recently completed works with Venetian themes. Glancing through the images in the exhibition catalog published by the Buschlen-Mowatt Fine Arts Gallery in Vancouver, it would have been hard to envision the emergence of the darker body of work that was currently developing in my studio. I was perplexed myself by the stark contrast between these two preoccupations, and I could certainly understand the shock of a viewer who was familiar with my earlier, more colorful work, when confronted with the bleak vision of the new. For myself, however, the difference resided primarily in the subject matter and in the reduced color palette. In other words, in terms of pure visual expression, the structural and compositional qualities I was looking for in my earlier work were no different in these homeless paintings, which were just as rich in dramatic engagement with the subject matter as in the houseboat series.

The first person to notice this dramatic engagement was Robert Whyte, the senior curator of the Museo Italo Americano, who came to see my new space. I had met Robert a few years earlier at an opening; he was a wonderful gentleman who liked the gestural aspect of my painting and who enjoyed the opportunity to practice his Italian with me on every possible occasion. "Marco," he asked, looking at some canvases stacked up against the back wall, "what are these pieces?"

"I'm painting the homeless," I told him.

"So how did this start?" he wanted to know. "How did it happen?"

I told him the whole story of my encounter with Willie, how I had chased him down to the Embarcadero and how, as a consequence, I became involved with drawing so many other people on the streets. Robert seemed very interested, so I told him more of how I met these individuals and inquired about their stories—how they ended up on the streets and how it affected them emotionally and mentally. I told him what I had discovered about their fears, and in many cases the progressive dementia that resulted from living in isolation from society. His eyes still captivated by one of the canvases, Robert described the impact these pieces had on him. This work, he said, was quite unlike anything I had done before. And, almost in the same breath, added that he would like to curate an exhibition of these paintings at the Museo Italo American in 1993 or 1994.

I remember well the turmoil of the following years that led up to the exhibition. My involvement on the streets was intensified by the need to find new faces every day. Some of the names are still with me: Mark Hollis, Rick Norman, Fred, Jeff, Dave, Marian, Linda, Joshua, Lorraine Austin, and dozens more. These were real people who posed for me, allowing me to capture a moment in their lives, a glimpse of the deprivation written on their foreheads. I felt privileged to be with them, to speak with them, sharing my experiences as a painter who had a genuine interest in their lives. Some were surprised and pleased, others confused yet still happy to receive the ten bucks. And hidden amongst these charcoal drawings there was *Massimo,* a self-portrait I made in a bathroom mirror, using my middle name as a disguise, so that I could actually be one of them.

I came to know this world well. I developed an eye, learned how to distinguish between the fake homeless and the real, the regular panhandlers, the winos, and the drug addicts. I came to understand an entire underclass of society much like our own but obviously very different. For long periods of time I would go out late in the morning and return to the studio at night, when the click of the key in the loft's deadbolt would resonate through the silence in the stairwell's dim light. Opening the door, I would blink into the darkness with visions remembered from my day amongst the homeless, and the sound of my own footsteps in the studio seemed to echo their loneliness. After a couple of years and a growing intimate understanding of life on the streets, my observations became consuming obsessions. The charcoal drawings were multiplying, with their images of internal desolation. Every morning I would see evidence of all of these beings all over the studio. They were everywhere. One in progress, always, resting on an easel; others piling up crazily on the floor. Then there were periods of painting, as I transformed my daily sketches into landscapes of brushstrokes, human landscapes that revealed the fragility of life.

Much of my early work had dealt with reflections in water; here the reflections gleamed through the translucence of so many watery eyes that mirrored anguish. I often discovered myself in these paintings. They felt like revelations. We are all accumulations of strokes. We accumulate these strokes through life. They become the baggage we carry within us from childhood, and most of the time we don't even know we are carrying baggage within us as the years progress. But then—and this can be frightening when it happens—an experience comes along and touches us deeply. We feel suddenly extra sensitive. We connect.

So these were emotional paintings, born of deep, hidden feelings. *Distances* was one of the more stressful pieces. It was conceived in 1991, and it explored the inequities of life through the presence of a pained figure in the foreground of the canvas, evoking at the same time intimations of death through the image of an abandoned mannequin. The rhythm of the brushstrokes intensified the aura of tragedy in a muted palette of gray-brown, pale ocher, and gray-ultramarine blue. And several other works elaborating on the theme of these bleak realities were in process as well.

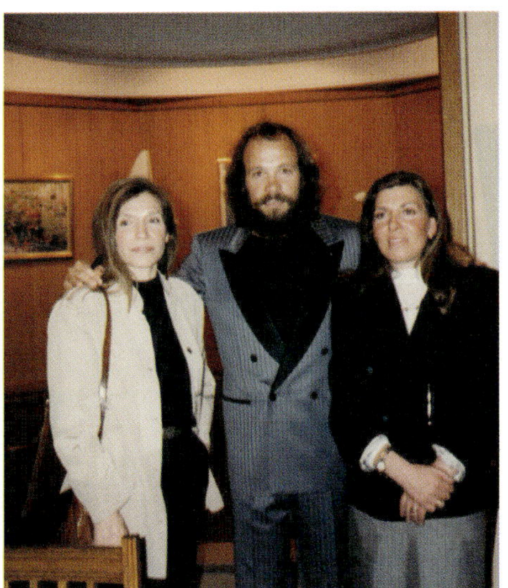

With my sisters Milly and Patrizia at my opening of the exhibition at Bernheim-Jeune in Paris, 1988. *Author's collection*

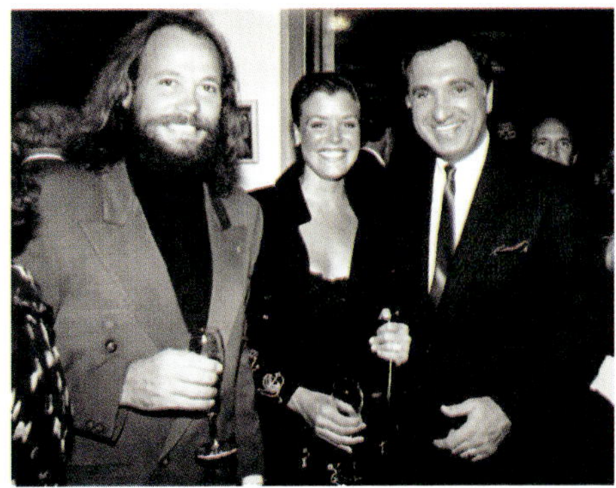

With Karen and San Francisco Mayor Art Agnos, 1989. *Author's collection*

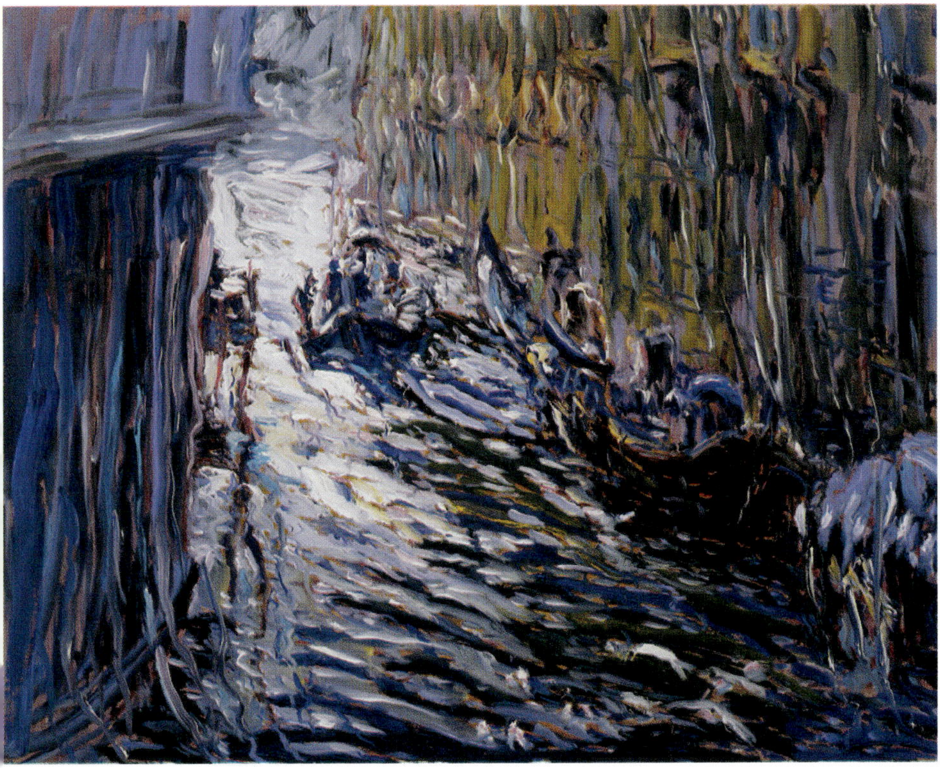

Barconi, oil on canvas, 1990. *Author's collection*

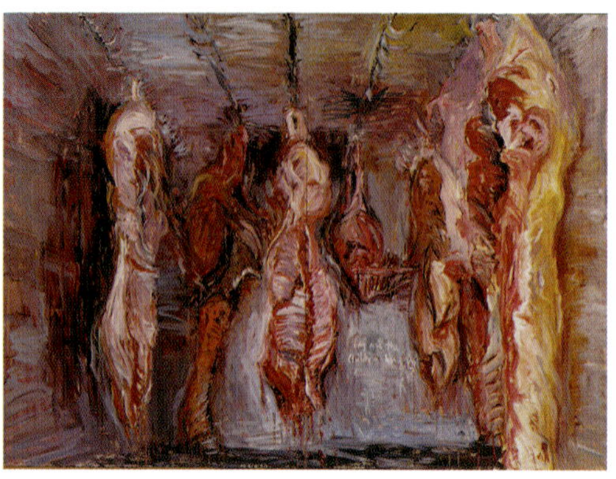

Why are the Children Hungry, oil on canvas, 1991.
Author's collection

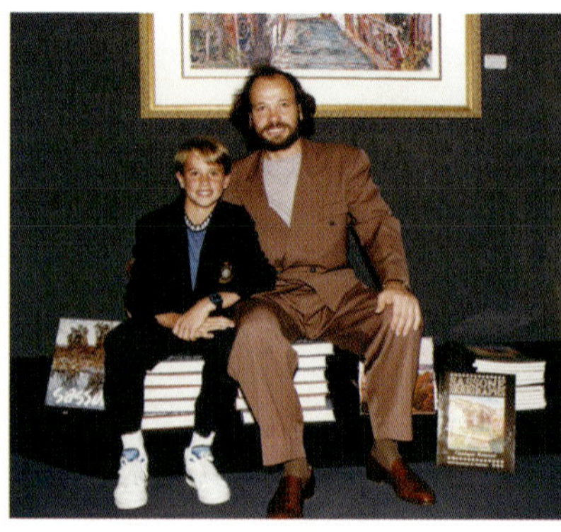

With Nicola sitting on a stack of my monographs in Chicago, 1991.
Author's collection

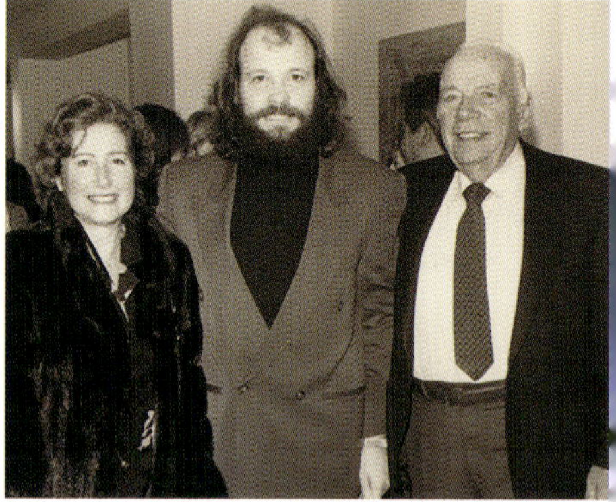

With Giulia and Oliviero at the opening of my exhibition at the Istituto Italiano di Cultura, San Francisco, 1989.
Author's collection

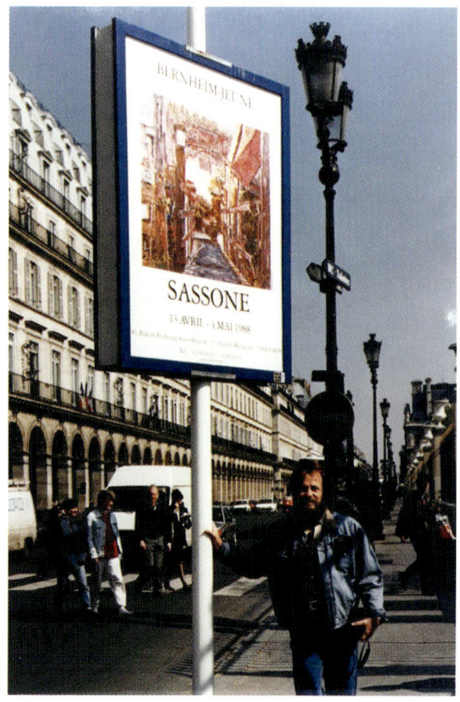

Me in Paris under one of the posters for my exhibition at Bernheim-Jeune, 1988.
Author's collection

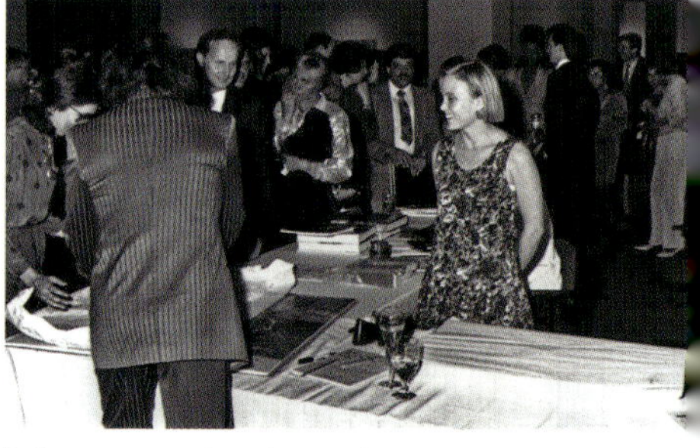

Me signing books and posters at the opening of my exhibition at the Los Angeles Municipal Art Gallery, 1988.
Author's collection / Photo by Lee Salem

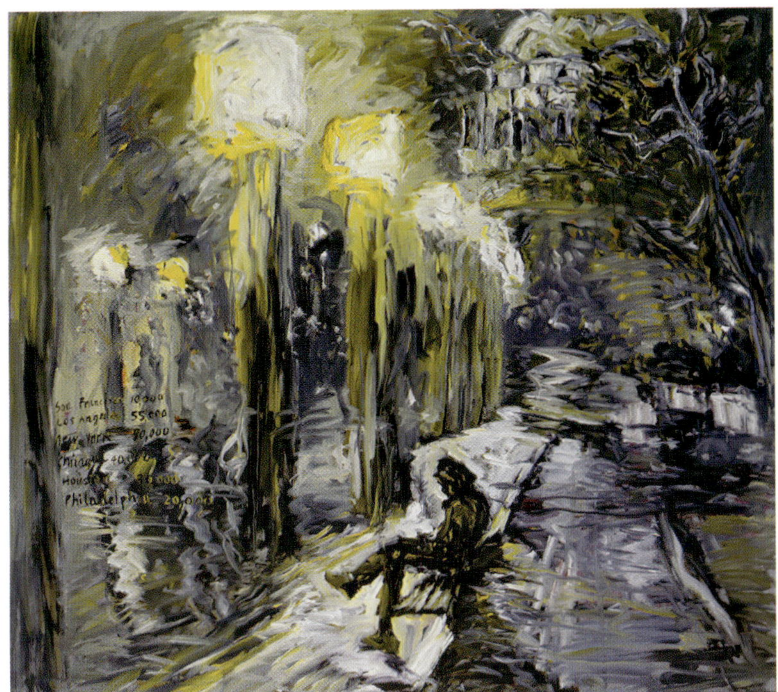

Untitled, oil on canvas, 1990. *Author's collection*

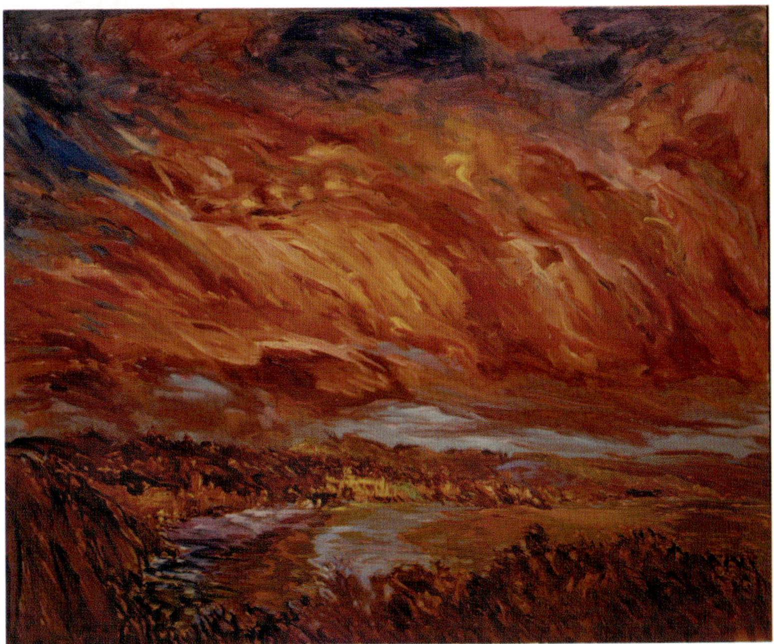

Tramonto, oil on canvas, 1991. This work was commissioned by the Ferrari-Carano estate in Sonoma County for the label of their Tresor, premium red wine. *Private collection, USA*

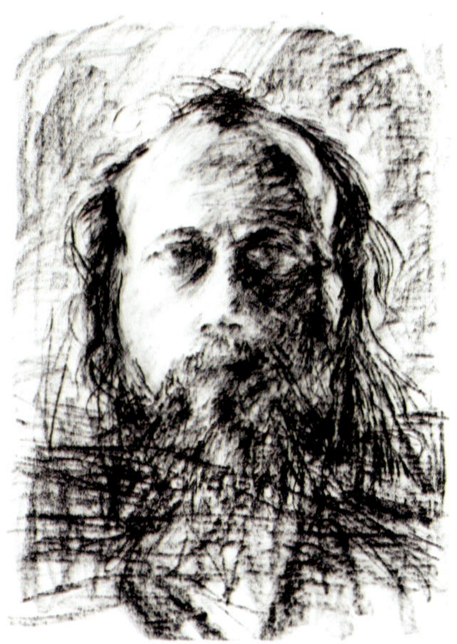

Massimo (self portrait), charcoal on paper, 1991.

Private collection, USA. ©Marco Sassone

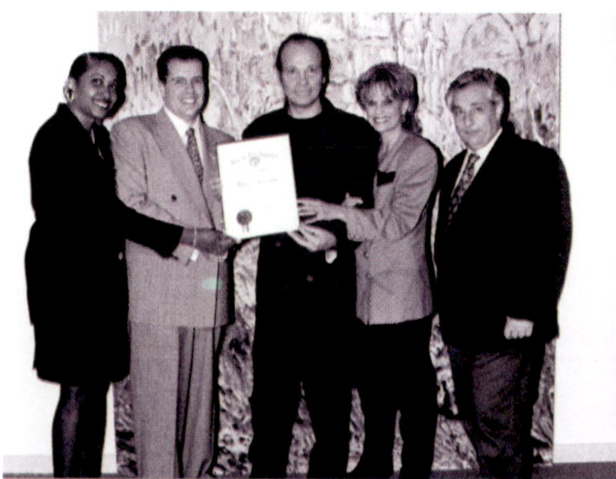

With (from left) two members of Los Angeles City Council, actress Mary Frann and Enzo Coniglio, Director, Italian Cultural Institute, 1996. *Author's collection*

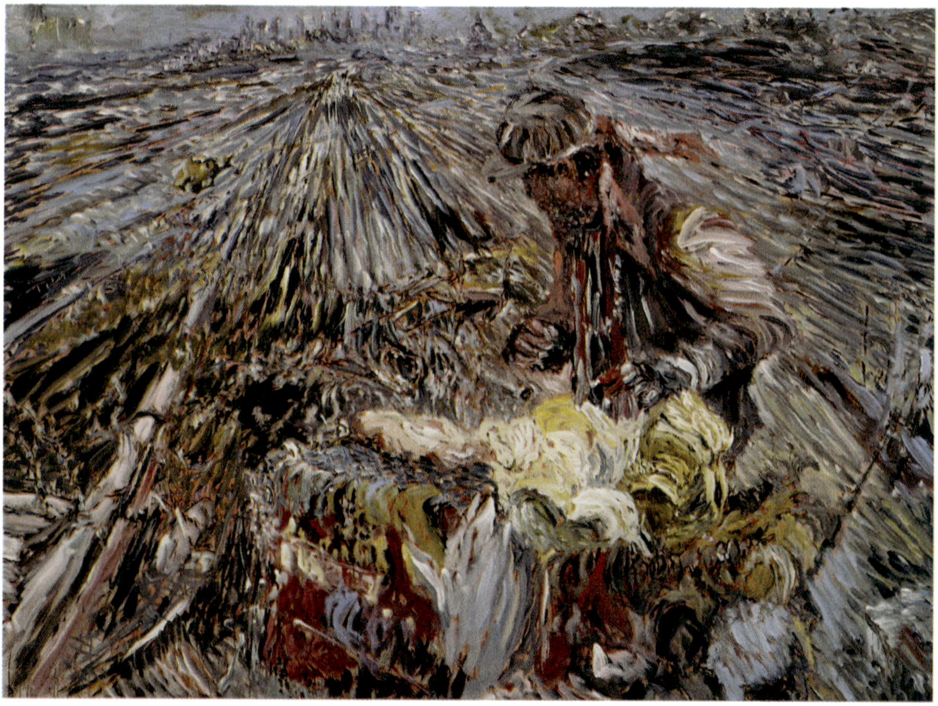

Willie, oil on canvas, 1992. *Author's collection*

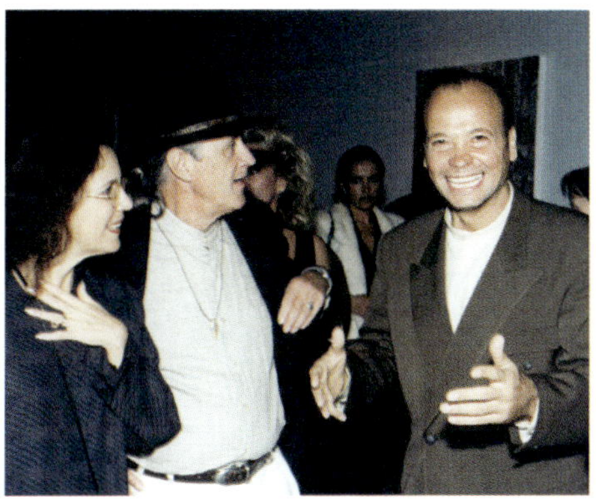

With author and art critic Peter Clothier (center) and his wife Ellie Blankfort at the opening of my exhibition at Diane Nelson Gallery, Laguna Beach, 1996.

Author's collection / Photo by Rick Lang

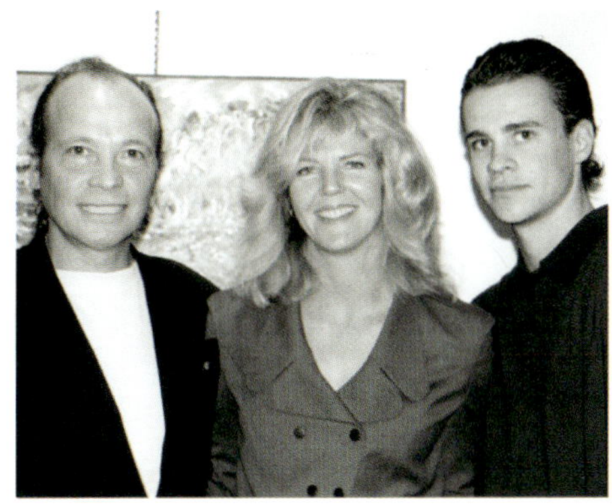

With Lee and Nicola, San Francisco, 1997.

Author's collection

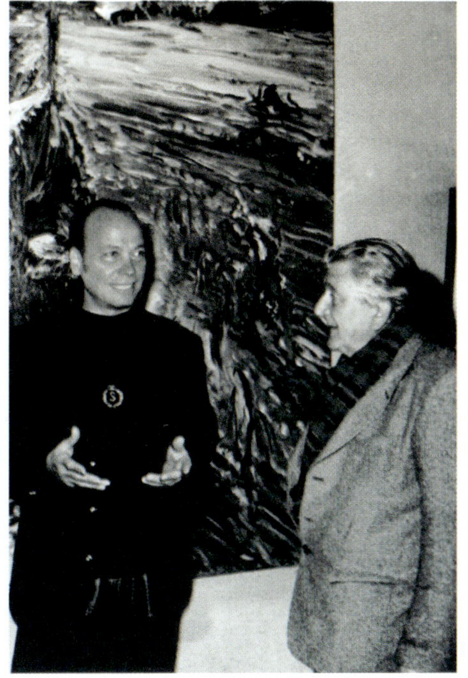

With Silvio Loffredo at the opening of Home on the Streets at the Church of Santa Croce, Florence, 1997.

Author's collection

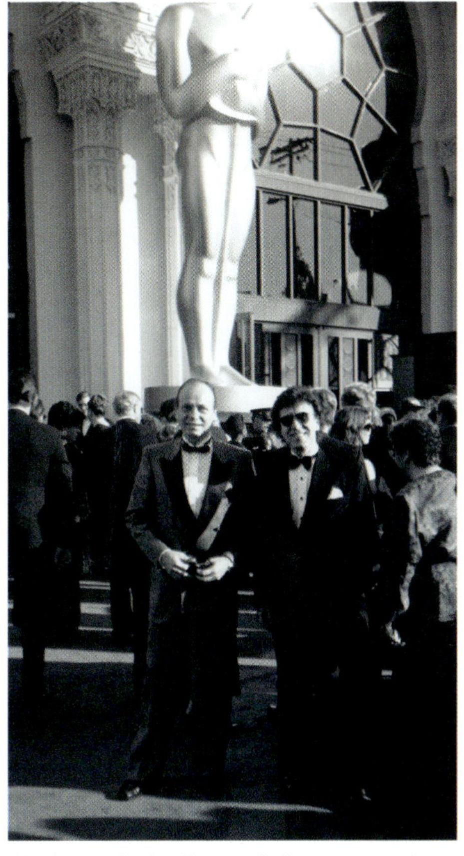

With my dealer Pasquale Iannetti at the Academy Awards, 1998. *Author's collection*

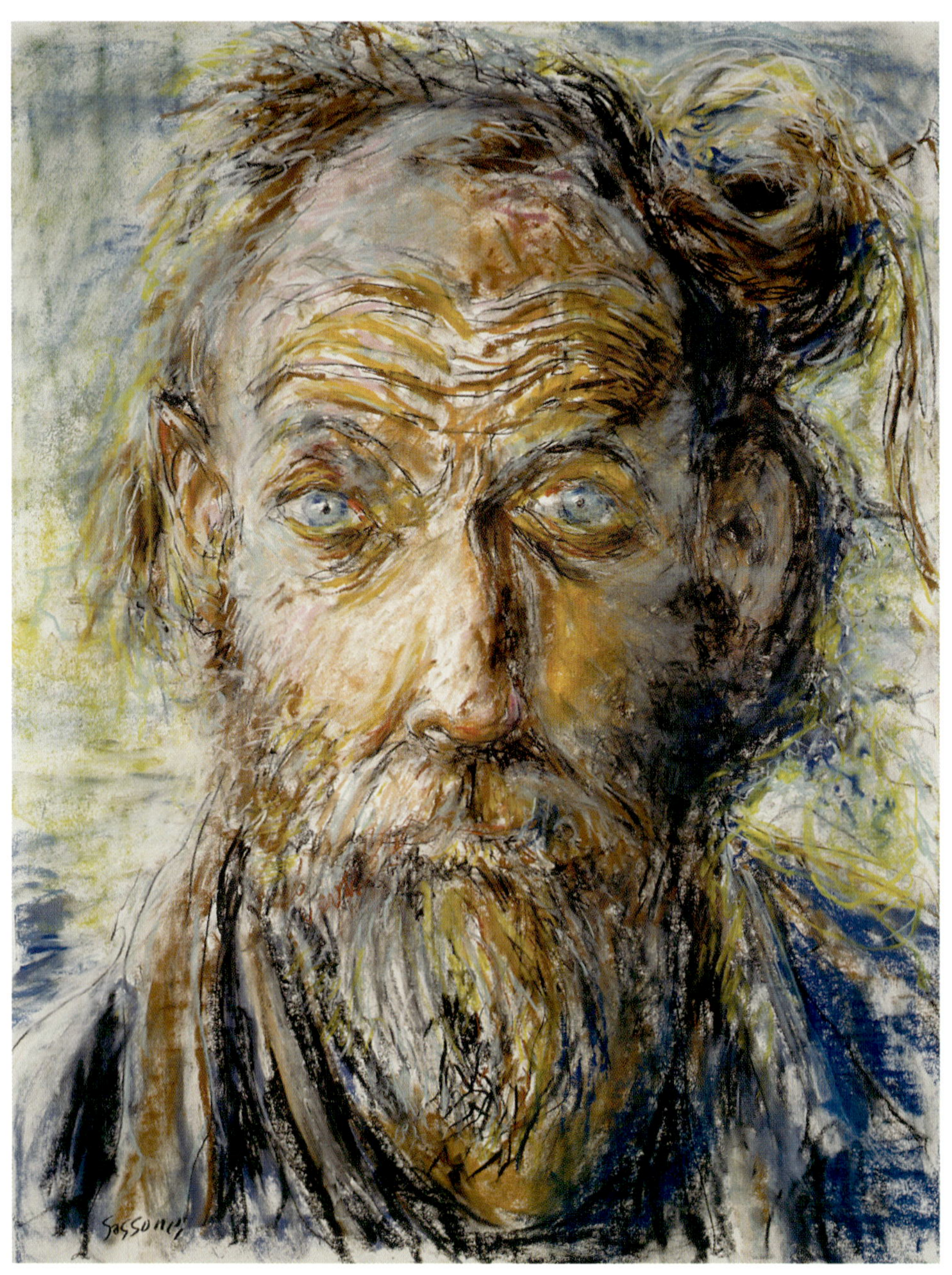

Man with Blue Eyes, pastel on paper, 2000. *Author's collection*

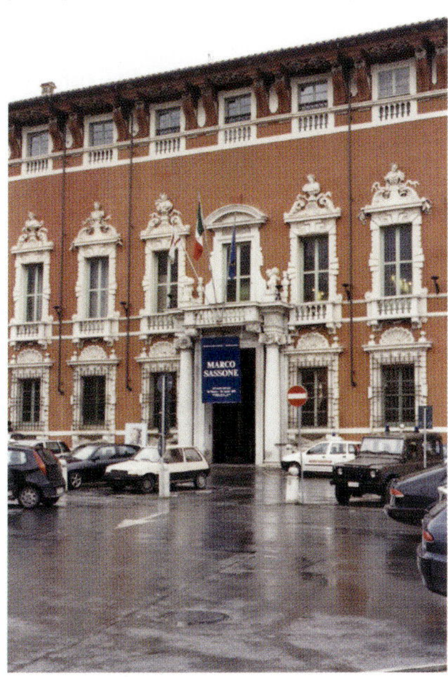

Palazzo Ducale, Massa-Carrara, presenting my retrospective exhibition in 2002. *Author's collection*

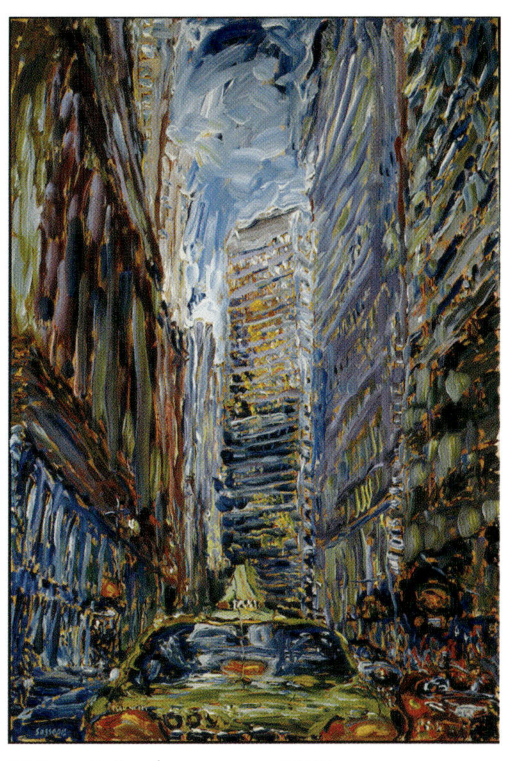

Yellow Cab, oil on canvas, 2000.
Private collection, Canada. ©Marco Sassone

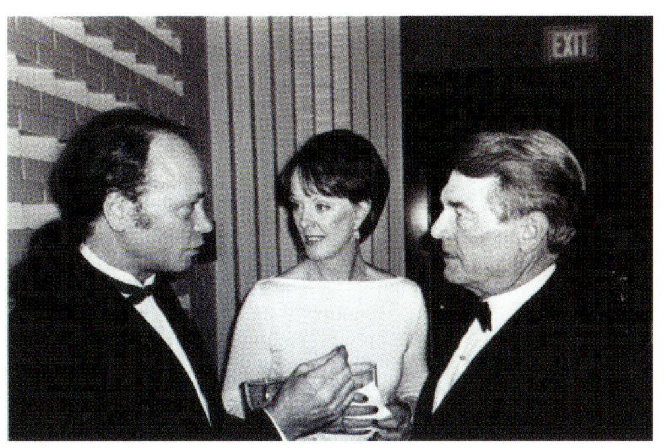

With Helen and Charles Schwab at San Francisco Museum of Modern Art, 2001.
Author collection / Photo by Anne Lawrence

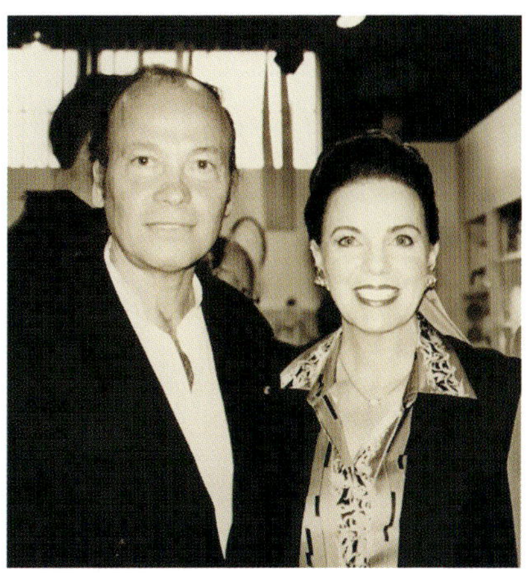

With Sylvia Bello at Museo Italo Americano, San Francisco, 2002.
Author's collection

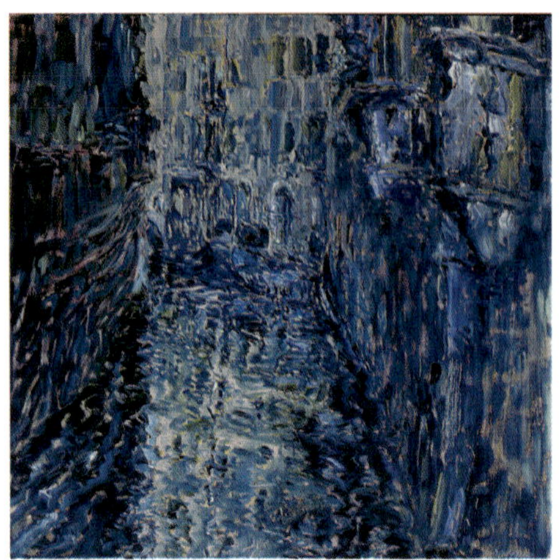

Venezia 75, oil on canvas, 2002.

Author's collection

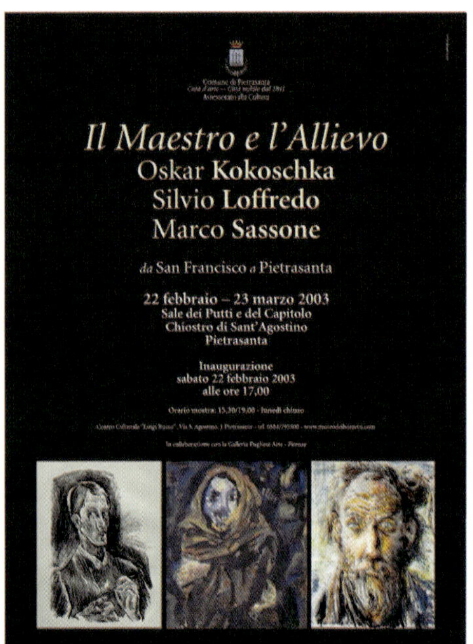

Poster for the exhibition Master and Pupil at the Pietrasanta Museum, Italy, 2003. *Author's collection*

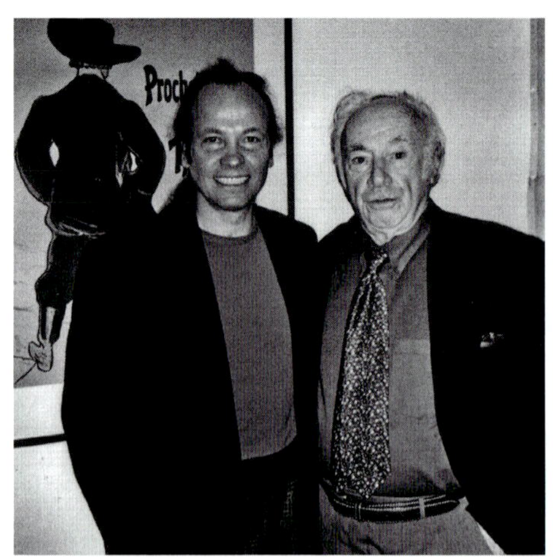

With author and art historian Peter Selz, San Francisco, 2002.

Author's collection / Photo by Anne Lawrence

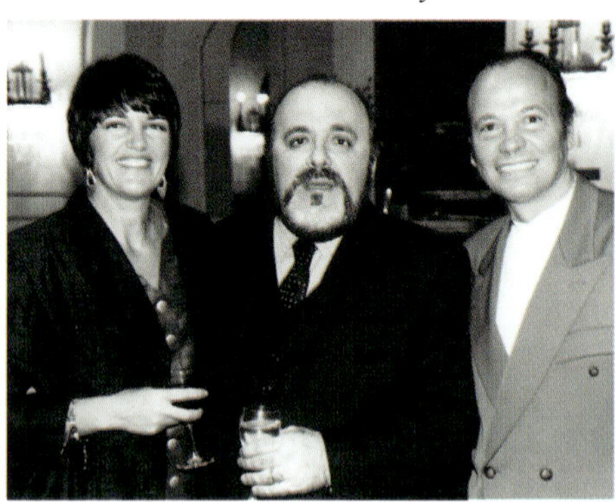

With Deborah and baritone Paolo Gavanelli, San Francisco, 2002.

Author's collection

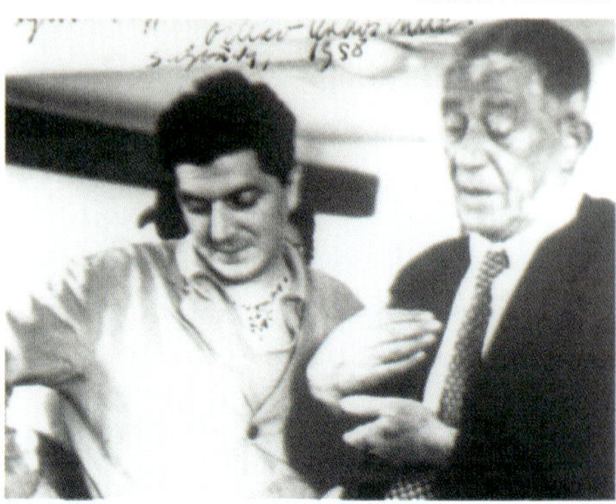

A vintage photo of my teacher Silvio Loffredo with Oskar Kokoschka in Salzburg, 1958. *Author's collection*

One night, surrounded by all my creatures, I came up with the title of the show: *Home on the Streets*, a choice that was warmly endorsed by both Robert Whyte at the museum and at my studio by my own assistants, who had been very helpful during those years with the logistics of my intense exhibition schedule. Meanwhile, the canvas for the projected painting of Willie had been waiting for a while on my largest easel. I had done some preliminary work on it, but I always seemed to end up completing other canvases instead. As with other cycles of paintings, I had several pieces in progress at the same time—some barely outlined, others more advanced with oil sketches and washes of various shapes and color. The charcoal studies with concepts for new paintings were never in short supply, but many of the studies would remain just studies. The ones that were eventually developed into paintings were selected via intuitive process. One choice might seem logical, another unpredictable. It's an organized madness that takes place in the studio, guided alternately by random thoughts and rational decisions. I never know for certain whether or not a study will become a painting.

The canvas for Willie had been prepared almost two years earlier, immediately after the relocation to my new studio. The easel, custom-made to accommodate large canvases, was placed directly below one of the large skylights that flooded the space with gorgeous natural light. My palette on wheels was readied with jars and cans of color ranging from pale, warm tones of red and yellow ocher to cool gray-blues of various tonalities. I began slowly to add structure to the outline of the figure, with the shopping cart in the center foreground. I kept looking at my original sketch, along with a few small photos pinned to the side of the easel. I wanted to maintain the freedom of the drawing, so I found myself approaching and retreating from the canvas in order to apply only the necessary elements to the surface. I started to elaborate on some of the shapes, applying spots, dots, and *staccato* dashes to suggest a center of energy beside the shopping cart; and as I moved to the left and right of the cluttered mass and the figure, I applied longer strokes, directed vertically toward a focal point in the distance, suggesting the convergence of the railroad tracks. At the very top, in bare outlines, I minimally sketched out the skyline of San Francisco.

I stood back frequently, watching this enormous piece in progress. I could sense the emergence of Willie from what appeared a wasteland, totally bereft of any other human presence. Days passed like moments, filled with anxiety each time I had to leave Willie alone, in progress, on the easel. I found myself going back to the massive foreground, applying a succession of small brushstrokes to portray some of the chaos that represented his whole life in the shopping cart. And each time I stepped backwards, I was affected by the image of the figure merging chromatically with his belongings. Then I approached the tracks on both sides of the cart with shades and tints of blue and brown, moving back and away from the foreground. I was deep inside the painting now as the pace picked up in a flurry of brushstrokes, paint dripping everywhere, working spontaneously with gray-blue converging lines that suggested hundreds of tracks running all the way to the top and vanishing into the skyline. Regaining my composure, I suddenly recognized a peculiar visual effect: the track on which Willie found himself appeared to move away from him at vertiginous speed. Emotionally exhausted, I continued painting. The pace of activity finally decreased on the uppermost area of the canvas while I started to address the tiny city structures with gray-cerulean tones, fading into a sliver of sky of similar coloration.

I have since often reflected on this piece as the expression of that vision of Willie I instantly connected with when I first glimpsed him through my studio windows two years prior.

During the years that followed, these visions continued to appear in a succession of images of persistent melancholy, images of homeless people living on the sidewalks of San Francisco, forced to sleep on bricks and cement. I needed to catch their spirit, their gaze with burning accuracy, with just a few marks grazing the surface of the paper, searching to uncover a truth which, like a curious fly, would remain entangled in their gossamer web. I saw an even more atavistic predator amongst them in *Hunger,* which became the title of a 1992 painting portraying a huge tangle of people almost swallowed up in a thick impasto of gray-blue paint. I saw existences that had no other prospect than to huddle down each evening along the sidewalks, their only hope the dawn of another abominable day. *Perspective* was the title of a very wide canvas, also dating from 1992, in which a human figure lay wrapped in a blanket with disheveled hair and ragged shoes, stretched out across the lines leading back toward a vanishing point—a fellow-human for whom there is no longer anything to hope for but the street. It's a street that leads nowhere in my painting, and one that offers no signpost to show the way but becomes the only world in which it is still possible to live.

Many of these paintings used the device of perspective to emphasize the tragic divide between the human figure in the foreground and the hint of civilization rendered with tiny city skylines in the distance—a vanishing point, a vortex, a place into which the human being disappears. *Doll-Land*, for instance, was conceived using the same element of perspective, but this time suggesting that almost anything, including dolls and children, could be homeless. I composed this work with three rows of mute doll figures facing the viewer, crowding the foreground in a frontal plane to underscore the confrontational nature of the painting. The palette of various accented tones of rust-reds and intense yellow ocher enhanced the nightmarish aspect of the canvas.

There were other works I created during these years related to the theme of homelessness but was not included in the series. One drawing that generated particular interest was selected for the exhibition *Issue of Choice*, at the Los Angeles Contemporary Exhibition (LACE) in 1992. I had rendered the interior of a church in pencil and charcoal, highlighting structures and details in the subtle chiaroscuro style that typified my early works in Florence. Far back in the church, the figures of two naked women were visible, one on either side of the altar, and one of the two was pregnant. Another work that attracted great attention, and one that directly challenged the viewer, was a canvas titled *Chinese Reds,* selected by the San Francisco Arts Commission Gallery for their exhibit *Body Politics* in 1993. The title derived from the name of one of my Lefranc & Bourgeois paints, but it was also a powerful reference to the subject of the work: Chinese policemen beating up a student in Tiananmen Square. The entire canvas was pervaded by various hues and tones of red, including the students' blood splattered everywhere, painted in with spots of Chinese red straight out of the tube. That same year, I was also invited to present an exhibition of watercolors called *Body of Water,* at the Pasquale Iannetti Art Gallery in San Francisco. The art writer Mariah Marvin struck a chord in me with her text for the catalog:

In some ways...[Sassone] portrays the chances he takes in his art as voyages by water, moving through mysterious ambiguity toward more light, more clarity."

"The chances he takes in his art" were words that truly resonated with me at night, within the confines of my studio, surrounded by the staring eyes of all my creatures.

And here, in my studio, the momentum for *Home on the Streets* was mounting as was the response to the upcoming show with the many letters of support I received from shelter organizations, mayors, senators, and members of the community, including letters from the State Capital and the White House. I kept pasting everything into a large scrap book—the sketches and charcoal portraits done on location, articles about the exhibition, and clippings of disturbing stories on the homeless from the *San Francisco Chronicle*. Some examples of the headlines in 1993 included "Homeless man set afire on Geary Street," "Homeless woman dies outside HUD office (in Washington)," and "138 homeless died this year in San Francisco," all of which served to underscore the relentless tragedy taking place every day on the streets of America. An earlier article in the *Chronicle* addressed the number of homeless people turned away from San Francisco shelters during the prior three-month period, with figures amounting to over three thousand per month. It was evident more work was needed from the government and each City Hall across the country. Our City Hall, unfortunately, embarked on one of the most contentious episodes in the history of homelessness in San Francisco: Mayor Jordan's Matrix Program and its unprecedented emphasis on the use of police force as a part of any solution. Without social service outreach programs in place, Matrix accomplished little to help those who were poor and homeless; instead, they were in essence targeted as criminals.

With these thoughts in mind, it was time to use the sketch I had made for a painting titled *City Hall.* I felt it in my bones late one morning as I approached a large, tall canvas that was already waiting with a skeleton of marks and strokes progressing upward from the foreground to the very top, 108 inches in all. For a few minutes I stared at the canvas; I didn't know where to begin, even though the vision was already clearly impressed on my mind. I approached it suddenly, a cluster of brushes in my hand, sketching out a whole intrigue of signs, some large, some narrow. They represented barbed wires twisting and turning through the mid-section of the painting like black and gray snakes entwined with each other in a frightening dance, suggesting an impenetrable barrier. Despite the rough texture of the surface, I was able to introduce some subtleties, with a variety of tones and tints ranging from blue-gray to pale gray-greens and with a pale reddish-ocher coming through. I continued working for a few days until this chaotic field began to reveal the complexity of its dimensions. I approached the enormous building of City Hall, partially visible through the rubble in the foreground. I climbed to the top of the ladder in order to reach the dome, shaping it with wide, flat brushstrokes of pale gray-ultramarine to match the coloration below.

Standing back, I was pleased with the roundness of the building looming over the rubble beneath. Now I assailed the entire blue-gray sky with countless heavy strokes of paint, laid on with speed and nervous accuracy, providing a rich meld of color that pervaded the canvas. But I was not done. I painted in the tiny figure of a homeless man, barely noticeable in the lower right corner of the canvas, placed precariously on the shaky, uneven terrain on the outside of the huge, snarled barrier. This painting, unlike others that would seem to take on a pictorial life of their own, emerged very close to my original concept. The message was clear: the tiny figure, representing the homeless population both in size and place, appeared to be marginalized, excluded by that huge government building occupied by our right-thinking society. But aside from its social commentary, this piece, like previous ones in the series, sprang to life. Its imagery was harsh and real, which contrasted with the fleeting, ephemeral presence of the human being. The power of a painting resides in its stasis, its capacity to capture and freeze a moment in time. In *Home on the Streets,* I felt that my work had acquired a density that underscored the materiality of the images, achieving a weight and palpable presence with which I felt entirely comfortable.

* * *

One late morning filled with crisp sunlight I was walking past the YMCA building in South of Market when I noticed from a distance the figure of a man sitting on the edge of a circular fountain. The area had just been renovated and was generally not populated by street people at all, but this person happened to be there, alone, staring into space. I walked towards him. His appearance was gentle, his looks extraordinary. I had no idea, at the time, how this encounter would affect my life and inspire my work for years to come. I said "Hi," but there was no reply. When I asked if I could do a sketch and handed him money, he quietly took the $10 bill and sat in silence. He made not the slightest move as I began to draw. His dirty blond hair was a total mess, spewing out in all directions, with a bun rolled up at his left temple. The wrinkles on his forehead were deep ridges, and a huge, unkempt, reddish-brown beard merged with the moustache that covered his mouth. His blue-gray clothes were shredded, his hands filthy with encrusted black spots of dirt. His eyes were sky blue, though, and he began to talk in spurts as I worked. He said he had been employed in a high-rise building as a secretary—gesturing up to the Cypress Leasing Corporation to his left—and then assured me that the revolution would be over soon. I asked his name. He could not remember. This sort of total amnesia was quite common among the homeless that I had encountered through the years, and, as a result, many of the drawings I made remained untitled. This time it was different. The title came to me spontaneously: *The Man with Blue Eyes.*

Back in the studio, I reflected on this man. How could we, as a society, let these human beings deteriorate before our eyes? This was a living person who was no longer able to fend for himself. I felt at once both defeated and inspired. I felt compelled to keep drawing this man's face; one small sketch on brown paper ended up on the cover of my scrapbook, and I picked out a large charcoal portrait for my *Home on the Streets* exhibition. The opening was now set for March 30, 1994, at the Museo Italo Americano with the show running through May 29th. The last painting I completed in time for the exhibition was a canvas called *Earth Man,* an imaginary vision of perhaps the first human, an anonymous man half-risen from Earth's bowels. Behind him loomed a huge expanse, a distance separating the subject from all other forms of life. With a palette that ranged from red-brown tones to pale Naples yellow and light peach tones, the canvas was flooded in soft light, accented with a variety of warm whites.

It is astonishing to think that the first painting chosen for this exhibition was *Aftermath,* painted in 1968 as a reminiscence of the flood of Florence, where a figure seen scavenging among the ruins is perhaps looking for food or searching amid the rubble for a family member, a home, a lover. The painting was executed in multiple variations of gray tones and was included by the curator, Robert Whyte, to trace the history of my connection with the show's theme, suggesting that twenty-six years earlier I had already started painting *Home on the Streets.* The series had pushed me to strip away the accumulation of tiny brushstrokes that typified earlier works in order to reveal my experiences and fears while applying paint to canvas. It also pushed me to examine the part of our human nature that can cause us to lose control at any moment, to fall through the cracks of society, to fall over the precipice and into the abyss. Despite the loneliness, the doubts, and the confrontations with my past in the course of those four years, I believe the process was necessary for me to become a better artist—and a better person.

As the date of the opening approached, I was looking to make some material change in my life, to mark this inner feeling of deliverance, this sense of liberation. So, on the morning of the opening, I called my ex-girlfriend Sheila, who owned a hair salon in town. She told me that she was planning to come to my opening with her husband, and I asked her if she would please come over to the studio to shave off the beard that I'd now worn for twenty-five years. She did. She also trimmed my hair and pulled it back into a ponytail. I looked like a new person.

And I felt like a new person as I drove my yellow Jaguar to the museum to attend the opening. I was alone. Of course, no relationship could have survived those years. There had been a few dates, and there was Lee, whom I met in 1991, and with whom I had pursued a tumultuous on-and-off affair that had ended recently. As I approached the entrance to the show, I heard a voice: "Hey, Buddy! There's a line here!" I had not even noticed the long line of people at the door. The voice barely registered as I hurried into the museum. I found myself gazing into the faces of the paintings that I knew so well, and they stared back at me, each one with individual identity, no longer faceless, unnoticed. I could see the huge paintings installed together for the first time, their surfaces standing out from the walls in fevered dreams of grays and browns, projecting in their intensity all the feelings and fears that went into their making.

"How close we all are in our fragile lives," I heard myself say. No one seemed to hear, no one seemed to notice. I was alone in the middle of a cavernous space packed with a crowd of people.

"Where's Marco?"

I heard the question repeated over and over, echoing through the crowd where I stood, invisible, surrounded by close friends. It was actually quite funny—and unsettling all at once. They were all there, my friends: Tom Bradley and his assistant Mary Ann; my friend Angela Aliolo, president of the board of supervisors at San Francisco City Hall; Robert Whyte, the curator; and all the museum staff I had come to know; my photographer, Evelyn Zappia; all my San Francisco friends and friends from out of town, including my close friend Sylvia Bello from Los Angeles; then, too, Lee, and other ex-girlfriends; my former wife Diane from Orange County; and Nicola, who was now fifteen years old. At one point, I looked at my son and whispered "Nicola, *sono qui.*" I am here. He looked at me and saw nothing. Then I whispered again, "Nicola, it's me." He turned, staring into my face, first questioning, and then with slow recognition.

"Papa?"

"Yes," I said, "It's me."

He was still in shock as we hugged each other. And suddenly the room was alive with curiosity and astonishment at the shocking transition in their midst.

The next thing I knew, I was crowded into the corner behind a counter, signing copies of the *Home on the Streets* catalog for guests. The cover, an edge-to-edge reproduction of the painting *Distance*s, gave a compelling contemporary look to the publication, sponsored by the Museo Italo Americano and funded by local businesses. There was a foreword by Tom Bradley, an introduction by Robert Whyte, and a text by Peter Clothier, art critic for *ArtNews* and whose writing I greatly admired. "In [Sassone's] desolate landscapes," he wrote, "man is most frequently seen alone, reduced to the struggle for survival in a universe that seems at once to swallow and reject him." The mayor of San Francisco, Frank Jordan, did not attend in person but sent a proclamation designating March 30th as "Marco Sassone Day in San Francisco." I was interviewed by

KGO-TV, channel 7, and a few days later Kenneth Baker, art critic for the *San Francisco Chronicle,* wrote in his review: "There is true technical brilliance here, especially in the sheets pasted into a large scrapbook near the show's entrance. In the drawings, [Sassone's] technique seems to discover fresh descriptive possibilities each time out. *Willy Frost* (1993) is almost Rembrandtine in its unsparing realism, while *Man with Blue Eyes* (1994) brings the woodcut portraits of E. L. Kirchner to mind."

The press coverage for *Home on the Streets* kept pouring in from publications throughout the Bay Area. But the single piece of writing that touched me the most was a letter, dated April 27th, from Amy Selwyn, assistant director of Strategic Planning for Associated Press (AP) in New York, who was in town to attend an AP Board Meeting. Of the many things she observed and experienced over a week's period, she wrote me, "Nothing struck me—or made such a lasting and forceful impression—as your work in the exhibit *Home on the Streets.*" She continued:

> *Home on the Streets* is brutal and unforgiving and, accordingly, unforgettable... After I left the exhibit, a bearded man with matted, filthy hair and torn clothes asked me if I could spare a dime... I gave this man some money and looked him in the eyes... The differences in our circumstances, the tragedy of his life and the comfort of mine opened me to a new level of compassion and, yes, anger, about the predicament of the homeless in this country. I am determined to become more involved and more

aware. I thought you might want to know the powerful effect your work has produced in a single human being."

13

THE OBSESSION WITH VENICE

1994 – 1995

One splendid sunny day with a few scattered clouds high above, I was driving south on Highway 101 in my Jaguar. A second exhibit of mine, running concurrently with *Home on the Streets,* was installed at the Olive Hyde Art Gallery, a public space operated by the City of Freemont, near San Jose. The show, *Italian Influence*, included twelve paintings, mostly from the Amalfi Coast series, along with a few watercolors painted between 1987 and 1993. I was actually looking forward to viewing a lighter version of my work again—one that portrayed more of a mix of light, sea, and sky reflected and refracted.

As I thought back on the previous four years of my life, Louis Stern came to mind. Whatever happened to him? I was concerned, of course, about his promise to represent me, and inquired several times through the years. But Louis always responded that he had not yet found a suitable space for his new gallery. His last communication to me was in the form of a brochure announcing a solo exhibition of small works by Marie-José Paz, an artist I was not familiar with, scheduled for November 1992, at his old office space in Beverly Hills. However, I later learned that he did finally move to a new location in West Hollywood to open his new gallery, Louis Stern Fine Arts. The fact that I had not heard anything from him was disturbing, and, obviously, his silence spoke volumes. It was clear that I was not invited to be part of the stable of artists in his new gallery, despite a wait of over ten years. It was at his suggestion that I left the Wally Findlay Galleries in 1982, in order to be represented by him. I had no way of knowing the motive for his decision, nor could I fathom his behavior.

Time passed quickly, as it always does. My life was full of excitement and hope. I enjoyed the affection that developed between the viewers and my work. I was passionately involved with my painting. But one can always sense when something is lost along the way, especially a friend with whom you have shared your thoughts and aspirations. A reliable source had recently pointed out the possible reasons for Louis' change of heart: for one, I had become too involved in instructing him on how to manage and market my work. I was too heavy-handed. Also, Louis disapproved of my association with my graphic publisher, worrying that it was too commercial. As I was driving, listening to Nina Simone play softly on the car's stereo system, I managed to wrap my head around the thought that he was probably correct about the first part. With regard to the "commercial" criticism, I always find it annoying when people insist on becoming self-appointed members of the discriminatory committee. This ludicrous thought pattern only affects visual artists, by the way. There seems to be no backlash against filmmakers, musicians, authors, or playwrights for creating successful works.

What does commercial mean anyway?

My publisher was distributing my original silkscreens just like any other publisher, and I'm sure Louis was aware that my output represented a fraction of the prints published for other artists, and in strictly limited editions. Andy Warhol, for instance, stopped personally making his artwork altogether, and his assistants created massive editions of silkscreen prints at his New York studio known as the Factory. I purchased one myself, a portrait of Mick Jagger signed by both Warhol and the rock star, in an edition of 250. His publishers marketed these prints very well.

Was this commercial?

Recently, Gerhard Richter, the acclaimed contemporary German artist, had a print for sale at a Christie's auction in New York. Titled *Bouquet*, it was numbered 254/500. The description indicated that it was a C-type print (known as a chromogenic print) of his painting *Bouquet,* painted several years earlier. In other words, the artist produced five hundred photographic reproductions of his painting. I submit that this is an excessive size for an edition, and that the result was not even original handmade prints. So here's my question: are Christie's auctions and Richter's publisher considered commercial?

In any case, people are entitled to believe in their own fantasies to justify their own intentions. That said, I found one plausible reason that could have made more sense while visiting the Louis Stern Fine Arts' website. "Louis Stern Fine Arts," his gallery statement read, "…offers a groundbreaking re-investigation of [...] West Coast abstract painters." Wikipedia basically concurred with this information, noting that the gallery "focuses on leading West Coast abstractionists." It would be reasonable for anyone to think that my work would never have fit in with this gallery orientation. Be that as it may, any or all of the above reasons may have contributed to Louis' decision. Still, whatever the case and whatever the reasons, we all have a responsibility in life to try to keep the other party informed of our intentions. When the other party happens to be your friend, I would think, informing him is a must. Failure to do so, failure to disclose the truth, is simply deceit. The worst disappointment in life happens when we are betrayed by our friends or family, and it pains me deeply to think back to this moment.

In retrospect, I cannot help but think that this entire sad episode was a mea culpa from the beginning: what had possessed me to leave the established Wally Findlay Galleries, with its locations in New York, Chicago, Beverly Hills, Palm Beach, and Paris, for a gallery that was not yet even in existence?

Preoccupied with these thoughts, I had almost reached my destination. I had been driving for about an hour and it seemed like no more than a few minutes. The Olive Hyde Art Gallery was a small, intimate space infused with soft light. My paintings were well installed. The director was not there when I arrived, but his friendly staff went out of their way to welcome me. I was handed a copy of two reviews of my show before heading back to San Francisco, both published in the *San Jose Mercury News*. In one article titled "Spots, Dots, Dashes Reflect Coastal Italy," art critic Robin Worthington seemed to have indulged her own fantasy when she wrote: "Much of the activity in the paintings springs from Sassone's thick, expressive brushwork. In *Southern Italy 3,* the strokes change from almost horizontal in the swelling seas at the base of the painting to arching strokes above, until they seem like feathers of a mythical bird brooding over the scene." This painting was eventually acquired by a collector in the South of France. Still now, when I look at the image, I cannot help but see a huge bird coveting the sky!

* * *

In September of 1994, I am sitting in Venice's Piazza San Marco one late afternoon at my favorite spot, the Caffè Florian, resting after an entire day spent wandering through this extraordinary city. This is not just a coffee shop. Caffè Florian has been an institution since its opening in 1720. One of the city's symbols, a meeting place for art and culture, this is where the Biennale di Venezia was first conceived in 1895. You don't sit here for just a cup of coffee; you are here instead to experience a unique vision of the past while engaging in Venice's contemporary life. That summer, at the end of my vacation, I had traveled north with my family from my base at the beach. I had been here in this marvelous water maze of the sinking Queen of the Adriatic many times before, and each time I retraced my steps it felt like a brand new visit.

It's incredible to think that Venice was constructed on water, built on more than one hundred thousand wooden stilts driven into mud like an upside down forest whose trees over time, and without oxygen, have become the stones upon which sits a city whose precarious and mysterious survival has, throughout the centuries, defied headlines of its imminent death. Venice continues to survive intact. To unravel the threads of memory of a city so rich in art, history, and traditions is a challenge, but it is necessary if we wish to avoid losing the culture of the past and the stories of the men who made the existence of this prodigy possible. Venice was the crossroads for people from all over the world who always found a secure shelter here. It was a bridge between Christianity and Islam, a meeting place to exchange in dialogue between all religions. No one could resist the enchantment of the City on the Lagoon, whose unbroken mirror offers the contemplation of a past, which has impressed its unique fascination on generations of writers, poets, artists, musicians, and illustrious travelers. Changes are minimal in Venice—a place that succeeds in delivering a sense of consolation one feels in knowing that, at least in some places in the world, modernity is unable to destroy or erase the past.

My obsession remains with the canals, especially the narrow, winding ones. Exploring their surfaces with the eyes induces a rapt, mysterious longing and, as you approach what appears from a distance to be a dead end, the canal will always surprise you with a new, unpredictable waterway that invites you to turn off into new directions, new discoveries.

Venice seduced me with my first visual discoveries, beckoning me forward into the perspective of a shadowy tunnel that stimulated my senses and provoked the evolution of my vision. I found myself returning constantly to familiar compositions with the reflective surfaces of the canals, tarnished and altered by the gradual loss of structures and literally dissolving into the sea. I would observe and draw the subtle movements of the moment. I came to believe that an artist's skill depends on attending carefully to the irreplaceable beauty of the present moment—taking note of the minutest detail while simultaneously stepping back from the world and staring as if into a mirror, allowing for some distance and eloquence of jest.

In Venice, I came to feel powerfully that painting was not about melancholy and regret. It was about this desire I felt, which caused me to relive with ecstatic delight all the years I had spent at the drawing board learning my artistic discipline, my craft, my dedication. Desires in Venice are never dormant; they are alive from the moment you set foot in this fountain of inspiration, visible through a fantastic mosaic of images rich in multiple meanings—meanings that often find in Venice a special place, where you are capable of daydreaming with eyes open. It helps to fine-tune your senses. We learn to see the invisible and listen to the inaudible—the stones, the light and dark, the undulating reflections, things that speak to us constantly. We observe the gondola, an object of unusual beauty as it glides silently, strangely, as if in a dream. When I am here, nothing is more beautiful. The subtlety of the senses, the ability to be conscious of the slightest nuances, even anguish—all of which I could find only in Venice. What surrounds me is filled with nobility. Even the rain in Venice is delightful. According to Friedrich Nietzsche, as he revealed his music predilections in *Ecce Homo,* Venice was the only place beyond the Alps. While his assertion makes little sense, I relate to the following words: "If I try to find a new word for music, I can never find any other than Venice." And with music in the air, it seems I could find, for a moment, all the answers right there in the water of the canals. The pull is so real, the attraction so strong. I feel I must have been here at some earlier time, and now, it seems, would be my chance to see what I had only glimpsed before, the strange delights I had discovered, or to see what had been hidden from me during previous visits; or, perhaps, to connect with the memory stream of our predecessors who passed through in previous centuries.

The emotions, imagination, and visualization of past events, the embedded history in the stones of the facades reflecting their innumerable images on the water below, all contribute to the awakening of my soul. I rediscover here the dual attraction of the ancient buildings and the water, with their endless manifestations of changing light. I respond to the peculiar coloration of mauves, rust reds, and roses—flesh tones—which possess a rich, deep resonance, often present in my earlier Venetian series. But I responded also to the blues and greens, tonalities that traditionally draw the mind toward the spiritual, reflecting a deeper, more internal process. I rediscover a sense of freedom and release my passion for a subject that I love to render on canvas in a succession of layers and marks, creating the visually compelling activity that constitutes both the surface of my consciousness and that of my finished painting.

Once back in the studio that year, I began to refer to my drawings and sketches. These were the images and shapes that expressed the world I was in, a mosaic of beauty that I was anxious to address through the act of painting, creating works that offered the viewer the immediate appeal of my personal experience. I wanted to create pictorial art that gathers colors and materials into a harmonic synthesis, that creates an *atmosphere* of beauty, not a representation—not a desire to copy a scene that is externally beautiful and can be exhausted by visual pleasure. Conversely, with my ongoing Venetian series, I wished to uncover the naked beauty, without superfluous adornment, without artificial makeup and embellishment, precisely as I have seen it and have known it. I had two paintings in the studio dating back to 1990 that captured the elements of that simple beauty in the moment: *Barconi*, a piece portraying large barges moving toward the confluence of a small waterway and the Grand Canal, rendered in gray-white accents and crisp, agitated blue-green strokes to accentuate movement. *Untitled* was the other canvas, produced similarly in nervous strokes but with a different coloration in reds, pinks, and ocher. It addressed the narrow perspective of a swift-moving canal in accents of cerulean blue beneath a turbulent and threatening sky.

Images of previous paintings return to me often when I embark on a new body of work. My eyes, this time, kept glancing back over various images that actually had little to do with Venice; one, in particular, stared back at me, a painting from 1992 titled *Big City Birds,* whose intense red-orange glow radiated over the entire surface. This work embodies a symbolic allegory fraught with enigmatic meaning. It represents a kind of wistful view of San Francisco, a city often seen at its best from a distance, whether from high up, as in previous urban landscapes, or from the water, when its impressive skyline is visible in all its majesty, embodying the city's ambition and energy. The bright red-pink birds, covering most of the canvas with their wings, contrast vividly with the blackness of the water below and the city structures, at once attractive and threatening. I find myself enraptured by this picture, the large birds in the foreground strangely fascinating, unexpected, as if returning to a place that was once theirs. They seem to confront the city with their own nature, their own spontaneous existence.

It was the coloration of this piece that inspired several of the paintings that I produced on my return from Venice. *Burano* was one such piece that retained the glow of *Big City Birds*, though this time on a canvas that reflected the natural pace of life on the island of Burano, located a few miles north of the Venetian Lagoon. The first time I saw Burano in the early 1970s, I was intrigued by the color of the houses everywhere on this tiny island and the reflection of their facades in the canals. I was also fascinated by the groups of local ladies socializing among themselves while tatting the Burano lace for which the island is known. Here, life seemed to have remained unchanged for centuries, along with time itself, like the water in this painting that provided a mirror for the activity in the housing complex. Unlike *Big City Birds,* however, the subject in *Burano* becomes secondary to the painting. The texture of the paint produces here an overall intensification of atmospheric color, with a surprisingly romantic light. The Venetian coloration in this piece and its mood of intimate tranquility seem to mark a dialectic contrast with the eccentric and overheated atmosphere of some of my earlier urban landscape paintings.

By the beginning of 1995, I found myself in a flow, painting a series of works projecting a mood of calmness, often in a variety of delicate hues ranging from rose and pale gold tints to earthy umber tones and light gray-greens. All these pieces felt close to my sensibilities at the time, paintings that seemed to me like subtly textured fabric. Conscious of their melting coloration, I sensed my freedom within their radiant surfaces.

When I think of radiance, there is only one person I have met who embodies this word, and when the Italian Consul Giulio Prigioni invited me to dinner with Sophia Loren, she was one of a few people for whom I would interrupt my love affair with Venice. "An Evening with Sophia" was scheduled in April of that year at the San Francisco Museum of Modern Art, an event sponsored by Armani and Bulgari. Giorgio Armani and the architect Mario Botta were honorary cochairs of the event. When the consul introduced me to the honoree, I definitely felt the magnitude of her presence. Her reputation in Hollywood preceded her: I once read in *Time* magazine that she could have swallowed most of her leading men with half a glass of water. Only a few of her costars had been able to match the energy she generated so effortlessly on screen. That evening, I felt a remarkable energy even before she arrived at our table. I noticed all the women at the event were prepared for the occasion, sporting their best wardrobe, their best jewelry, makeup, and hairdos. They radiated feminine beauty. But when Sophia walked into the room, there was no question that she belonged on a different plateau. Yes, as she approached the table, she was radiant and stunning. Sixty years old already at the time, she still projected an exuberant elegance. She was not one to initiate conversation, but she was never slow in offering a prompt or pertinent reply.

I, myself, am not proficient at small talk. Normally, I tend to speak only when I can no longer remain silent, or if I have something of value to contribute to the topic being discussed. Fortunately, Papa came to mind. He lived in Naples before moving to Florence during the war, and Sophia Loren was born near Naples, in the small town of Pozzuoli. So that offered me some common ground, and we shared an interesting exchange that included my father's talent as a lyric tenor during his directorship of the Teatro Dante in Campi Bisenzio, near Florence where I was born. Then there was also my military service in Naples, where I discovered for the first time the extraordinary beauty of the Amalfi Coast. Sophia was excited to be in San Francisco, where people were happy to express their warmth and affection for her—though she found the city very gloomy! She talked about her favorite films—*Gold of Naples, Yesterday, Today and Tomorrow, Marriage Italian Style,* and *A Special Day*—and what a wonderful time in her life it was working on them with the great Italian actor-director Vittorio De Sica. They were films that I remember well from growing up in Italy, stories that touched and inspired an entire generation at the time.

That evening I received a gift from Sophia Loren, a CD of her film, *Two Women,* for which she had won an Academy Award. But there was more that came back with me to the studio that night. As I turned on the lights, though nothing had moved, my space came alive. I always enjoy these moments. It feels as if you are dropping in unannounced, observing everything as an outsider. There were things all over the place, an orderly mess: my huge, 10-foot long table covered in sketches, pencils, and notes everywhere, including references for paintings with color indications and stickers from my assistant Lee. The painting table offered a spectacular view of brushes in dozens of different containers; ceramic bowls with small tubes and mountains of large tubes; next to them, an array of paint sticks placed upright—hundreds of them, looking like an intricate sculpture made up of intersecting sticks leaning into each other. This sight is the first thing that captivates visitors to my studio, and I explain that these are brushes with paint dried out over the years, still serving a purpose for stirring and mixing pigment in the bowls.

On that particular night there were paintings talking to me from a variety of different easels. Some large canvases, some small, some completed, and many more in progress. And they all related to each other in coloration and subject matter. They all spoke of Venice. As I stood, silent and alone, in the middle of this wonderful chaos, still dressed in my black suit, still holding the gift from Sophia Loren in my hands, I understood that life was full of dreams that can be fulfilled. I sensed a new motivation—more drive and enthusiasm. As I kept gazing at a painting of a winding, narrow canal with its deep perspective, I felt myself pulled into its reflective surface, moving, searching, riding the surface of the water toward the end of the canal. And in that moment, I knew that around the corner there would be something marvelous awaiting me.

14

THE MAN WITH BLUE EYES

1994–2001

I remember with great pleasure when that body of work left the studio for my November 1995 solo show—*Back Home: Marco Sassone's Venice Paintings*—at the Diane Nelson Gallery in Southern California. Several other exhibitions were scheduled in the course of the mid-1990s, including the installation of the entire *Home on the Streets* series that traveled to Los Angeles under the auspices of the city's cultural affairs department. In the catalog, I dedicated the show to Tom Bradley, who, as mayor of Los Angeles for two decades, always saw the homeless as human beings. As much as he wished to be present at the opening, he was unable to attend, having suffered a stroke that impaired his ability to speak. I had visited him recently at the hospital, and he made a great effort to communicate with me by writing out sentences on a notepad. I wished him well, and when I left I could not help but reflect on the circumstances and the fragility of our lives, which we so often take for granted.

Having come back in touch with *Home on the Streets* at the opening of that show, I began spontaneously working on the portraits again. It was not with the same intensity of social consciousness that I'd worked a few years earlier, but with the memory of those same looks, staring at me, as subjects which I now felt compelled to paint. There was one face I could never forget, a face that haunted me, a face with no name: the man with blue eyes. I started making sketches in charcoal again and later dove into painting in oil, trying to capture this man in full color with brushstrokes and restless dabs to render the thickness of his skin, upon which time had weighed so heavily. The first portrait I completed was particularly significant to me. *Man with Blue Eyes* managed to capture the unquenchable pride that marked his gaze. Pride in both his misery and his defeat, like distant suffering that was no longer painful yet contained only the memory of pain. I felt that I had caught on to some vital visual truth in his stare into space, his wrinkled face, his glassy blue eyes seized in a moment between reflection and surrender. The point here is not necessarily that I had penetrated the character of this man, rather that I had seen everything evenly, transmitting the creative detachment between my gaze and his lack of response. I wanted everything to be there, down to the shadow cast on his face by the disheveled tangles of hair around his ears, the creases above his eyes, his scruffy beard, his silent intensity.

Sometimes I wonder if the images of paintings, realist paintings, can still contend with the innumerable images of other visual media such as film, photography, and television.

The relationship between painting and these media, especially photography, has long been a matter of debate, and I sense that the expressive power of painting has changed—not necessarily for the better—as a result of the vast proliferation of photographic and digital images. An artist who uses a snapshot as the basis of a composition is making the assumption that painting and its direct conversion of light into brushstrokes is still what's important. Andy Warhol's reiteration of a photographed image a hundred times on canvas also takes for granted that photographs are the primary tools of an artist's popular appeal. He suggests that culture and nature have reversed themselves, that the photograph or the image on the television screen is what counts most in our comprehension of the world. It makes no difference if one disagrees with him or not, Warhol greets it with the blissful certitude of an apostle.

Back in 1964, Arthur Danto, an art critic and professor of philosophy, attempted to read significant philosophical purpose into mundane images like Warhol's *Brillo Boxes*. Warhol's own description, however, insisted that the emptiness of his unemotional, repetitive work was neither a philosophical reflection nor an ironic comment on the nature of art, but rather a direct reflection of his own troubled psychology. "Everything is nothing," he wrote. "The reason I am painting this way," he told an interviewer, "is that I want to be a machine."

There is little an artist can do given the vast influence of mass media, especially since the audience for the art world is relatively small. Mass media is the reality we live with, and we would all do better to keep this in mind. It is precisely on this ground that many of the so-called "stellar" contemporary reputations find their footing. Contemporary artist Damien Hirst, for example, shared in an interview that he wished he were able to paint but had "tried it and . . . couldn't do it." When faced with a bare, white canvas he said, "I don't know what the hell to do."

Like Hirst, a whole generation of promising artists have successfully completed art degrees with no actual art instruction, and they are inundating the leading museums and galleries with their videos, photographic images, and installation pieces. We are trapped in the idea that this new visual media has a vast sway over the way we see and feel about the world around us. No painting can ever be experienced by as many viewers as a news broadcast. But this should make no difference to a painter. What is significant is the lasting power with which a painting can embody a lived experience rather than an empty concept. There is no great work of art without an experiential core, a sense that the mind is working on the primal matter of existence. Painting is, I affirm, precisely what visual media is not: an intimate, intrinsic engagement, not a mass seduction. This is painting's relevance. It is a world reshaped by the unmediated, time-intensive subtlety of the painter's eye. Painting offers an option to the unfelt, the merely conceptual, the derivative, or the pretentious sublime.

I tried to paint *Man with Blue Eyes* as a work of steely concision and deep intention, an assertion of the advantage of scrutiny over stage, without regarding the body and face as merely inventory of potentially abstract forms. I tried to render him with pores, orifices, and saggy flesh—with all the humanity he possessed.

In each of my homeless subjects I tried to get beneath the skin, to articulate their rage and impotence, their complex suffering. I learned how to attune myself to the subjective experience of these outcasts who haunted the streets of San Francisco, lost souls like the man with blue eyes. My approach was to embrace the perhaps romantic attitude that nothing human should be alien to another human being. *Man with Blue Eyes* confronts the spectator with the strangeness of his existence, epitomized by his piercing eyes. This apparitional figure looks mad, as so many of the homeless are in San Francisco. I was interested in faithfully representing the physical bodies of the homeless—their skin—which records both sensations from within and the wear and tear from the outside. I needed to draw on my integrity and artistic competence to convince the viewer of the truth of this particular vision, even when it became outrageous enough to convey this man's delusion and loss of contact with reality, which is especially evident in those intense blue eyes.

I had done the first portrait of the *Man with Blue Eyes* in charcoal in 1994, sketching his face at great length and then followed up with numerous drawings as studies for possible paintings. These portraits progressed through the years into an entire series, completed in different mediums and sizes. Some of the oil portraits were based on a careful observation of the nuances that evoked his tenacious humanity, employing a succession of brushstrokes that let the color drip and flake. Other canvases were painted later with shorter, more flexible strokes and brief textural touches that seemed to accentuate the throbbing of his flesh and nerves. There were also long periods of time when I turned to the softness of pastel to render his face and figure, often exploiting chalk marks that seemed to slice into his flesh like a pitiless scalpel of suffering.

Man with Blue Eyes extended the theme of homelessness that ran through my life and work, starting with the memory of my first encounter with a *clochard* when I was in grammar school, then the vivid recollection of the flood in 1966, and my own experience living on the edge shortly after my arrival in California in 1967. The series not only probed the disturbing emotions I had personally experienced during those periods, but it also offered an engaging subject that challenged me as an artist. It addressed an anxious moment, and a puzzling one, in my relationship with street people. His crazed appearance and his delusional state set this man apart from every other encounter during my four-year obsession with painting on the streets of San Francisco. The entire body of work also expanded on my evolving iconography and provided me with an immediate, contemporary setting for the art of portraiture.

Over the years I have tried to understand the popular response to *Man with Blue Eyes.* The startling subject matter itself was enough to garner attention. Some of my previous work had similar appeal, but here the viewer was confronted with a more complex and disturbing reality that stimulated a diverse range of feelings. When I recall how I made the series—the process I went through at the time—the series felt like nothing I had ever done. I had no prepared notes to follow, no preplanned color palette to work with. There were no questions about composition. No wondering about how to construct these pictures and no hesitation on the approach.

There are some painters who stand in front of a blank canvas with no idea of what to paint. This has never been the case with me. I always have an idea, since it is precisely what drives me to paint in the first place. So I may have a variety of impulses and indecisions to start out with, but once I begin to paint, the need to follow through drives me. If I start to paint a still life of a bowl of fruit, let's say, I don't end up with an image of figures on a bed. For me, painting is not a casual endeavor. I admire artists who are able to change their work as they proceed, adding and removing as they go along. But I cannot delete anything. Everything that is on the canvas must remain there, including preliminary sketches and drawings, stray marks, and spontaneous strokes; all of me and all my peculiarities are a part of the work, a part of the creative process. It's a process that remains as unpredictable today as it did when I began my journey fifty years ago. As I work, I love to be lost in the moment, painting quickly, intuitively, and reacting to any subtle nuance in the process itself, ready to capture a revelation or something unexpected. The *Man with Blue Eyes* offered me a new revelation in each portrait. I took a passionate interest in every aspect of this work. I felt compelled to paint with care and affection. The attraction to my subject was total, as was the challenge to paint him, trying to render on canvas his slightly diverse expressions with fresh descriptive possibilities each time. Following the oil portraits, this delightful madness continued up until 2001 with a series of pastels on paper, including one titled *Man with Blue Eyes Sitting,* which managed to capture some of his more individual gestures.

But it was the first pastel, *Man With Blue Eyes,* a full frontal portrait of his face, that was eventually chosen for the catalog cover of my museum retrospective in Italy, as well as the illustration for the large exhibition poster. It also ended up in numerous publications and online articles. These portraits were born in a sequence, one after the other, almost as if to answer my own internal questions through the act of painting them. Later, though, I came to believe that these images did not provide answers at all; they only prompted further questions of both the artist and the viewer.

During this process, I felt overwhelmed at times, which aroused some difficult and puzzling feelings within me. Was I painting myself as I painted this man with blue eyes? Could that even be possible? But no, I told myself, this is the man with blue eyes, a man I met on the streets by chance, simply a face I felt compelled to paint. And yet... the emotions kept coming, flooding in as I worked from one portrait to the next. I was captivated by the man's gaze as if it addressed me personally. I sensed his pain—and my own. There was some reflection of myself in the painting, I thought. No matter the confusion in my heart and mind, the work continued to comfort me. Perhaps the act of painting these portraits was a way of soothing my old deep wounds of a life in exile from my home country. Or the wound of feeling excluded from an elitist contemporary art world at this time, even though I was warmly embraced by the public. Nonetheless, I had created a life full of painting. I had embarked on a vibrant journey in which I was drawn to the real—the raw and the genuine—rather than to the world of abstract concepts.

15

MY RETURN TO TUSCANY

1997–2002

My personal life seemed to pose ulterior questions as well. It was evident that I had been incapable thus far of maintaining a long-term relationship, and at my tender age I often wondered if I would ever be able to resolve this problem. The studio, however, kept me grounded in my work, with so many ongoing projects made possible by the help of my faithful assistants. I never experienced any problems with them and had always managed to maintain a good working relationship with them, including with Lee, my current assistant and former girlfriend. Life is unpredictable, and I was impressed that we could arrive at this resolution. We discovered a different sort of relationship, in which the studio became a fertile terrain for communication that provided us both with pleasure over the course of many years. Lee ended up being a devoted aide, someone I could trust completely to take care of things whenever I was away in Italy for long periods of time.

The late '90s were marked by a substantial increase in professional activity. I was pleased to have established a greater demand for my work in general, along with more invitations to lecture, more commissions, and an intense schedule of solo shows that were slated for San Francisco, Los Angeles, New York, Toronto, Tokyo, and Milan. There were also three museum exhibitions in Tuscany.

* * *

"You know, we're getting very excited about Marco Sassone's return to the Galleria d'Arte Mentana after thirty years," Laura exclaimed on the phone one day in the spring of 1997, calling from the gallery in Florence where my career first started. "I just got off the phone with Santa Croce. The Franciscans are looking forward to hosting an exhibition at the Cloister's Museum," she added.

"I am so glad to hear that," I said, managing to interject a few words while she kept rattling on about the logistics of two concurrent exhibitions in Florence: *Home on the Streets* at the church of Santa Croce and *Opere:1987–1997*, a survey of ten years' work at her gallery.

I was genuinely excited about my return to Tuscany and was delighted when the huge crates were finally unloaded in the Piazza Santa Croce, near the steps to the entrance of the church. They were soon moved into a small courtyard beneath a colonnade, where workers began carefully carrying them by hand into the museum under the direction of the monks. The labels attached to the plywood surfaces of the packing crates were evidence that my paintings of the homeless had traveled a long way from the streets of San Francisco.

All the pieces from the museum exhibition three years earlier were here. The press' reaction to *Home on the Streets* had been challenging and intense. The public had responded with shock—and with some discomfort—but for anyone who saw this work, the homeless would never be invisible again. Yet, the paintings had become an orphan collection: none had sold, with the exception of the self-portrait, *Massimo*, but their impact was nonetheless significant. In Los Angeles, the public was again simultaneously moved by the artworks and disturbed by their content. The proceeds from the sales of catalogs and posters had been donated to City Light, a women's outreach program sponsored by Mrs. Kirk Douglas.

Now, on this April morning in 1997, the art was being installed in the most appropriate of spaces, the Cloisters of Santa Croce. Not only a dramatic Renaissance setting for *Home on the Streets*, it was also the epicenter of the most humanitarian of religious orders, the friars of Saint Francis. Meanwhile, several blocks away toward the Arno River, Laura Adreani, the owner-director of Galleria d'Arte Mentana, was similarly occupied with the unpacking and installation of the collection of thirty-nine works she had selected for the show, including oil paintings, watercolors, and drawings. The exhibition was accompanied by a catalog titled *The Roots of Marco Sassone* by Tommaso Paloscia, a senior Florentine art critic, who had already been known to me thirty years ago, before I left for America.

The air that came whistling between the columns and arches of the portico was damp and chilly that opening night at Santa

Croce. Swirling gusts of wind animated the brown robes of the Franciscan monks in the courtyard as people crowded into the Cloisters Museum. I was overwhelmed. A multitude of faces—many familiar to me that night—were busy examining the huge canvases and the charcoal portraits of the homeless. There were people flipping through the pages of my scrapbook, displayed on a table in the center of the exhibition, caught up in the stories, the newspaper clippings, the sketches I had made on the streets, and in the journey that had brought all these art works to this place. And in the middle of it all, stood my old professor and friend Silvio Loffredo, who introduced me to those in attendance on a television monitor. Most of the time I spent holding the arm of la mamma. At one point, Silvio stopped by to whisper just three words in my ear: *Ci vuole coraggio*—"It takes courage."

The reception at the Galleria d'Arte Mentana was equally well attended and perhaps even more lively. Walking there from Santa Croce through the maze of familiar medieval streets, I stepped into the gallery and was greeted by a posse of art students bursting with questions about the large body of work on the gallery walls. Their spontaneous greeting, "*Maestro, buona sera!*" brought Laura to the entrance of the gallery. "Marco, yes," she said, "they've been waiting for you… But come to the back when you can, there is a gentleman from "Speciale Regione"—Italia 7 TV waiting to interview you." A short while later, with the interview in progress, I caught sight of my father out of the corner of my eye, with a catalog in his hands, talking excitedly with la mamma. He had just opened the catalog to discover that the exhibition was dedicated to him, and he was completely overcome with emotion. The first page in the catalog read: *A Papà.*

A few days after the two openings, a review appeared in *La Nazione,* Florence's major newspaper: "Sassone's Homeless—Desperate Cries of Loneliness," by Paola Bortolotti. She wrote:

> Two exhibitions appearing concurrently … present Florence with a broad pictorial spectrum bearing the signature of Marco Sassone. The more impressive, both in terms of scope and theme, is the exhibit in the Cloisters of Santa Croce. [Sassone's] is a painting style which is powerful and agitated, as expressionistic as that of Kiefer or Kossoff, in which the contemporary element is a distortion of perspective that adds a sense of disconnectedness to the uneasiness the images inspire … The persistent theme … is not the protest against a social problem; this merely provides a pretext to allow the urgency of brushstrokes, heavy with color and light, to spill out on the canvas. This becomes more evident in the second exhibit, at Galleria d'Arte Mentana … Here the subjects of Sassone's paintings are bright Venetian panoramas … in which it is the water that becomes the turbulent element, distressed by the vestiges of shapes and shadows cast by the buildings that are reflected in it …

The high notes of Florence were echoed, literally, in San Francisco the following month, in 1997, at an event at the Palace Hotel where I met Luciano Pavarotti. A dinner in his honor had been created by Gualtiero Marchesi, a Michelin three-star chef, who had flown in from Italy for the occasion to create a special menu. The moment Pavarotti arrived at the party, of course, he attracted the television news cameras. "I need makeup," he sang out—and every woman in attendance started searching in her purse, eager to lend him blush and other things. All of which set the stage for a wonderful evening, but when I met him, all he wanted to talk about was painting. At the time of my 1988 Paris exhibition, after a close friend of his in the U.S. had acquired one of my paintings, the great tenor had requested a copy of my monograph. Now he had an idea: "We could trade painting lessons for voice lessons," he suggested. "But I can't even hold a tune!" I replied.

Apparently, though, he had already indirectly taken lessons from me, using images in my book to hone his skills. I once came across a painting by Pavarotti at a New York Art Expo in the early '90s, at the booth of a dealer who represented celebrities who were also amateur painters, and it looked like an exact replica of one of mine. In addition to Pavarotti, the dealer was showing works by Tony Bennett and Prince Charles. I was flattered that he was inspired by my work... but took care not to mention anything to him that evening.

"Painting!" he exclaimed. "It's my secret passion!" His earliest ambition, he told me, was to become a painter. And even with dozens of people waiting in line to shake his hand, he refused to interrupt our conversation. "Painters are the real artists," he declared. "They create their work... As for me, I just interpret what others have created."

"I understand the concept," I said. "But your voice, isn't that the art?"

"God gave it to me," he replied. What an amazing moment, to see him standing there in front of me, larger than life!

* * *

Back in the studio, I resumed work on several preparatory drawings I'd been making for a commission of a mural in an upscale restaurant in downtown San Francisco. The theme was the name of the restaurant, Il Palio, which referred to a medieval pageant with a barebacked horse race in the city of Siena. I produced a final study to scale for the space, painted in oil on several pieces of cardboard, and set off for a meeting with Mr. and Mrs. Gianni Fassio, owners of the restaurant. We sat at a table in the middle of the large dining room where the commission was to be installed. The couple was evidently surprised not to see me with what they imagined would be a large-scale study of their mural. Instead, unpacking the seven pieces of brown cardboard I had brought with me, I proceeded to build a scale model of the very room we sat in, using the four larger pieces to create three walls and a floor, intersecting the sections with a tongue and groove system that I had devised. Now they could see where I was going with this—but where was the study? As far as they could tell, the other three smaller pieces of cardboard were also brown, until I flipped them one by one to reveal the painted side, inserting them into the construction of cardboard walls, where I had made slots to secure each one of them. Now the projected mural was visible in color and to scale, and the couple could see exactly how it would appear when installed.

At the end of the presentation, Mrs. Fassio had only one question: "Will the mural look like this maquette (model)?"

"Yes," I replied. "Exactly. Just a bit bigger!"

The finished work, measuring 75 x 350 inches and painted on five panels, was installed in February of the following year. Most commissions deal with specific themes, and I'm always concerned when these begin to feel like burdensome restrictions. However, once I get comfortable with the subject while making my preliminary studies, the developing vision begins to open up to the pictorial elements needed for the inspirational aspect of the project that I'm working on. This was the case with Il Palio.

I have enjoyed working on all the commissions that I have accepted. The work is always *felt*, and despite—perhaps because of—the challenges, I proceed with care and enthusiasm, aware that the process itself will generate the distinctive emotions that I need. A commission completed in the early '90s, for instance, dealt only with a color scheme. The Ferrari-Carano Winery wanted a "red painting" for the label of their 1988 reserve, "to reflect the depth, complexity, and richness" of their Meritage red wine, as they stated later on the label. This was a project I welcomed, as I recall. Still, when the agent for the winery initially approached me, my first reaction was to ask if the wine was any good, since I was not familiar with the winery at the time. In response, the owners—who had requested a painting by Sassone for their label—took matters into their own hands, packed a box with a variety of their wines and drove down from Sonoma County to San Francisco. So it was that I found myself sitting down one afternoon with Mr. and Mrs. Carano and their wines in the lobby of a downtown hotel. It was an interesting encounter, I must say, having a wine tasting in the middle of the afternoon. They were wonderful people and we later became friends. And the wine was excellent. I often wondered how I could have been so uninformed!

As a result of our meeting, I presented them with three finished canvases. Their choice was one titled *Tramonto* (Sunset)—an intense landscape of burgundy reds and oranges, with pale gold accents—which was reproduced for their Ferrari-Carano label with the name Tresor below the image. One of the vintages of Tresor, I heard later, was also selected by the White House. This project had been great fun. I was impressed by the designer's function in this instance, allowing the art to make the primary statement. The result was a label of intense red coloration that made a striking statement on a custom embossed black bottle. I was astonished to see how such a large canvas could be visually reduced to a small scale and still produce an impact. At a single glance it seemed to condense the image of the whole universe. It's also a great pleasure to know that my work was used to represent the Tresor brand in the pages of a splendid book, *Icon—Art of the Wine Label,* which documents one hundred and twenty labels worldwide on life size bottles.

Another commission I was immediately inspired to accept was *Saint Francis,* a work for the National Shrine of Saint Francis of Assisi, in San Francisco. As I remember, it occurred to me during the process, that this was the first commission I would create as an American for I had just become a U.S. citizen on December 1, 1998, after living in California for thirty-one years. I also reflected on my connection with St. Francis as a result of my experience with the homeless, and the work evolved quite naturally into a canvas that incorporated the figure of the saint over the background of the city I had grown to know so well. I was very moved by the text in the book whose cover illustrated this commission:

> Marco Sassone seems to have dipped his brush into Franciscan thought and brought to life a world of poverty and heartache that few see. He reminds us of the less fortunate, of the severity of urban poverty, while at the same time he thrills us with a portrait of Saint Francis worthy of a church wall.

My schedule continued to be intense during the late '90s and into the year 2000 with an exhibition in Toronto at the gallery of Odon Wagner—who would eventually become my Canadian dealer—and later a solo show at MB Modern in New York City. I attended both openings. Odon Wagner, a leading dealer in Toronto, presented an installation of twenty-five recent paintings that he had personally selected at my studio in San Francisco. I felt truly welcomed when I arrived for my first exhibition at his gallery, where the show was accompanied by a catalog, *Marco Sassone: A Way Back Home,* with a passage in the foreword by Peter Clothier:

> That this journey is for [Sassone] a matter of passion shows clearly in the turmoil of his painted surfaces. Their affect is a complex of the full range of human emotions: if we find in them the joy of coming home and the ecstasy of creation, we also find, if we attune ourselves with clear attention, the rage of anger and the shiver of fear which artists bring to their work when they are in touch with the fullness of their humanity.

I left for California, I recall, with a pleasant feeling about Toronto, a city I had just discovered for the first time and thought I wouldn't mind returning to. Back at the studio I resumed work on a series of urban landscape paintings that approached the city, this time, from a street perspective. I had several of them already in progress, and they kept me feeling as edgy and excited as the movement I was trying to convey on the two-dimensional surface of each canvas. *California Street East View* reflected the chaotic feeling of any downtown metropolis. The contemporary street scene was rendered in blue-green tonalities, punctuated with a multitude of highlights that suggested movement everywhere.

Immediately after this one was completed, I started work on a tall canvas, loosely sketching out a narrow receding perspective, something like a Venetian canal. Walls of buildings lined the sides of the composition, framing a distant skyscraper with a narrow strip of sky above. Following the flow of the previous painting, I began to test the same color scheme on the massive wall of the buildings on the left, and at midpoint on the canvas, bringing the color down gradually, almost to street level. The strokes were broad, long, and flat, depositing a range of darker alizarin and tones of rust brown, merging with gray-blue brushstrokes at the lower end. Moving on to the opposite side of the canvas, I started to delineate the walls of the buildings on the right, using gray and muted purple tones with shorter strokes in a diagonal pattern to suggest an inward perspective. Soon the momentum picked up and I was working rapidly. I filled in the spaces in a random pattern, while the images gradually emerged against an under painting of rose and terracotta hues, part of which would remain visible in the finished work.

For a couple of days, in breaks between the action, the anxiety began to mount. I'm always edgy when the process is interrupted, edgy as I get back to work and try to rebuild the pace I had previously established. I had done some work on the skyscraper at the front edge of the background, contrasting dark tones at the bottom and light hues at the top. I now moved to the lower part of the canvas, center foreground, painting the previously outlined shape of a taxicab in gold and pale yellow tints, with blue-gray highlights. Dominating the foreground, the yellow glow of the taxi, seen as if through the rear window of another car, now continued up to an area where I applied a succession of fluid brushstrokes that seemed to reflect back in the glass of the distant skyscraper. That done, without further debate, I approached the remaining higher end of the canvas to render the sky with large, flat brushstrokes of dark blue-gray at the very top, merging with lighter tints of blue that blended with the skyscrapers and the buildings to each side.

Yellow Cab was part of the show in New York, along with a series of Italian landscapes that Louis Newman, the director of MB Modern, had selected for the exhibit. The gallery was located in the Fuller Building on 57th Street. Louis produced a small-format exhibition catalog that is still one of my favorites, illustrating some of these pieces and including text by Maria Porges, an art critic for *Art Forum* and *Art in America,* who made this interesting observation:

> These places are seen from the distance of affection mixed with longing, of memory mixed with

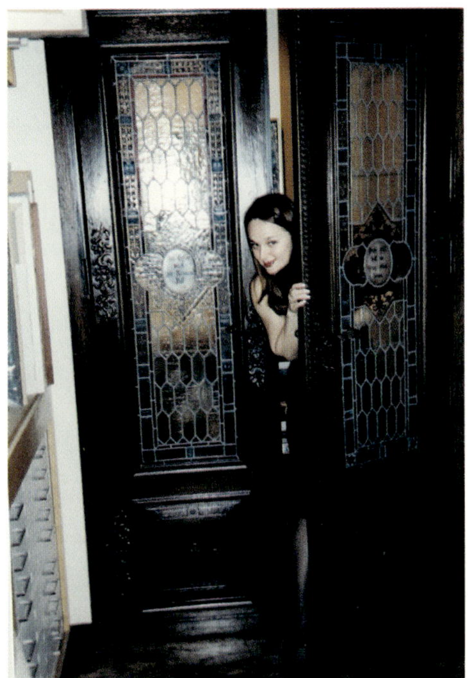

San Francisco Studio—she came through a door I didn't know I left open, 2003.

Author's collection

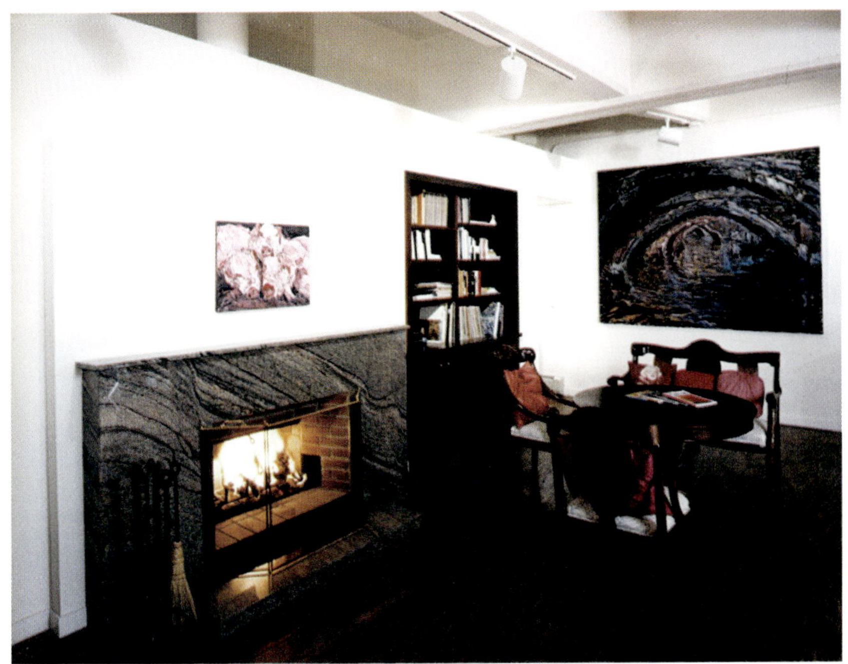

San Francisco studio, 2003. *Author's collection*

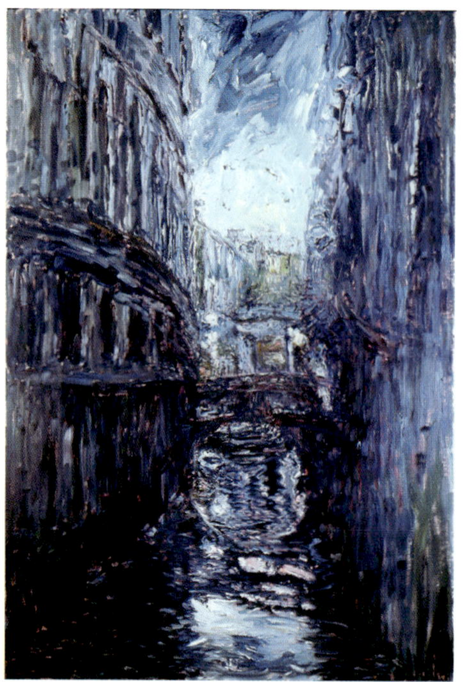

Venezia 79, oil on canvas, 2003.
Private collection, USA. ©Marco Sassone

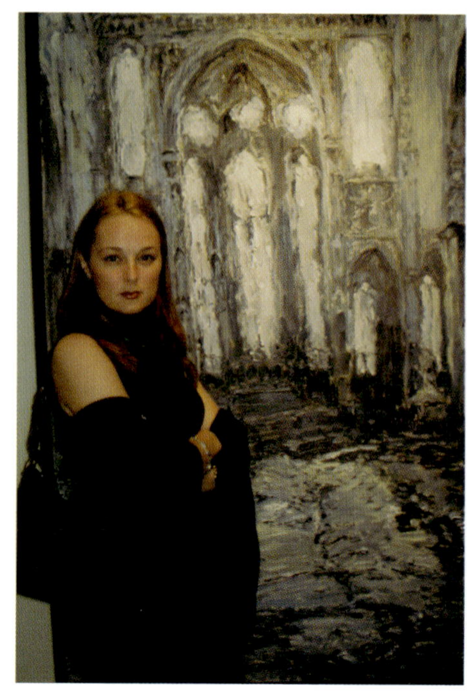

Emily, an image of beauty in my San Francisco studio, 2003. *Author's collection*

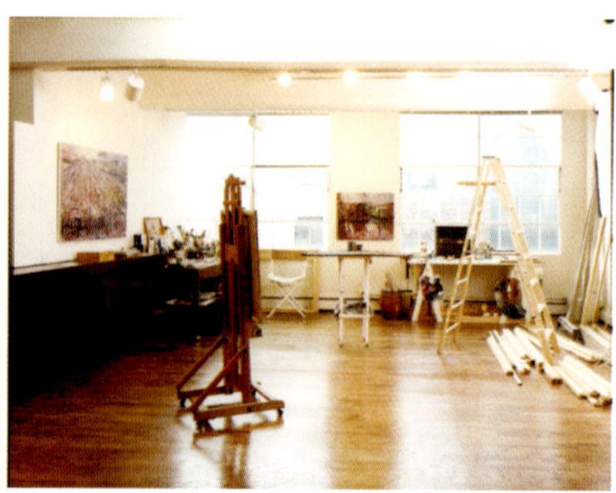

My San Francisco studio, 2003.
Author's collection

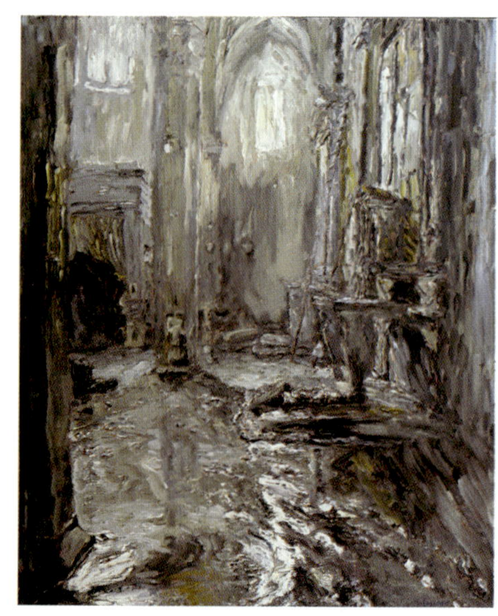

San Remigio, oil on canvas, 2003.
Private collection, Canada. ©Marco Sassone

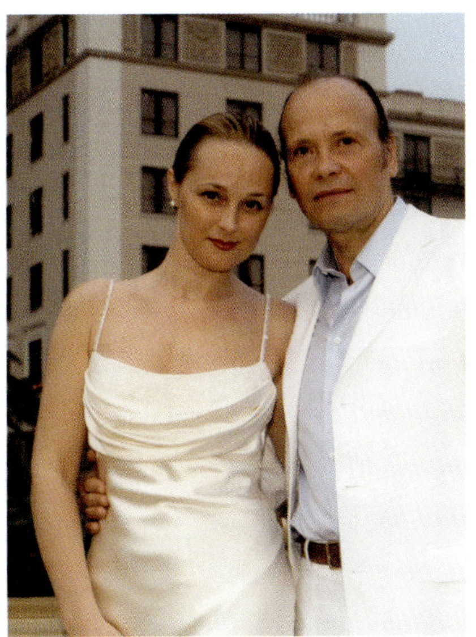

With Emily at our wedding reception in Palm Beach, Florida, 2006.

Author collection

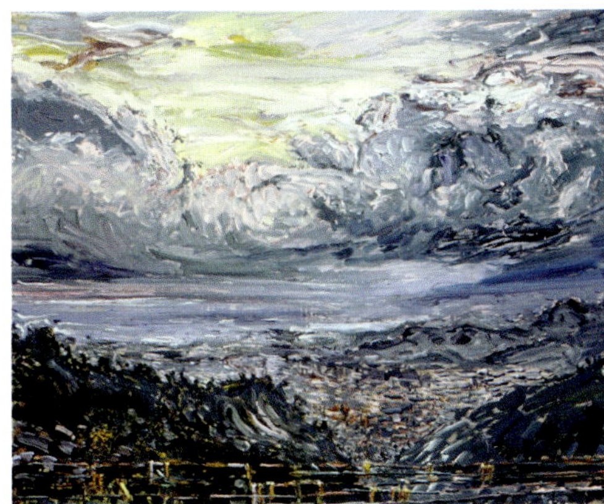

Le Mollette, oil on canvas, 2004.

Private collection, Canada. ©Marco Sassone

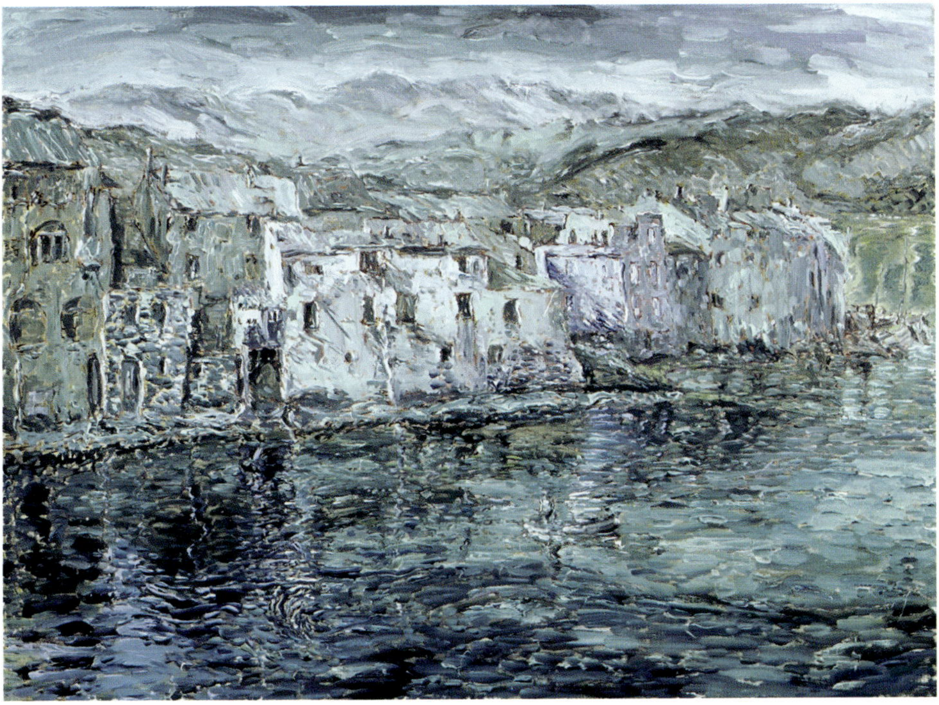

Saint Florent, oil on canvas, 2005.

Private collection, Canada. ©Marco Sassone

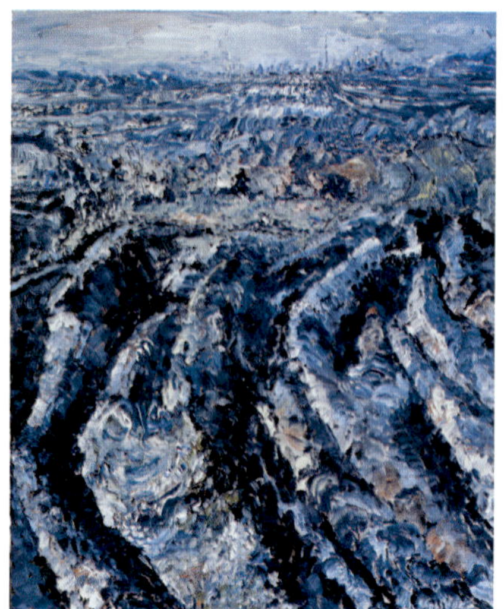

Border Crossing, oil on canvas, 2008.
Author's collection

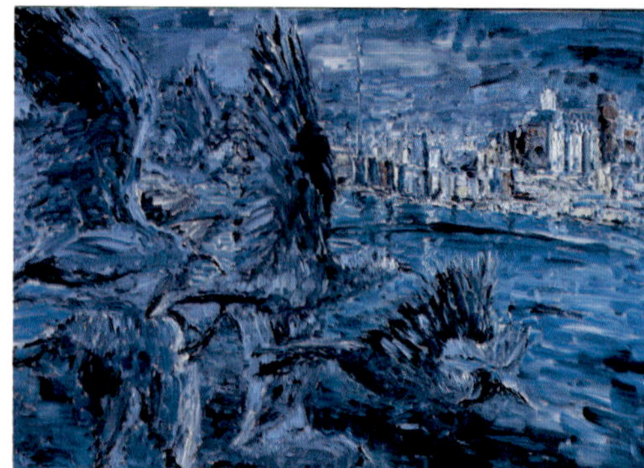

Big City Birds, oil on canvas, 2008.
Author's collection

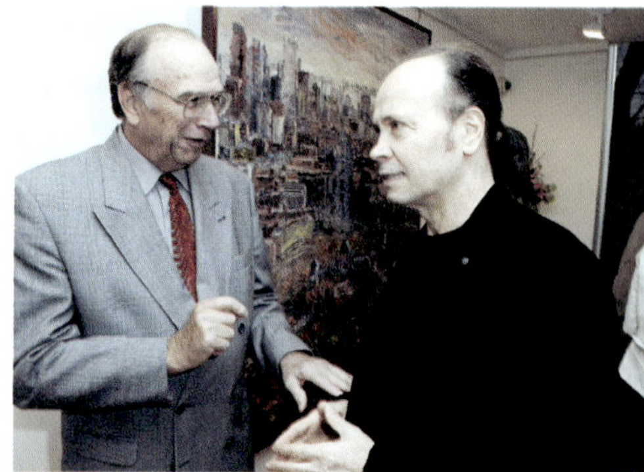

With Elvio Del Zotto at the opening of my exhibition at Odon Wagner Contemporary, Toronto, 2008. *Author's collection*

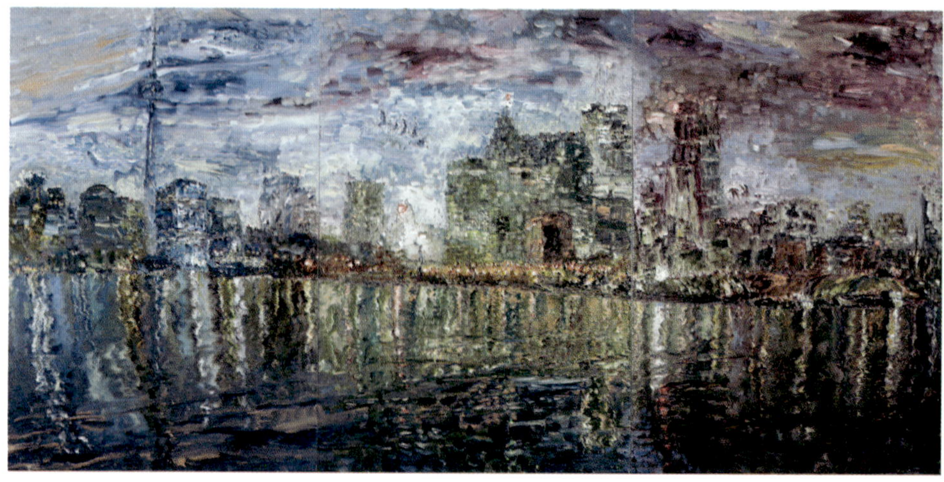

Waterfront, oil on canvas, 2009. *Commissioned for the Bellagio on Bloor, Toronto. ©Marco Sassone*

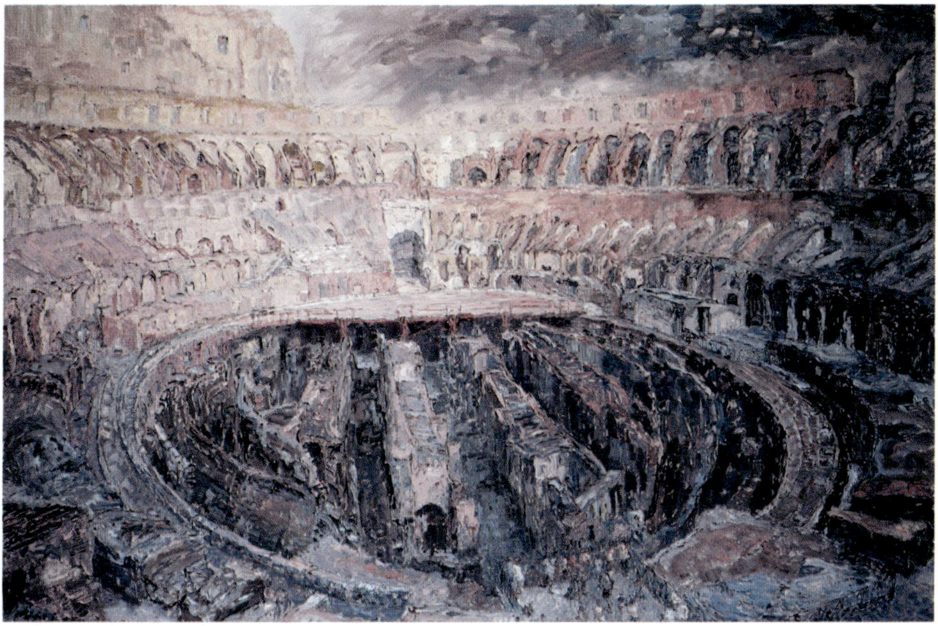

Colosseum, oil on canvas, 2009. *Author's collection*

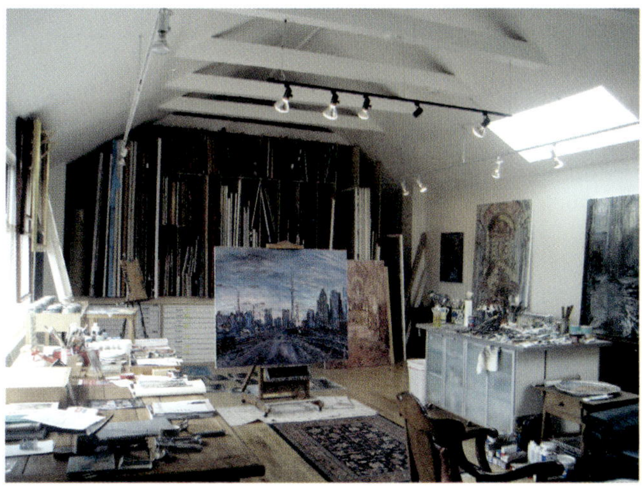

My Toronto studio, 2009. *Author's collection*

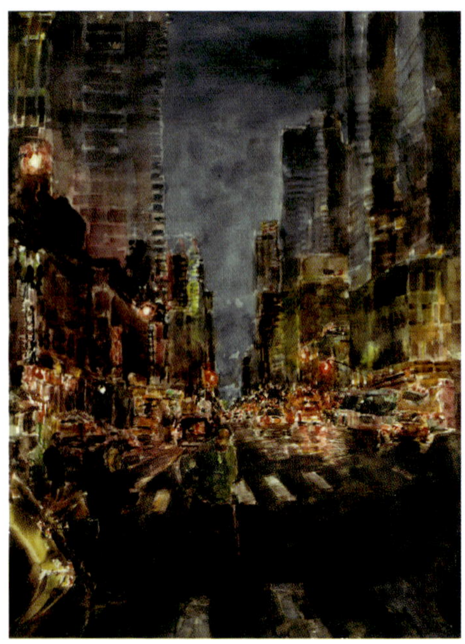

Moment, watercolor on paper, 2011.

Author's collection

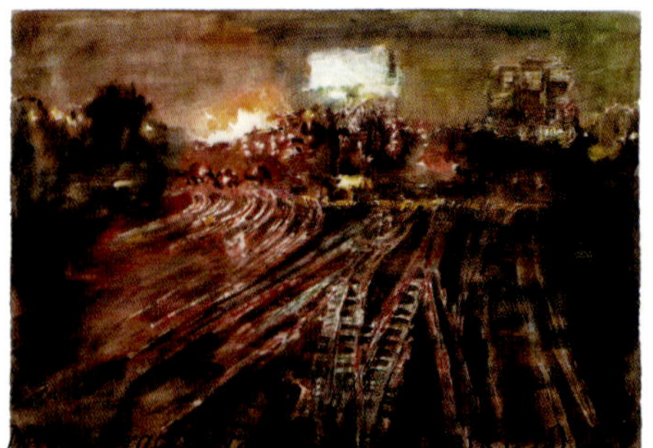

Private collection, Canada. ©Marco Sassone

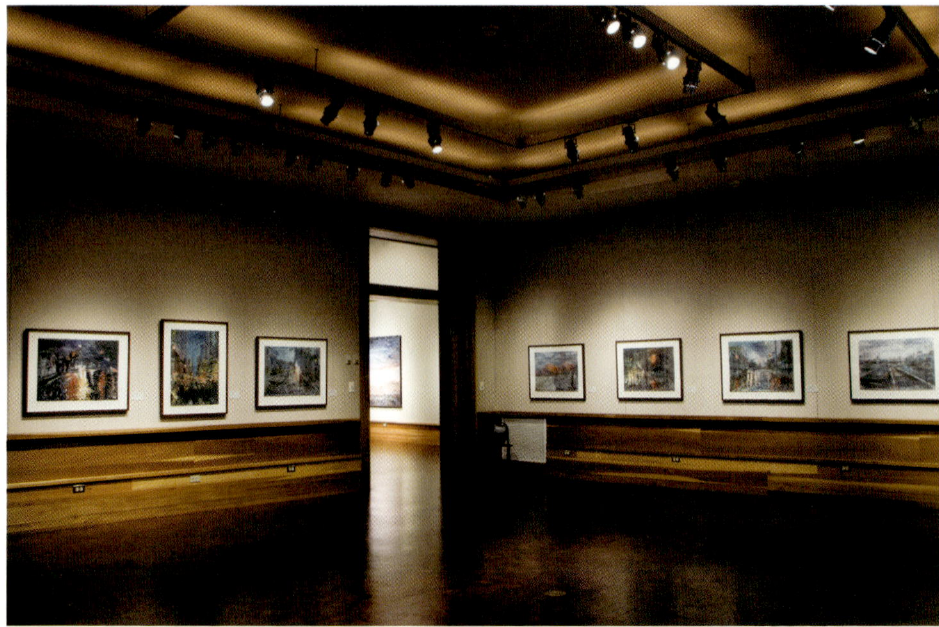

Installation of my exhibition at San Angelo Museum of Fine Art, Texas, 2013.

Author's Collection

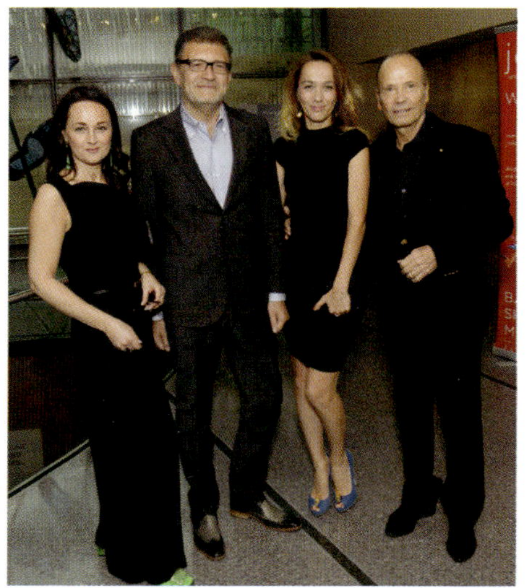

With Emily, Director Emanuele Lepri, and Lella Satie at the opening of my site specific Installation at Bata Shoe Museum, 2016.

Author's collection / Photo by Steven Blackburn

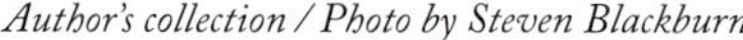

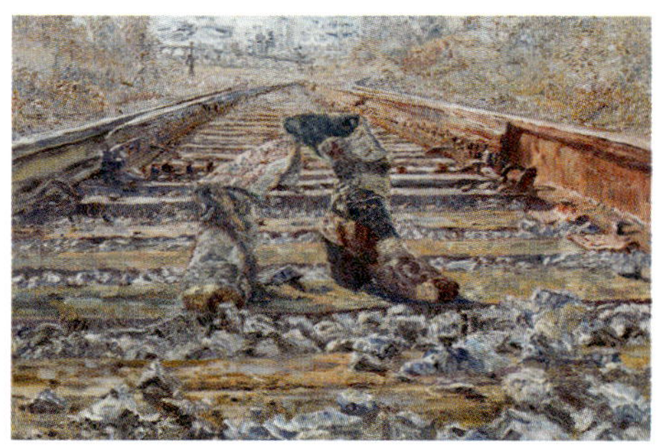

Journey, oil on canvas, 2015.

Private collection, USA ©Marco Sassone

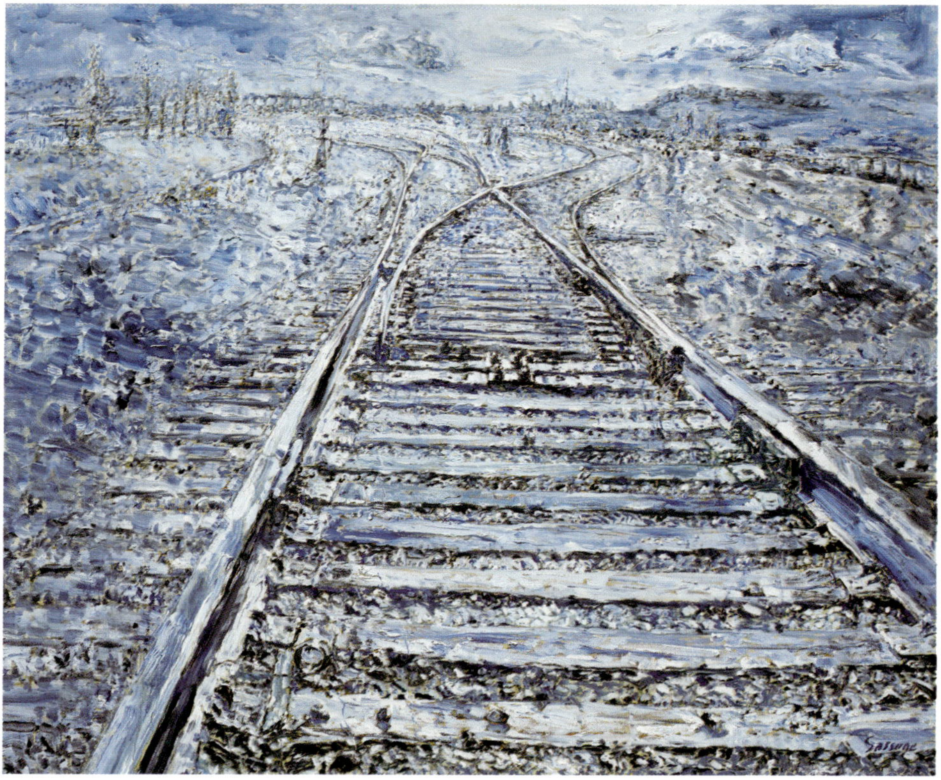

Blue Tracks, oil on canvas, 2016.

Private collection, USA. ©Marco Sassone

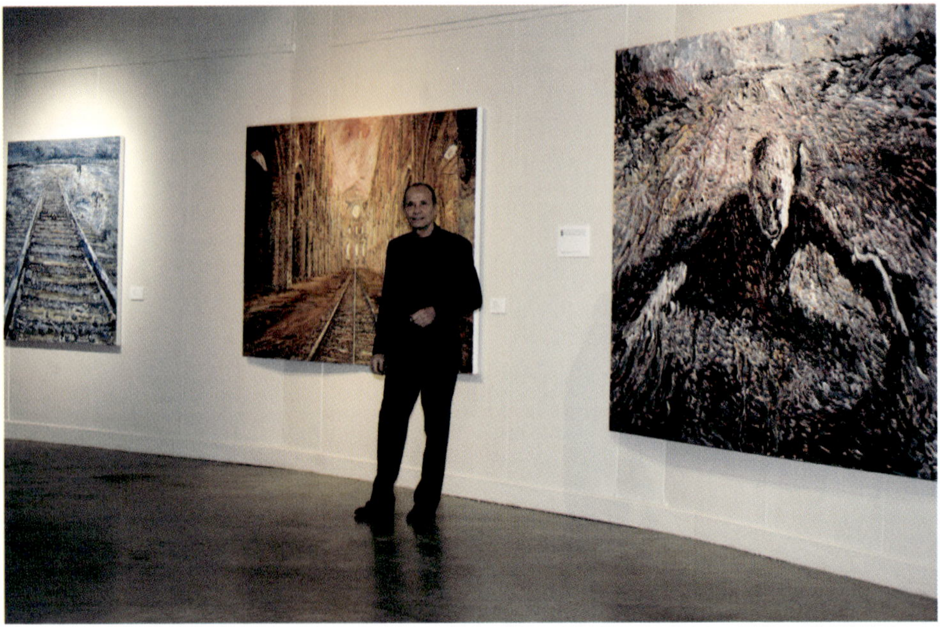

Me at the Columbus Centre installation of my exhibition Home on the Streets, Toronto, 2019.

Author's collection

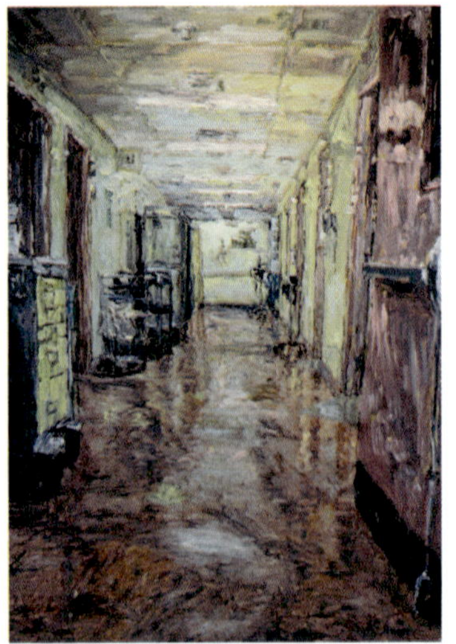

Corridor, oil on canvas, 2019.

Author's collection

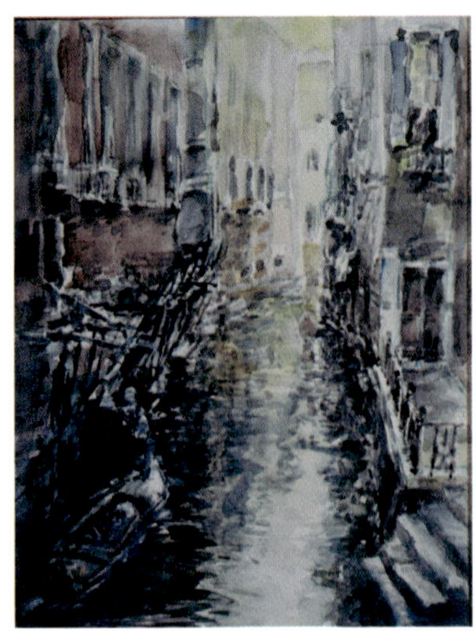

Venezia 5, watercolor on paper, 2021. Part of a series of works painted during the lockdown in Toronto.

Private collection, USA. © Marco Sassone

> the immediacy of everyday experience. Through Sassone's vision of the two worlds in which he will always live, we can experience what it is like to find ourselves far from where we started, yet be at home wherever we are.

It was one of these pieces painted with "affection" and "longing" that became the center of a wonderful episode, enough in itself to count the show a success. It started on my return to the studio with an email, dated January 12, 2001, that I received from a collector in San Francisco. We had met in the mid 1980s at a Los Angeles art fair, where he "wanted desperately" to purchase one of my paintings but couldn't afford it at the time. As he followed my career, he wrote, the thought of owning "one of your paintings has never left my mind." His wife gave him a book signed by me for Christmas in 1996. They were both planning to be in New York at the time of the MB Modern exhibition and—as the letter continued—he took the invitation with him and visited the gallery on Saturday, December 2nd, just after the show was installed. Walking in from the street, he was "overwhelmed by *Costiera Amalfitana XIII*" and immediately began to wonder how he could acquire the painting. He told his story to the gallery staff and was so excited that he went to get his wife, who was shopping further down the street, and brought her back to the gallery. He left obsessed with thoughts about how he could raise the funds to buy the painting.

"But in my typical fashion," he wrote, "I decided to wait until another show." Still, the story had a great ending: without his knowledge, his email continued, his wife "had secretly arranged ... to purchase the painting. She had it shipped to our neighbor's house and gave it to me for Christmas ... It is the best Christmas present I have ever received ... I am your number one fan."

I have given a lot of thought as to how an artist should measure success, and it's clear to me that money is not the measuring stick. The notion of success goes beyond bank accounts; it goes to the core of what it means to pursue a career in the arts. To this day, that simple piece of email correspondence truly touches me. It's a story that validates the reason why I paint, and one that gives genuine meaning to my definition of success. It saddens me that art, more and more in recent years, has assumed a secondary position to the business of art, and that the value and significance of a painting has been displaced by this new standard. A proliferation of splashy products and objects extracted from the detritus of popular culture has arrived to dominate the marketplace, and the "art world," with its record-setting auction prices, its extravagant projects and sensational events, has risked becoming a mere extension of the entertainment industry.

My friend Anne Lawrence, a writer for the *San Francisco Examiner*, once persuaded me to attend a much-hyped contemporary art event with her. I had no interest in seeing Jeff Koons or his slide presentation but went for the pleasure of escorting Anne. The artist had flown into town to entertain three hundred and fifty prominent art patrons belonging to the Director's Circle—donors contributing $10,000 or more annually to the San Francisco Museum of Modern Art, so Anne informed me. The then director of the museum, David Ross, introduced Koons as "an artist who always pushes our visual envelopes," which the artist himself proceeded to do in a presentation that included large examples of his *Made in Heaven* paintings, made by gallery assistants and displaying magnified images of himself engaged in explicit sexual acts. Meanwhile, in real life, the genius himself looked and acted more like a conservative Midwesterner than an avant-garde artist.

"We all have sexual parts," he explained disingenuously. "And there is no reason to keep them private."

I thought the whole thing surreal. When the director announced that we had time for just one question for Mr. Koons before moving on to dinner, no one raised their hand. It seemed the museum patrons were still in shock. A long silence ensued. It didn't look particularly good, I thought, that no one in the audience was sufficiently inspired to ask a single question, so in my own spontaneous way, I decided to come to the rescue. I raised my hand without even knowing what I was going to ask, and the entire auditorium turned in my direction.

"Given your presentation of inflated erotic balloons and other explicit sexual images," I said, "would you agree that your former wife, La Cicciolina, has had an influence on this work?"

Very few people in that crowd knew what I was talking about, or that La Cicciolina was the working name of the Hungarian-born porn star Ilona Staller, who later became a member of the Italian Parliament in the late 1980s. There followed a few moments of awkward silence before the artist began to answer my question in his slow monotone, and even then he fudged the answer. It appeared Koons did not wish to give credit to his ex-wife, suggesting that the inspiration for this work preceded her—even though it's widely known that the *Made in Heaven* series dates from after the time they met.

The whole art world was there that evening, from Richard Oldenberg, the head of Sotheby's, to the painter Chuck Close and the hundred million dollar donor, Phyllis Wattis, along with an A-list of glamorous San Francisco socialites. The subject of my question was echoed in numerous conversations among patrons on our way to dinner. I found myself talking, among others, with Helen and Charles Schwab, Kenneth Baker, the art critic for the *San Francisco Chronicle*, and with Jeff Koons himself, who seemed eager to offer me more of his own innocent clarifications.

It all seemed to me like smoke and mirrors. Come to think of it, a lot of the art I see these days in museums and galleries is mostly smoke and mirrors—flashy things that appeal to the superficial eye. Too many artists today seem ready to abandon the kind of content that encourages you to reflect profoundly on your life and instead play with objects in which you merely see your own reflection. Maybe that is the point. Maybe I'm just being invited to see some shallow part of myself reflected in this art, some narcissistic aspect of the modern consumer culture. But if that's the message, I find myself in full agreement with the late art critic Robert Hughes, who observed that Koons "... was the last art star to be cranked out by the Manhattan mechanism... a starry-eyed opportunist, whose ambitions took him right through kitsch and out to the other side into a vulgarity so syrupy, gross, and numbing, that collectors felt challenged by it."

The business of art is a challenge for any artist. I was fortunate to have inherited something of my grandfather's business acumen, but even that was not enough to thrive in this new, vast canvas of art commerce. There was nothing I could do about the kind of art that had become popular with patrons and tickled the public's fancy, dictating what was relevant and collectible. Some of this "shock-art" had been popularized by a group of young British artists, initially supported by the prominent collector Charles Saatchi. The first name that comes to mind, of course, is Damien Hirst, whose work seems to be about the trite, yet unsettling reality that all living things decay after death. This artist's most notorious installation was a tank fabricated out of glass and steel in which he suspended a 14-foot tiger shark—that is, the cadaver of a shark, of the kind you can see in any natural history museum. Now placed in the context of a gallery, it may have been supposed to take on some sort of symbolic value as death incarnate.

By contrast, there is one British artist who has been as obsessed as Hirst with the mortal flesh. I'm thinking of Lucian Freud, a painter who can totally engage your heart and mind when you simply look at one of his portraits. I can scarcely talk about Freud in the same paragraph as an artist like Hirst, whose shock tactic images fail to engage either my intellect or my emotions. Lucian Freud was, in my opinion, the greatest realist painter of the modern era. In his work, the tradition of Ingres flows seamlessly together with the representational mastery of Renaissance art in a completely contemporary framework. His portraits possess a hauntingly human quality, conveyed by his accomplished skill in evoking the texture and vulnerability of skin and flesh.

The story of Hirst's shark piece had an interesting twist following the sale of this "fish trophy" to a collector for many millions of dollars. The shark began to decompose just a year after its manufacture. When the artist replaced the old shark with a new one, it obviously raised the issue of whether the collector now owned an original art piece or a copy. Hirst claimed that neither the physical object nor its replacement mattered, since he was a conceptual artist. It was his idea, in other words, that was important, not the object itself. This notion, as I see it, is a perfect example of the classic distortion of the essence of art, which holds that artworks are indispensable and specific, while ideas belong to the field of philosophy. There is only one *David.* All the other sculptures or images are imitations. It is through the magical process of art that one unique piece is created, and the process of its creation cannot be reproduced. When we travel to Florence to see Michelangelo's *David*, we are not going there to see Michelangelo's idea of *David.*

* * *

That year, in 2001, I spent my August vacation by the sea in Tuscany as usual, and traveled to Florence at the beginning of September. On September 11th I walked from my house in the historic center to the Hotel Balestri to meet a collector from Rome, my friend Carlo Eletti, who had come to visit me. It was a beautiful Sunday afternoon, and I couldn't have ever imagined that I would witness a terrifying event that would change the entire world in the space of no more than a few minutes. I entered the hotel lobby to find the television on, with the image of one of the familiar World Trade Center towers flaming out like an enormous column of wood. An electrical short circuit? A plane that lost direction and altitude? A bomb? An act of terrorism? Frozen, momentarily, in place, I could not take my eyes from the scene; and even as I asked myself these questions, an airplane appeared on the screen—an airplane flying extremely low, directed toward the second tower as though aiming at a target.

Now, suddenly horrified, I understood. The airplane sliced into the second tower like a blade into a cardboard box. It was just after 3:00 p.m. in Florence. A quick calculation told me that in New York it had to be shortly after 9: 00 a.m., but nothing else came to mind. I had no idea what to think or feel. My brain froze, and I could only watch in horror as people leaped from the highest floors of the skyscraper, gesticulating in despair, in order not to be burned alive. I had never before seen people deliberately choose death. Then the towers fell—the first, as though collapsing into itself; the second, seeming to liquefy. In the ensuing silence that surrounded me, I felt a surge of rage, the sudden urge to exchange my paintbrush for a sword. Then came the news of the third plane crashing into the Pentagon, and the fourth one falling to the ground in Pennsylvania.

I was startled into the recognition that even America was vulnerable. The more open and democratic a society, the more exposed it is to terrorism. America's vulnerability lies exactly in its strength, in its capitalism, in its multi-ethnic core, in its tolerance. Fifteen of the nineteen hijackers were born in Saudi Arabia, and all went to Al Qaeda training camps in Afghanistan. A few million Americans are Arab-Muslim, and when someone from Afghanistan comes to visit a relative in the U.S., nothing prevents him from attending a flight school in San Diego or enrolling in a university to study chemistry and biology.

I wanted to talk to those individuals who—after seeing the images of September 11th—disdainfully chuckled and indulged in such comments as, "Good, Americans got it this time." But I wanted even more to speak to the ones who ignorantly deluded themselves in devotion or doubt, or those who feared to speak the truth for fear of sounding racist—the people blinded by the foolishness of insisting on being "politically correct."

I myself had chosen exile. By that I mean, self-exile in San Francisco where an ocean separated me from my "politically correct" compatriots. It may sound strange, but when the exile's home is a disenchanted and injured soul, geographical location does not matter. The feeling of detachment is the same, as is the sense of loss. Besides, San Francisco has always been a haven for immigrants. I just happened to move there. In any event, the exile tends to seek order and continuity, and out of a respect for order and continuity I have chosen to remain silent.

It appeared that extremists, such as those who attacked the World Trade Center, considered themselves entitled to kill infidels, if only because we drink wine, because we go to the theater and the movies, because we love music, because we dance, because we wear shorts, because women at the beach sunbathe nearly naked, because we make love when we want to, because women are allowed to drive, because gays and lesbians have fun at nightclubs. The western world lives with those threats while Islam's historical past provides a fertile ground from which to condemn the present. Meanwhile, terror attacks continue at the hands of not only people with fake or legal passports, but even from those who live legally within our borders.

* * *

Having had to postpone my departure from Florence by a week as my original return ticket was booked for September 12th, when flights to the U.S. were still grounded, I finally arrived back in San Francisco. A somber mood pervaded the city amid tension and fear generated by reports that two bridges on the West Coast had been on the terrorists' target list. I did not have it in me to fly again for a while and decided regretfully not to attend the opening of my upcoming exhibition in Tokyo that October. Instead, I slowly found my way back into the studio in preparation for a December show at my dealer Pasquale Iannetti's gallery in San Francisco. I had picked out a selection of paintings and pastels in small format, most of them composed in a coloration of evanescent blue, with diminishing perspectives over the Venetian Lagoon; and I was able to add a few more pieces before the opening, knowing that Pasquale was particularly receptive to my work on paper. The exhibition was well attended and well received, notably by the art critic David Bonetti in a review that appeared in the *San Francisco Chronicle* a few days later.

By now my return to Tuscany was imminent. The museum show at Palazzo Ducale in Massa-Carrara, scheduled to open March 23, 2002, was to be my largest retrospective to date, counting eighty-three works that included paintings, watercolors, pastels, and drawings. So, after attending a reception in Pasadena, California, where I had sent four large canvases to a group show titled *Facing the City* at D.N.F.A. Gallery, I departed for Italy again. Once there, I set up a working studio at Villa Oliviero, about thirty minutes from Massa-Carrara, a province in northern Tuscany characterized by an extensive coastal area and the Apuan Alps. Their peaks of powder-white perfection could be seen from the seashore below, and in the heart of these mountains exists the spectacular site of the Carrara marble quarries. I found it humbling to be in their presence, to feel my own smallness in the face of such greatness.

I was excited to be in Massa-Carrara and looked forward to participating in the installation of my show—paintings selected from various cycles, including a series of works on paper to which the curator, Massimo Bertozzi, had assigned an additional gallery space. He had written an in-depth critical essay, *With Heart and Mind: Reality and Fantasy in Marco Sassone's Painting*, for a catalog which illustrated each of the works in the exhibition. I was not surprised to see the image of *Man with Blue Eyes* on the cover, bled to the edges and cropped at the top and sides in order to magnify his intensity. This was a portrait that Massimo responded to and that he used for the museum posters. They were not only pasted up on the walls all over town, as is customary in Italy to promote cultural events, but throughout the province and all the way to Florence, two hours away. Anticipation of the exhibition continued to mount up until opening night, when the Mayor of Massa cut a blue ribbon in front of the grand entrance. Guests had traveled from both Northern and Southern Italy; family members arrived from Milan, Rome, and Florence; and, much to my pleasure, collectors came from Germany and California. I also felt very much at home and embraced by a local crowd that surged into the museum to discover who was behind the *Man with Blue Eyes*. It continued to attract visitors like a magnet for the entire run of the exhibition.

The installation spanned several series of works, with a good representation of portraits in both oils and pastels. There were paintings of the Venetian Lagoon dating from the late 1980s to 2000, including *Barconi,*1990; a few pieces from the Amalfi Coast series; a few urban landscapes, including *Yellow Cab,* 2000; several canvases from the Houseboat series of the late 1980s; and six large canvases from the homeless era, including the 1968 painting *Aftermath,* which the curator described as a work uniquely mine in terms of its poetic feeling and its explicit declaration of intent. Included also were two canvases from 1991, from a series I called "Socio-Political realities": *City Pigs* was rendered in tones of pink and red but without any grays or warmth, as if to conceal behind the huge forms of the hogs a city swallowed up in attrition and distress; *Why are the Children Hungry?* was a depiction of quartered beef hanging from hooks, also dominated by pink and red tones.

The reception was remarkable. The public, both shocked and challenged by the clash of themes that my homeless canvases introduced, seemed to gravitate instead to the air and light of the Venice paintings and the spacious deep blue of the sea in my Amalfi Coast pieces. The press published numerous reviews in both local and national newspapers, including *La Nazione* and *La Repubblica,* where Ilaria Bonuccelli wrote: "The *Man with Blue Eyes* stares out at you. No concessions made. He offers you—perhaps forces upon you—a magnified view of trashed humanity... His pupils gape at an interior world which he invites you to enter, without knocking."

But once again, I was more affected by what the general public had to say, people who simply managed to get lost in the artwork—people like the butcher at the supermarket, who was busy questioning, discussing, and projecting his own opinion of the huge and varied body of work he had seen at Palazzo Ducale—all while slicing my order of Prosciutto di Parma.

My love for this part of the world led me on numerous expeditions up into the hills above the museum. The area reminded me, in a way, of the terrain of the Cinque Terre, with villages carved into the mountainside, vantage points from which you could make out, in the distance, the thin, blue strip of the Mediterranean Sea. I would park the car some place and stroll up the narrow, twisting country lanes that led me to an infinite variety of views of the landscape below, roads with double rows of chestnut trees and, beyond, mossy pathways dense with yellow dotted butterflies. It was up here one day, in the village of Ca' di Cecco, that I bought a home studio with a shingled red roof, green wooden shutters, and a small garden with wild rosemary and bougainvillea. Here, looking out over the vast landscape from the second floor balcony, I could sketch the valley immediately below, where it reached out gradually toward the city of Massa in the far distance; it seemed to sit in the middle of a green carpet, merging further on, in softer colors, with a glimpse of the Mediterranean on the horizon. Above, cloud formations would change from moment to moment, filled with the atmospheric turmoil of immense skies, their crisp colors settling over the coastline at dusk. It felt to me like I was here to stay.

My work that year continued with more openings in Italy—Milan in May and Venice in June—before I returned to California, where I began to work on ceramics for a brief period of time. I greatly enjoyed the process of painting the largest bisque platters I could find with special ceramic pigments that reminded me of the fluidity of watercolor, though covering the painted surface with glaze for firing proved at first a bit traumatic. However, the joy returned with the wonderful surprise that was revealed each time a piece would be recovered from the kiln.

Despite this unexpected and pleasurable distraction, I soon found myself once again absorbed in my ongoing series of the Venetian Lagoon. The soul of Venice has reappeared periodically in my work, often portrayed in the murky waters of its canals, where the day-to-day toil of living wears on, where houses and palazzi are blended and consumed, as shown in two paintings from 2000, *Venezia 40* and *Men at Work*. I have sometimes found it difficult to identify the pull I feel toward this subject, the origin of that feeling of total rapture with which I would infuse my Venetian paintings. This time, returning to the subject after a break of two years, I noticed a new element that had begun to permeate my work, a monochromatic tonality that first appeared in *Venezia 75*, a canvas I was just then completing. When I laid down the brushes, I felt exhausted by my total surrender to the process and the drive to bring the painting to completion. This surrender unleashed a vitality all its own but also reflected my internal agitation at the time. There was a sense of mystery in this square canvas. The innumerable deep shades of blue seemed to evanesce and spread out in the air, allowing the material form to be swallowed up in a kind of soundless chaos.

This monochromatic palette persisted through that year and the beginning of the next. *Venezia 79* was a tall canvas imbued with a similar glow of blue strokes, dissolving from the sky into the sea. It evoked a mysterious sense of longing, as though seeking to reach beyond the vanishing point of the canal, whose unfocused periphery was reflected into the same blue-gray water.

I vividly remember the melancholy that would overwhelm me as I stood before these paintings, mentally whispering goodbye to the studio when I left for Tuscany yet again—this time to attend the opening of a very special exhibition and one in which I felt particularly honored to be included called *Master and Pupil: Oscar Kokoschka, Silvio Loffredo, Marco Sassone,* at the Pietrasanta Museum.

The elegant installation of this exhibition in the Cloister of St. Agostino of Pietrasanta was accompanied by a museum catalog with a cover image of the splendid 1957 Kokoschka painting, *London, Chelsea Reach.* The text was written by Peter Selz with a black and white photo printed next to the introduction illustrating what was, for me, a truly poignant moment, with the young Silvio Loffredo—later to become my mentor—standing next to the great master Oscar Kokoschka in Salzburg, in 1958. Peter Selz, the former curator of painting and sculpture at the Museum of Modern Art in New York and the first director of the UC Berkeley art museum, had authored several books on German Expressionism. In his text for the current exhibition, he described what he saw as the thread that connected the two artists: "The relationship between master and pupil in the arts can take innumerable permutations from servile imitation to outright rejection. In the case of San Francisco painter Marco Sassone, his teacher, the Florentine artist Silvio Loffredo and his mentor the Austrian master Oscar Kokoschka, we find a transmission from one generation to the next of an Expressionist visualization." Writing specifically about my work, he noted, "A canvas like *Chinese Reds*

(1990) in its scarlet color relates to the chromatic scheme of his teacher's *Angel of Death* (1998), while alarming paintings like *Marlboro Country* (1990) . . . or *Coit Tower Night* (1998) . . . elicit a fervent emotion, comparable to the sensations evoked by the canvases of Kokoschka himself."

The affinity that united the artists in terms of both form and content was also noted in a number of reviews of the show. It was particularly revealing to me, as an observer this time, to track the parallel artistic paths of the three of us, side by side, both in often overlapping subject matter—sacred art, for instance, the sense of death—and in the particular visual passion we each poured into our paintings.

Master and Pupil offered me a unique opportunity to immerse myself in paintings united by a distinctive artistic continuity and a subtle harmonic thread, expressing an emotional and spiritual experience of reality in the form of powerful chromatic marks. Marks that triggered the memory of time spent in the studio of professor Loffredo, whose intuitive approach to his art instilled in me the great lesson of humility through his gentle and affectionate teachings and through his ever-present grace.

16

THIS WOMAN

2003–2005

Whenever I spent time in Italy, I would often feel guilty about the distance I had created between my life there and my beloved studio in San Francisco. I had gone back and forth between the two for a while, and by mid-April 2003 I was once again ready to embark for a return to California, following an extended period in Tuscany. My mixed emotions and affection for both places were echoed in the words of the art critic Maria Porges, who noted in her essay about my New York exhibition in 2000, that I am always destined to live in these two worlds.

So soon enough, here I was back home in San Francisco, still suffering from my perennial feelings of displacement, like a nomad wandering from one location to the other, biding my time before comfort and complacency would eventually set in. I was back in the stomach of the whale—as I called my studio—trying to cope with the present while reflecting on my recent past.

It was unnaturally quiet for days. Then one morning, I was wandering around my space examining things, looking at paintings as usual, one by one, especially recent work, attempting to rediscover the mood and the working pattern I had left behind. Ravel's *Bolero* permeated the air, a musical rhythm barely audible at the start of the melody, when the phone rang. It sounded particularly loud on that spring day. "Good afternoon, Maestro," said a familiar voice. It was my friend and dealer Pasquale. He had called to remind me of the opening of the Francis Bacon exhibition that evening. "We would really love to see you at the reception," he continued. It was Thursday, April 24. I managed to pull myself together, and still in a daze I made my way to the Pasquale Iannetti Gallery on Sutter Street, not imagining for a moment that my life was about to be change forever. I made my way through the main floor of the exhibition, packed with guests, and found myself in the open doorway of a viewing room whose main wall held my canvas, *Venezia 75*, in a warm embrace. It had only recently been picked up at the studio by the gallery. While I stood there, staring at my painting, I heard a silvery voice beside me: "Can I help you?"

I turned and replied, with a smile, "If I need help, I'll be sure to ask you."

The owner of the voice looked at me for a moment, and I was struck by her unusual attractiveness. But then, seconds later, armed with a neat stack of papers, she vanished into the crowd. It was only after a few minutes that Pasquale reappeared with her. "Marco," he told me, "there's someone who'd like to meet you. Emily, this is Marco Sassone."

I had to laugh, and Emily, surprised and a little embarrassed by our previous exchange, stumbled over some unnecessary apology. We spoke only briefly that evening, and I was delighted when she told me that my work—especially that painting—was the reason she had asked to be introduced to the artist.

Returning to the studio, I felt genuinely moved to have met this woman, but I did not think much about it at the moment, although I was impressed by the excellent touch with which she had organized the details of the Francis Bacon installation. Still, my curiosity was aroused, so two days later, on a Saturday afternoon, I returned to the gallery. My apparent reason to return was to see the show again, but the truth was—and she knew it the moment she saw me—I wanted to see her, to check things out in the light of day. And things still seemed beautiful and intriguing. I walked up to her desk and sat with her there for a moment, so that my interest would not seem too obvious to the curious gallery staff. We made a date to see each other a few days later at the end of her workday, at six o'clock in the evening, in a hotel lobby on Union Square—which proved interesting because Emily went to the Sir Francis Drake Hotel instead, while I was waiting for her at the Saint Francis Hotel! Eventually, we managed to meet up and sat down to talk intensely for a couple of hours. As we left, we promised to contact each other very soon. It was actually she who called first: could we go together to see a painting by Leonardo da Vinci, currently on exhibit at the Legion of Honor Museum? I was impressed. The usual date is for a drink, a cup of coffee, or possibly for lunch or dinner. But no, this time the date was for a museum exhibition. I really liked that. It felt special. The exhibition, *Leonardo da Vinci and the Splendor of Poland*, had traveled to San Francisco from the Milwaukee Art Museum and was running through May 18. I, unfortunately, had to postpone our date twice at the beginning of that month, but we finally made it on a Sunday, the last day of the show.

"What kind of a car do you drive?" Emily asked.

"It's a Jaguar and it's yellow," I said. When I picked her up downtown, she was surprised by the color—as most people are. We walked through the exhibit quickly, anxious to get to what we had come to see, the only painting by Leonardo. I was familiar with *The Lady With the Ermine,* a small painting on a wood panel, approximately 20 x 16 inches, supposedly portraying Cecilia Gallerani, mistress of Duke Ludovico Sforza. The beauty of her image is pictorially mesmerizing as she cradles an exotic pet in her arms. We both gazed at the portrait for many long minutes, marveling at its perfection. It seemed like the pet was following the woman's gesture, as she appeared engaged with something or someone beyond the picture frame. We left the museum talking about Leonardo's skill with the human figure and bodily gestures, and how a pose is able to express the sitter's inner thoughts.

My own thoughts, though, began to drift beyond our conversation. I began to realize that an image of beauty was walking with me to the car. This woman was striking in a natural, modern way. She possessed an elegant presence. Her classic, chiseled face was extraordinary. Her fair skin looked like porcelain. When she smiled, it was disarming. I was not quite sure what might be happening between us, but after that Sunday afternoon we met frequently, mostly at my studio for dinner.

And that's how the knocking at the door began, metaphorically, with this young, attractive gallery lady. Even though some part of me insisted on keeping her at a distance, another part definitely wanted to open the door. We had known each other for over a month now, and each encounter had been significant and exquisite. Curiously, I was content simply with kissing her on the cheek upon arrival and departure. There was a sense of mystery to this woman; her personal history would unravel slowly, I thought, at the appropriate time—quite unlike so many others, eager to disclose life, death, and miracles all at once.

I remember Emily's first visit. There was a knock at the door that resonated with great anticipation in the studio. She came in with sunflowers in her hand and an expression of pleased surprise as we stood together for a moment at the entrance, in front of the antique-stained glass doors that led into the large open space. The contrast between the rough exterior of the building and the refined interior of my loft was a surprise to many people. She didn't remark on it immediately but seemed to be taking it all in with a sense of relief. Perhaps the rough exterior had scared her. Little did she know, I had my own delightful fear to contend with from within.

Late at night, after her visits, I would drive her to the Bart Station at Powell and Market, so she could return to her home in Walnut Creek, a town in the East Bay, thirty minutes from San Francisco. We would hug and kiss before she went on her way—looking back at her from afar—and vanishing in an instant.

This woman was on my mind constantly. I don't know how, but I managed to keep painting. I was working on a couple of canvases of Italian church interiors at the time. I'm not sure how I arrived at this subject. Perhaps it was the recurring memory of churches during the flood of Florence, a part of my intense dialogue with the past, and perhaps also because they felt like window frames looking out over monochromatic canals. There was a powerful attraction to working on these pieces. I envisioned the interiors melting chromatically as I described the evanescent shapes within, converging toward the focal point of a main altar in the lower center. This was the case in *Santa Croce,* a canvas whose gray-blue tonality infiltrated the space with a cool light that glowed through the tall, arched windows above to a paved floor below, inundated with watery mud imprinted with random footsteps, the only reminder of a human presence.

Emily's presence, however, was increasingly felt each time her footsteps resonated as she entered my studio. She brought with her a smile, enthusiasm, energy, and an incomparable glow of beauty. One evening in the studio while I was watching her recline on the green leather sofa in a black silk dress, she crossed her legs in a gesture of casual seduction. It was like watching a scene from a 1930s movie—and yet it seemed neither of us was ready to change the exquisite state of things: chaste kisses and delicate caresses.

It was already the middle of June. The air was warm in the studio, and the skylights wide open throughout. Upon the completion of *Santa Croce,* I found myself moving on immediately to the next piece, a similar church interior, yet dissimilar in composition and tonality. Here, the main altar was positioned on the right side of the image, balanced out by a tall, slender column on the left, reaching from top to bottom. The canvas was also wider. The viewer's eye was invited to enter into the composition with ease, absorbed into a pervasive spatial light that was reflected throughout. The interior objects were evanescent, as before, but flooded this time in a grayish pearl-blue-green tonality that was reflected below in the muddy water on the floor. The title was *San Remigio,* the name of a small church I had first visited in November of 1966 and whose impression had inspired me throughout my career. Both canvases held a special significance for me. They represented a pictorial achievement, a compendium of technical and artistic qualities, harmoniously developed through many phases of painting in a life devoted to art.

Was it a coincidence that I met this woman now? Perhaps, I imagined, she was the one who could take me further in my life. Meanwhile, our secluded encounters continued over dinner with spaghetti al pomodoro, wine, flowers, music, dreams, and respect.

By Friday, July 11, 2003, I had known Emily for two and a half months. That evening, I was preparing dinner as I had done many times before. She called ahead to tell me she was looking forward to seeing me, but that she would be a half hour late. She knocked on the door. Her subtle perfume preceded her as she entered, her mouth reddened by Parisian lip rouge. With a smile she announced that she was here to stay the night.

I was instantly overcome with both excitement and anxiety. Dinner and wine served to calm my internal tremors just a bit. But the tremors persisted as we prepared to settle down for the night together. Normally I perform an entire ritual of dental hygiene before bed and decided this time would be no exception. It would help me calm my nerves and keep my cool. I turned off the light. Her scent was hypnotic. The open skylight creaked as a soft breeze drifted in the air. The stars were shining and a faint glow filtered in from above. Emily melted into my arms. There were tender kisses, languid caresses, and I trembled with anticipation as the sculpted forms unraveled from the folds of her black silk nightgown.

These intimate encounters continued, each time an adventure in words, in the stars and the heavens above, where I was searching for fortitude and direction. The end of July was all too soon upon us, and I was tormented by the rapidly approaching date of my scheduled departure for Italy. My summer plans that year included spending my birthday with family. I still don't know how I managed to make the trip, but I did—despite the dreadful anguish of saying goodbye to Emily. Even then, I didn't really feel the void until I arrived at my destination. We talked for hours over the phone late at night, despite the nine-hour time difference, and at least twice a day, no matter where I was—whether riding my bike along the coastline or walking on the main drag of Forte dei Marmi.

"He disappeared again," Papa would say at the dinner table or at the outdoor cafe in Pietrasanta, under the marble plaque testifying that Michelangelo had been at this very place in 1518. In fact, as I told Emily, Michelangelo made so many trips here that he seemed to have left his tracks everywhere behind him. Though his most magnificent works are found in Florence and Rome, his mark as an artisan and sculptor is ever present in any one of the tiny side streets in Pietrasanta. He came here first in search of the ultimate stone in the marble quarries of the nearby Apuan Alps. Many sculptors followed him here through the centuries, including some of the well-known modern masters like Henry Moore, Isamu Noguchi, and Jean Arp. They came not only for the white marble but also for the famous stone workers' craftsmanship, who did the work to the artist's specifications.

"But didn't you have an exhibition at the Pietrasanta Museum?" Emily interjected once, excitedly. And yes, I did, just last February, but at that moment it felt like years ago. Often, we would both forget we were talking on the phone, and any place seemed appropriate if only I could hear the sound of her voice. She talked to me about my paintings in the gallery in San Francisco, how not only collectors but tourists, too, were attracted to my images. She talked about the pleasure she felt in dealing with artwork to which she felt emotionally connected. And one night, ten days into my vacation, we found ourselves agreeing sadly that the prospect of another twenty-nine days before my return to San Francisco was excruciatingly painful. I decided on the spot to shorten my time in Italy by a week, the longest amount of time I could consider without upsetting la mamma and the rest of the family. I had never before left earlier than planned.

* * *

She was waiting for me at the airport—her image even more beautiful than I remembered. She studied my face silently and stared at length into the depths of my eyes. We embraced lightly at first, then I hugged her tighter; as we kissed, it was as if the entire world had entered into a gentle twilight. In that instant, I wished everyone in the world could embrace each other the way we did.

And yet, my internal monologues continued. The ghosts of my past reappeared in the present. I had never before been able to fully accept being in a relationship. I would tell myself that I valued my independence. But then perhaps it was not so much independence I prized, but rather space, more of a dream space, a fantasy space, a kind of breathing room. I equated independence with being alone, and in that I was mistaken. This is probably why any lasting relationship had eluded me until now. But I could not deny that something new was happening within me at that very moment.

One day, playfully I thought, shortly after my return from Italy, I asked Emily what she really wanted from me. These are the kinds of questions—often prompted by a glass of wine—to which you do not usually expect an immediate answer. But Emily's reply did not take long. It came in five wonderful pages, written by hand on the cream-colored stationary of the Pasquale Ianetti Gallery, with the title "What do I want from you? Besides you?" This was Emily at her best, I soon discovered: there were thirty-four answers to my question, and they resonated and touched me in a way I had never felt before.

* * *

Fragments of rainbows floated up everywhere while white flashes of ascending spray filled the air, flying up from the mass of cascading crystal water below. Hand in hand, Emily and I were leaning over the railing of Horseshoe Falls, the immense, steep curve of Niagara Falls on the Canadian side. It was my first visit, and we were both absorbing the spectacular sight, surrounded by the exquisite colors of autumn permeated with rare subtle perfumes. Looking back, behind us as we walked, the Niagara River by contrast seemed calm and tranquil, rolling magnificently between the towering cliffs that rise on either side of its banks. It was late October. We were attending the Toronto Art Fair on the invitation of my dealer, and Emily was excited to show me her favorite natural wonder in Canada.

Our time there passed rapidly—six days so dense with emotion they seemed only a few moments—and we returned to San Francisco enthralled with each other. After our return, a thank you note arrived promptly with a message in her signature style on a delicately embossed pale ocher card. The last words of her note said everything: "My lips were petrified by the terror of missing love until they met yours . . . I miss you constantly."

The following Sunday afternoon, as she was preparing to return home, words came out of my mouth before I knew what I was saying: "I thought this was your home!" I told her playfully.

Nothing further needed to be said. In early December Emily moved in with me at the studio. This was a remarkable moment, I thought—a moment in which I had decided to follow my heart after more than twenty years of living alone.

The holiday season of 2003 was celebrated with spiritual warmth and a tall Christmas tree by the fireplace, decorated only with blue globes. This was Emily's idea but finding dozens of blue globes in the city proved to be a story all its own, because the stores were selling them only in boxes of mixed colors. We drove everywhere for an entire day, only to discover later, much to our relief, that they were readily available at a Walgreens store on Fillmore Street, practically next door to the studio. It was important for her to find blue—because blue was the color of trust, she said, and honesty and loyalty; a color that evokes peace, tranquility, and inspires higher ideals. I was aware that blue tonalities draw the mind toward the spiritual, but all the other symbolic attributes that were important to Emily had eluded me up to that moment. Our majestic blue Christmas tree seemed also to suggest an inner security, a reason she loved as well.

In the new year, I found myself increasingly engaged in a new series of Tuscan landscapes inspired by my house high up in the hills of Massa. As a way of getting into the process, dozens of sketches already cluttered the floor and the large worktable. At the same time, I was preparing a number of canvases with preliminary compositional sketches in oil. I interrupted the work briefly to take Emily to Hawaii for a special anniversary—to celebrate one year since we first met in the gallery in San Francisco on April 24, 2003—and resumed painting upon my return to the studio. In these paintings I felt a connection to earlier periods of my work, only this time there were additional benefits—the experience acquired through the years had brought with it multiple facets of vision, greater technical skills, and subtler chromatic effects. In essence, I was approaching the universal subject of beauty with a more fully developed sense of life. There was a mood of contemplative affection in this *Ca' di Cecco* series; some of these landscapes were envisioned at dawn or at dusk, but always at a moment when the relationship between light and darkness seemed at its most complex and indefinite. It is a moment in which they meld even as they divide, when the sky is layered with colors; a moment characterized by the portentous expectancy of *Le Mollette* ("the clothes-pins"), in which I rendered multiple rows of clotheslines from left to right in the immediate foreground, suggesting an invisible terrace from which the massive sloping landscape opens to reveal in the distance clusters of housing in the city of Massa below and merges with a glimpse of the Mediterranean beyond. Above, an immense sky fills two-thirds of the pictorial space, with heavy cloud formations threatening the expanse of land below.

I had gladly surrendered to these colors and forms. My eye was ravished by the formal qualities of these vistas and their beauty, a beauty that invariably prompts a profound aesthetic experience. This is a concept, I believe, that is not readily accepted in modern art, at least in the opinion of modernist painters like Barnett Newman, who held that a completely new art was needed. He wanted art to represent fundamental truths, not some sentimental and artificial beauty. In other words, as Newman himself once stated, modern art was the desire to destroy beauty, to discard Renaissance notions of beauty. It was an art that was abstract and intellectual. As for me, I wonder who can believe that beauty is merely sentimental and artificial and that Renaissance notions are just notions rather than sophisticated knowledge. I wonder, too, whether conceptual art, as it is pleased to call itself, has any truly noteworthy notions or ideas. Read, for example, American artist Sol Le Witt's *Sentences on Conceptual Art*, in which he argues that concept doesn't matter! And speaking of truths, how could I avoid mentioning French-American artist Duchamp, who wanted to enlist art in the service of the mind, making the ridiculous assertion that any foolish thing can be a work of art if only some clever "artist" convinces the ingenuous that it is so?

Certainly these notions leave much room for dispute. Newman, for instance, appears to be ignorant of Renaissance art and contemptuous of the artist's responsibility to beauty. Perhaps in this context it would be valid to explore whether or not external beauty is the counterpart of the expression of internal beauty. I, myself, would rather believe that natural beauty reflects and manifests the inner beauty of the soul. A painting, as I see it, is especially moving when it leaves us waiting anxiously for a reply, which it declines to give. Specifically, it embodies a feud between the beauty of matter and the beauty of the soul in their most subtle forms, suggesting their apparent incompatibility even while encouraging the belief that, with true and honest sensitivity, they can be reunited. Which means being receptive at once to nature and to one's own inner self and understanding that they somehow mirror one another, each being the unforeseen spirit of the other.

Several pieces from the *Ca' di Cecco* series had been picked out for show at the Odon Wagner Gallery in Toronto, opening in November. Emily had taken over discussions with the gallery as to the scheduling and organization of the exhibit. Five new canvases, including *Le Mollette*, were illustrated in the catalog *Marco Sassone: New Work*. Emily and I flew to Toronto before the opening, staying in the splendid home of her friends Mirella and Vito, whom I had met during our trip the previous year. Later, with their help, we located an apartment on the nineteenth floor of a downtown tower overlooking a vast green expanse called the Rosedale Ravine. I decided to maintain a base in Toronto, since Emily had a special fondness for this city where she had spent many years. Following the opening we resumed our travels, arriving in Florence to spend Christmas and New Year's with family and friends.

Emily had captured my imagination with her intellect and her love. My natural propensity for the feminine side had endowed me with a deep respect for women. I was always fascinated by the psychological aspects of human nature and by introspective insights into the human soul, which, in the case of women, meant I was searching for a classic and mysterious woman. Emily embodied—with regard to the sense of mystery that a woman can have in the eyes of a man—the essence and synthesis of everything I see, understand, and love about the opposite sex. I realized now there had long been quiet dreams and aspirations haunting me from within that I had been too distracted and professionally involved to recognize, or too afraid to acknowledge and pursue. As I began to awaken to the authenticity of my heart's true desires, a miracle took place: I felt happier, and my life felt complete. I missed Emily whenever we were not together. Our exchange of love notes continued for Valentine's Day, birthdays, and even for no reason at all. In San Francisco for our two-year anniversary, she again expressed her feelings with great eloquence: "When a human soul reaches another one similar to its own, their shadows create a spirit. A spirit of power and belonging. It seems like you never knew yourself before ..." And shortly following those words—too soon it seemed—she left for Toronto while I remained in San Francisco, in the studio working, surrounded by my world, my colors, my dreams, and missing her yet not alone any longer. I was aware that I had entered a new chapter of a book on whose first page appeared the words: Here begins a new life. I followed her a short time later to our new retreat in Toronto, and soon thereafter we returned together to San Francisco.

The back and forth travel, however, had disadvantages. This became clear to me in late May of 2005 as I was working on *Saint Florent*, a monochromatic painting of land and water painted in muted blues—blues melting and merging into a variety of turquoise and pale greens, with subtle accents rendered on the faded facades of an ancient village mirrored in the water below. It was an image that elicited a deep range of emotions in me as I applied the finishing touches. And it was here, precisely, immersed in this fantasy landscape of evanescent colors, that I experienced an epiphany. I decided at that very instant of completion, after twenty-four years in San Francisco, that it was time to relocate my life to be with Emily in Canada.

17

TRACKS

2005–2013

The mood in the studio that summer of 2005 was one of excitement and melancholy. Emotions were running high. In my own spontaneous way, I decided to relocate to Canada without fully realizing the magnitude of the decision. I had moved many times before—from Florence to London and to America and now to Canada—for different reasons. This time, however, I was moving for a woman. I was fully conscious of it, and I was excited. But packing and shipping an entire studio—a place that had been my sanctuary for the last twenty-five years—proved to be an emotional rollercoaster that I would never forget. But I was moving forward, believing in my destiny, a destiny that I had created for myself time and time again.

And so it was on August 15th that I finally departed for Toronto. Emily was already there, waiting for me. The search for a new studio began immediately, even as I gazed around me at a city that I knew little about. This vast industrial metropolis looked intriguing with its dynamic, muscular routes merging into the heart of the downtown area, on the north side of Lake Ontario. But it was still too soon for me to surrender entirely, as I recall, and the sights of the city by the bay were pulling me back. In January of 2006, I flew to San Francisco with Emily for her birthday and proposed to her on the wild shores of the Pacific in Half Moon Bay. We returned to Toronto engaged and were married a few months later in an intimate ceremony at The Breakers Hotel in Palm Beach, Florida.

On July 1, 2006, la mamma passed away in Florence at the age of eighty-five. She had been sick for only a few months. I had just visited her a week earlier on a false alarm, and she welcomed me with her familiar smile, thanking me for my red roses and a card with the words, "I am always with you." That was the last time I saw her alive. On my next trip to Florence I was able to join my family only during the service at the church of San Remigio, where I stroked her head and kissed her goodbye. La mamma left an unbridgeable void in all of us. The family was never the same. My two sisters, Milly and Patrizia, would not talk to each other for years after her departure. For them, it was a life-altering and profoundly emotional experience—not only the fact that my mother died, but also bearing witness to her final hours. They were the caregivers, a role that becomes part of your identity, like becoming a mother. It seemed their suffering was compounded when that role came to an end. As for myself, I reacted differently, from a distance, and during my trips back and forth to Florence. The void in my heart was alleviated by memories of life and love, not loss. I chose to see in it a way of bringing comfort and guidance to those who were not in the same stage of life's journey as myself.

La mamma was the sweetest, kindest person I have ever known. Her mind was truly enchanting. While relearning how to live in the world without her, I felt things that I had almost forgotten. I experienced acute nostalgia, a longing for a time lost, but still flooded with memories. She became ingrained in my soul. Grief emanated out of my pores and into the world that surrounded me.

In the winter of that year a snowstorm hit Toronto that lasted several days. For hours I watched the snow drift down, the sky go gray, then eerily dark, with nighttime snow resembling flakes of ash. A white mantle covered everything in a mood of grief. A sense of loss pervaded the atmosphere. Like the snow, we are always falling toward the ground, though we often forget it. Grief infiltrates the external world. One common experience of those who grieve seems to be to try to bring back the dead, not literally, but rather to see or seek signs of them in the landscape of life. People often go through periods in which they see the dead person in objects or animals and sometimes construct a false reality, a reality where their loved one is simply hiding out or absent. La mamma was present for me in the form of a ladybug. How could I think otherwise when a ladybug was waiting for me on my pillow in the bedroom upon my return from Florence? We live on the nineteenth floor! And during the weeks that followed, a ladybug would appear constantly on the inside of the large windows of the living room.

During this time I felt that life expected me to absorb the loss and move forward, like some kind of emotional warrior.

The recurring question of "how are you?" seems to be an expression of concern, but it shouldn't always be taken for an actual inquiry. As I reflected on the struggle to accept the loss of my mother, I realized that her absence became a presence. The grief I felt reoriented me toward myself, a paradox of mortality and the awareness of my own impermanence. It is not only a question of getting over the absence of a loved one and healing; it is also a question of learning to live with this transformation.

One day I went for a run. I dislike running in the cold, but after a long period spent indoors in the dead of winter, I was filled with exuberance. One of my favorite pathways is accessible by going down ninety-five wooden steps below the glass tower we live in, through woods and foliage, and ending up on a large expanse of grass where I usually pick up the pace before turning back. That afternoon the air was crisp, and I felt myself float up off the ground. The world came alive. The brightness of the snow and the trees intensified. Behind the vanishing point of the treescape, I sensed worlds beyond my perception. La mamma was out there, inaccessible to me yet indelible. The blood moved faster through my veins. Suffused with this glow of emotions, I stopped for a moment to stand still in the middle of the pathway, feeling disoriented for no reason, or for reasons I didn't need to know. Then I sprinted up the wooden steps to the top and as the adrenaline rushed out the clarity vanished.

I'd had a similar experience before, as a child in Campi Bisenzio where I was born, near Florence. I was walking from the house to open the gate to the garden. It was springtime. As I placed my hand on the gate, the world went ablaze as bright as the multitude of flowers before me, and I felt I was lifted out of myself and realized that I was part of a grandiose book. What I knew of life was a small version of a larger reality, the pages of which had already been written. What I would pursue in life and how I would do it was already known. I stood there, my heart palpitating.

I think about la mamma every day but not in the same manner as I used to. She goes through my mind like a swallow flying back home: sudden, radiant, magical, gone. And the ladybugs continue to visit me periodically.

* * *

With the assistance of a new real estate agent I'd met in our building, I located a wonderful space for studio in the film district on the east side of the city. I saw several lofts in that area and decided on one on the top floor of an old Colgate factory that had original hardwood floors, high ceilings, skylights, and large paneled windows facing northeast. But it was the large terrace on the rooftop that convinced me to purchase the loft immediately. I began remodeling the raw space with a local carpenter, adding wood cabinets, a new kitchen, a huge rack for storing paintings, and installed my stained-glass double doors from the 1800s to separate the entrance from the interior space, just as they had done in my studio in San Francisco. These doors followed me everywhere I moved. I had developed an affection for them since acquiring them from an antique dealer in California, who showed me photographs of an Austrian castle with interior fixtures, wood panels, and other exquisite objects available for sale. I love antiques placed in contemporary settings.

Everything felt new at the time—a distinct sensation to which I had become accustomed through the years—but the contents of my old studio offered the comfort of familiarity as I resumed life and work in yet another part of the world. My assistant, Sarah, was also new. She came highly recommended by Barbara Edwards, the director of the former Sable-Castelli Gallery in Toronto, whom I had met at a reception at the Italian Consulate. Having previously worked as assistant director of a fine arts gallery, Sarah brought with her experience, attention to detail, and a well-suited personality that I truly admired.

I continued to become familiar with my surroundings. I was attracted to the freeways, underpasses, railroad tracks, and all of the city's arteries. I was intuitively driven to these spots, where perspective exercised its magical pull on me; it's a feeling, an instinctive need to look, to see, and discover that guides you to a specific place for no specific reason, or for reasons you don't fully understand. From a painter's point of view, it seems like the subject matter selects you. In 1989, following my encounter with Willie, my first homeless subject, I had produced numerous sketches on location on an abandoned track near the Embarcadero in San Francisco. I thought it was the figure of the man himself who attracted me, but when I returned to the studio, I found myself painting a watercolor of a track without Willie in it. My immediate reaction in that moment of curiosity and reflection was to give birth to an entire series on the homeless, which I did. Now, many years later, this marvelous vision of tracks resurged with a force and conviction that led me into a whole new exploration of my personal journey.

From the time I was a child growing up in Italy, I always felt a strong desire to go, to depart, to arrive in some other place. I still remember the excitement I felt when my family announced that we were moving from the small town of Campi Bisenzio to Florence. I was ten years old at the time and not at all afraid of losing my school friends. The prospect of the departure eventually overshadowed any other affectionate feelings I had for my birthplace. Florence was the world of art, and I became a modest practitioner in this overwhelming city of the Renaissance. However, the desire to get away from the weight of the city's towering history was ever-present.

Art is a creature that inhabits every part of me. Naturally, my inner nature manifests itself in the art, and when I paint it is often autobiographical. My journey reveals itself in my attachment to a perspective of converging lines that becomes synonymous with railroad tracks. And those tracks led me further into a dramatic engagement with my past in terms of departures and arrivals. They came to connote a sense of ruin and corrosion too.

Abandoned tracks also suggest the trains that once rode these iron paths with passengers departing and arriving. They lure my imagination into stories of people fussing with the details of their journey, caught up in the plot of their own lives and the accidental confluence of characters, as if it were my own heart beating beneath their clothes. The train reunites us after a summer apart. It serves as the perfect place for bonding, where passengers exchange stories of their adventures and update each other on their lives. Being on a train allows us to face others when conversing, to discuss something as we gaze out the window or while having a meal in the restaurant car.

As an adolescent I rode the train on my own from Florence to Milan during several late summers. I loved to visit my maternal grandparents. For me, it was a great adventure that sparked my youthful imagination. It was the train itself where the adventure took place. I saw the train as a magnificent monster that unleashed itself over ocean and earth, gleaming and smoking like a volcano overtaking mountains and devouring landscapes, gliding over canyons, disappearing into hidden tunnels and charging out fearlessly, expelling its extraordinary, ear-piercing scream in sudden bursts. It was the journey that helped relieve my doubts and instill confidence, making me realize that anything can happen if we believe it possible.

An abandoned track, as sad and lonely as it appears, offers me each time the vision of a wonderfully rich metaphor for the endless parallels of life.

So here I was in my studio, inundated by a multitude of sketches, notes, and preparatory studies in pencil, watercolor, and pastel—all images of tracks and other urban routes offering a similar vision of vanishing perspective lines. A momentum was building. You travel as you paint. The canvases that now began to emerge reflected my new investigations into a color relationship that originated in a more monochromatic palette. The work, I was sure, had reached a level of maturity that was an accurate measure of the progress in my painting over the previous several years, during which I had arrived at a consolidation of the technical and intellectual elements that had been developing for over forty years.

I shared my thoughts about this new series of paintings with my dealer, Odon Wagner, when he visited my studio in late 2006. He reacted with a subtle enthusiasm and picked up two canvases immediately to be shown at the gallery. I later learned that the paintings were placed in the collection of the

Royal Bank of Canada, and Odon, given this initial success with my new work, booked a solo exhibit for me, scheduled to open in 2008.

I felt this work was truly my own and reflected the evolution that had taken place in my own life. It takes a lifetime of work to reach your core, I thought. These canvases of railroad tracks felt like the focus of my existence as they came to life in a magical rhythm of succession. A flow of strokes synthesizing all of the ideas taken from a myriad of sources fell into place and formed a cohesive whole: a palette of somber hues, with curving tracks and switches that drew the viewer's eye into unseen, converging focal points. A portrayal of steel beams that literally railroad the vision to vanishing points that terminate in faint city skylines standing above an expanse of wasteland, totally bereft of human presence. At the same time, I felt myself in some of these canvases—as the observer—the invisible and implied presence of the dispossessed, wandering along these tracks and stepping across them in their own aimless journey.

My flow continued uninterrupted through 2007 and part of the following year. During this time I produced two additional canvases that made it into the show just before the opening in April of 2008. *Border Crossing* elaborated on the characteristics and coloration that appeared in previous works in the series, but this time I opted to omit the railroad tracks in favor of large curving furrows in the foreground, gradually leading further up the painting into a chaotic noman's land of blasted landscape. It suggested a feeling of transience with more crevices merging with the miniscule vanishing skyline of a city and then winding its way across the top of the canvas, weary under a sliver of pale gray sky. *Emilia,* the given name of my wife Emily, is the title of the other painting, a canvas that resumes the theme of tracks, only this time in a vertical format. I intended this work to address a higher plane of existence: the vertical thrust originates in the human, earthly realm, rising compellingly toward the horizontal. The railroad tracks separate near the top, approaching a faint suggestion of the Toronto skyline at the horizon. It is a painting, as I see it, where all movement is essentially variable. The track appears to emphasize both the idea of moving horizontally across the land and a vertical propulsion. At times I see the track, too, as descending from above, descending perhaps from "Emilia," the name inscribed on the top of the cityscape, in an intuitive pictorial gesture, discovered suddenly during the act of painting and symbolizing my journey to reach the woman who is now my wife.

The opening at the Odon Wagner Contemporary was a success. The show was accompanied by an exhibition catalog with a text by Jonathan Goodman, art critic for *Art in America. The Globe and Mail,* Canada's national newspaper, published a review by the art critic Gary Michael Dault, who offered this description of the series:

> In these persuasively lonely and poignant paintings, the gray-blue tracks... begin in the foreground and wander off into the distance. They thread themselves this way and that through foggy gray middle grounds and out into oblivion, the flecking and dabbing of Sassone's brush reading now as

> the rusting, flaking and slow ruin that comes with abandonment.

After two years of work devoted to this project, I was gratified with the response. But there was more. This time I also sensed within me a feeling of accomplishment emanating from Emily, an evolution of my own human qualities that brought me here, similar to intuition in a flow of painting. I couldn't take my eyes off her at the opening, as she illuminated the reception with her wonderful, magnetic presence.

* * *

The summer in Toronto came and went in an instant. Then the winter felt the same as if it had never left. And through my large windows overlooking the morning mist, I felt right at home and realized I had been here before—all my life in the studio, engaged in work—in work that didn't feel like work but more like care of the soul.

I sometimes think that even the most ordinary activities, performed with thoughtfulness, have an effect far beyond their apparent insignificance. At times, we may lose an opportunity to reward the soul by skipping ahead to final solutions without pausing to enjoy the process. There is something wonderful inside the nature of things, in the experience that transforms our lives by giving us more complexity and depth. The seed of spirituality often blossoms in the mundane and is nurtured in the small daily activities. It is through mystery and madness that the soul reveals itself, and the journey is not only about acquiring experiences, but about deeply felt, risky, and unpredictable explorations of our existence. Art, I think, is more compelling than reason. For one thing, images precede language and are closer to feelings. The entire process of art is not about the expression of talent or making pretty things. It is about the conservation and contentment of the soul. It is about arresting life and making it available for observation. Art captures the eternal in the everyday, and in turn feeds the soul.

I had been painting straight for several weeks—more canvases of railroad tracks with a monochromatic palette of gray-blue tones or rust reds. I interrupted my workflow for the installation of a commission I had received several months earlier for the lobby of the Bellagio, a glass tower in downtown Toronto. It was finally coming to fruition. The mural had been approved long before by the board of directors from a set of charcoal drawings I had presented, along with a final study in soft pastels, made to scale for the space. The completed work was titled *Waterfront* and comprised three panels measuring 72 x 144 inches overall. It was unveiled in late October of 2008.

Back at the studio one morning in early December, I received an email that truly touched me. It came from Chelsea, a social worker and student at the University of Southern California in Los Angeles. The message in the subject box read: "Man with blue eyes." I could never have anticipated what I was about to read. The man with blue eyes had a name, John. After being homeless for over twenty years, he was now rehabilitated and living in Venice Beach. Chelsea was delighted to report that her professor had discovered my portraits of street people. "John is taking much better care of himself since his days in San Francisco," she wrote. "Although, his appearance hasn't changed much his personality sure has ... The paintings are so dead-on to the man I know, it's scary." This news, among other sensations, took me back fourteen years in an instant, as I was reminded of my poignant time spent on the streets of San Francisco. This man had been a key figure in my series of paintings for the exhibition *Home on the Streets.* His tale is a journey of human survival, and his portraits illustrated the cover of my books, posters, and inspired Chapter 14 of this memoir.

Coincidentally, other reminders kept recurring during this period of time. I had been invited to give a lecture at the largest homeless shelter in Toronto called Seaton House, where I had the privilege and pleasure of speaking to an audience hungry for more images of my art and to hear more about my life as an artist. This was to an audience of people who were homeless, who came from all types of social backgrounds and former walks of life, who gathered temporarily under one roof, still bearing visible scars of their struggles. A short time later, a book was delivered to my studio door. Published in 2009 by the Canadian government, it was entitled *Guide to Services for People Who Are Homeless.* Illustrated on the glossy cover was one of my portraits staring back at me—the vivid image of a man with desperation in his eyes—a vibrant reminder of these people's unshakable humanity, where resignation and defeat already felt exhausted, yet distant flashes of a former pride still burned.

In 2009 I enjoyed a studio visit from a distinguished New York dealer, Louis Newman, director of the David Findlay Jr. Gallery. He came to select work for two shows he was curating at the gallery and for the Palm Beach Art Fair in Florida. My exhibition schedule during this period of time intensified. Ironically, the paintings of railroad tracks were taking me places. On October 1, 2010, I attended the opening of my San Francisco exhibition in the splendid space of the Shrine of St.

Francis, and a few days later I traveled to Rome for the October 12 inauguration of my solo show at Palazzo Dell'Informazione. Both events generated extensive public and media interest. One item, however, that captured my sensibility and still resonates today was the title of a video interview produced by the Italian news agency Adnkronos in Rome: *Marco Sassone: When the Soul is Nailed to the Canvas.* The words made me reflect on memories of a city where one culture is built over another over millennia.

You cannot help but be inspired by Rome. You can literally breathe in the differences between Italian and American culture—their attitudes toward aging and mortality—as seen in the architecture of the two countries. Rome's glorious architecture is truly integrated with the art. In the course of this trip, I felt compelled to revisit a couple of majestic sights. The first was the Mausoleum of Augustus—the giant circular tomb of Rome's first emperor, built in 28 BC, and one of the most remarkable monuments of that time. As I was standing there, hand in hand with Emily, inhaling the air emanating from this space, we both felt overwhelmed by the feeling of the passage of time and by an indescribable sensation surrounding a site that houses the ashes of numerous illustrious people and emperors, in addition to Augustus. Then the Pantheon—one of the best preserved buildings in all of ancient Rome—and the one I am drawn to see again whenever I am in the Eternal City. Built originally during the reign of Augustus, the Pantheon, as we see it today, was completed one hundred years later. What a glorious sight, this mysterious space constructed as a temple to honor every god, an inspiration to both Renaissance and modern architects. I can remain inside for hours, staring up through the circular central opening, an eye to the sky. It's incredible to realize that this structure built two thousand years ago remains to this day the largest unreinforced concrete dome.

On my return to Canada, I made a series of drawings set in ruined cathedrals. In these images, the shadows and dark spaces shaped by architecture soared above a track, placed in the middle of the floor, moving up from the foreground and dissolving into the back wall of the church. These studies led me into a canvas painted in somber tones with highlights of sepia color. I titled it *Terminus,* suggesting the final arrival at the end of the line. The church was stripped of its ceiling, exposing a dense and muted gray-blue sky. I next returned to another large picture in progress, *Colosseum,* a work that Emily referred to later as "open heart surgery." It was also painted in sepia and rust reds. My intention was to convey the layers of ancient civilizations that once packed the largest amphitheater ever built—a sensation of intricate human crossings and deep crevices that converged in a circular motion toward the center of the image.

My work continued with a large cycle of watercolors depicting the nocturnal imagery of urban landscapes and railroad tracks that resulted in my 2012 exhibition at Berenson Fine Art in Toronto. In *Through a Glass Darkly*, an essay published in the *Huffington Post* on March 27, 2012, the critic Peter Clothier suggested, "These dark paintings are, after all, not primarily about the darkness that pervades them, but about the light that manages to shine through." That same year I was invited to present a solo show at Price Tower Arts Center, a museum designed by Frank Lloyd Wright in Oklahoma. Back in Toronto, Berenson hosted a retrospective, *Marco Sassone:*

1968-2013, curated in part with works lent by private and public collections. This exhibition was the source of a flood of intense emotions and vivid memories for me, tracing my path back through time and exploring every phase and evolution in my journey as a painter—strong sensations that persist longer in the subconscious depths of the soul than in the conscious memory itself. A mere spectator, this time, I was both humbled and delighted to be witness to a body of work in which the multiple images of a disparate past coalesced convincingly in a fully unified pictorial language.

In 2014 a selection of current works from my ongoing series of cityscapes and railroad tracks was also the subject of a show titled *Oil and Water: Paintings by Marco Sassone*, installed at the San Angelo Museum of Fine Art in Texas.

18

FORGED

2014–2021

Through the years I have received Google alerts for "Marco Sassone" to catch any mention of myself or my work when it appears online. One late afternoon in October of 2014, I received an alert that turned my life upside down. It announced simply: "Original Signed Lithograph by Artist Marco Sassone," for sale at auction. It claimed to come with a certificate of authenticity. My first thought was that this must be an error as I have never produced lithographs. I had seen this sort of mistake online before, describing my serigraphs as lithographs, so I left this item up on the computer for later inspection and carried on with my day. That night, however, when I went back to the computer, I noticed that the so-called "lithograph" was not an image from any of the sixty-two editions of serigraphs I had produced. It was the reproduction of a painting, an early landscape, but

I could not identify the image immediately. What caught my attention instead was the auction information: "Value estimated at $4000–$4200," with a starting online bid of $275. Something was definitely wrong here. Then I read the title of the piece, *View of Avalon,* circa 1976, and stared at the image again. My antennas went up this time, and I went over right away to the coffee table to consult my large book, *Sassone,* published in 1980. I knew that the painting in question was illustrated here among more than one hundred other images. I found it immediately on page 38. Then I went back to the screen and enlarged the Sassone signature on this alleged lithograph.

For the next few moments, I was in a state of complete shock. My signature had been forged!

So the print was in fact a lithograph, but a forged lithograph. I didn't know what to think. It was evident that the fake was an exact replica of the printed illustration, captured illegally by some photographic process, then enlarged and reprinted on paper. For the following few weeks I was glued to the computer, investigating the auction houses that were selling these counterfeit prints with fake signatures and fake certificates. I discovered dozens of these lithographs coming up for sale. By now, I was becoming more proficient on the computer and kept downloading the information I found. I discovered two major online platforms used by individual auction houses to post their merchandise: icollector.com from Canada and liveauctioneers.com from the U.S. The forged lithographs were appearing on both of these platforms, posted by several auction houses under a variety of names. I wondered how many Sassone prints had sold so far and received my answer right away when I clicked on the button "Sold Items." The result was one thousand items on icollector.com and over three hundred on liveauctioneers.com! I was overwhelmed. I continued downloading information to my computer, fearing what I was seeing online might eventually be erased. Meanwhile, every day there were more fake lithographs for sale. I knew of over fifty different images that had been forged. I knew the title and the year of each image, since they had all been copied from illustrations in *Sassone*. Basically, each image had been photographed from the book, then enlarged and printed on white paper. Margins were left all around the image, and my signature was forged in pencil on the right bottom corner in the margin.

Painting has guided me through my own path of self-discovery. It is a search that renews itself in innumerable ways as I've found the essence of life within a world of color, light, and nuance. It has taught me how to go deep into matter, how to investigate the subjects close to my heart in order to continue my journey. But this time I was embarking on a distinctly different voyage of discovery. I needed to know who was copying my artwork, who was forging my name, and I realized that I was committed to this task with an intensity equal to my painting. After all, it was my work that was being abused so blatantly and in broad daylight, where anyone can look, yet few understand what it is that they're seeing. What could I say if I were to call the police? I was sure they would need proof, which I did not yet have. So who was going to unravel this thing, if not myself? Given my ignorance about such matters, I knew it was going to be a challenge, but I was set to go. Some friends were telling me to just let it go. Just paint, they told me. I would have loved to go back into the studio, but I could not let this go. What about all those people who were getting scammed in my name, I worried, who thought they were buying an original Sassone lithograph? There were thousands of them, and that number was continuously growing. So should I just sit there and take it?

No, I thought; this is not who I am. I was never one to sit still and take it. But how could I find out who was behind this storm of criminal activity? Who was responsible for it? This was the question that tormented me. How could we put a stop to this forgery of my work?

One idea came to mind immediately: in order to at least find out where the prints originated, I would need to order some. So I asked a couple of friends—my former assistant Sarah in Toronto and Diane in California—to purchase the prints online. At the same time, I started to investigate the names of the individual auction houses posting my prints for sale: Fine Art Online Auction; Wholesale Art Auction; Wilson Fine Art and Antiques; Art and Jewelry Auction House; and Buy Art Auction. When I googled their addresses, I could find no clear information as to whether these businesses existed. I noticed that two of them were in Colorado: Fine Art Online Auction in Denver and Wilson Fine Art and Antiques in Boulder. Both of these companies listed Mary Wilson as the contact person. I called Franco, an old friend of mine, in Boulder. We were in school together in Florence and he was immediately ready to help me with my plan. He drove to both addresses and called me back. "There are no auction houses at these locations," he told me. "There is an office building at one address and a gas station at the other!" He added that "Mary Wilson" was nowhere to be found, which gave me a good laugh. I could not believe it. But then he made a return visit to the building at 1942 Broadway in Boulder and discovered a receptionist in Suite 314C for the Colorado-based "Registered Agents Inc." So, Mary Wilson, if the name was even real, had two companies registered under her name but no actual place of business as purported online. The same was true for the other names: fake addresses or the addresses only of their registered agents. Either way, there was not an auction house at any of these locations.

I decided to purchase two more counterfeit lithographs with the assistance of my friend Lella in Toronto and Collin in San Francisco, a close friend of my son Nicola.

The first two prints I had arranged to purchase arrived in mid-December via FedEx. They had been advertised online by two different auction houses, Wholesale Art Auction in Murray, Utah, and Fine Art Online Auction in Denver, Colorado. However, both prints were shipped from the same PostalAnnex in Las Vegas. Okay, I thought, I was getting somewhere. The invoices indicated that the artwork had been picked up at an auction house. I decided at this point to contact the Royal Canadian Mounted Police in Toronto, since icollector.com's headquarters for these multiple auction houses was in Canada. So I spoke to my friends and neighbors, Donald and Caroline, across the hall from me. Caroline is a superior court judge in Toronto and Donald is a senior assistant deputy minister in Ottawa. He commutes constantly. Don proved to be very helpful. On December 17th he put me in touch with Inspector John Shoemaker, who in turn assigned my case to Inspector Ann Koenig. I exchanged a few emails with Inspector Koenig, who informed me that we could meet only after the holidays in early January.

Well, I spent a lot of time on the computer during the holiday. I knew now Las Vegas was the place to investigate and systematically began to check the websites of each individual auction house. I checked their registrations and was not surprised to discover that they were all registered in Las Vegas. Some websites were even registered by the same web company. But one auction house, Art and Jewelry, stood out from the other ones, even though this company did not have a website; they instead used the icollector.com website. Their place of business, however, was listed at 6130 Flamingo Road, Las Vegas. PostalAnnex was also located at the same address, according to a commercial invoice that included the name of Darryl McCullough as the contact person. All of a sudden Flamingo Road appeared to be a very busy place. Two other names showed up online at that address as well: Colonel's Auction House and Daniel's Auction House, both listing the name of a "Colonel Coker" as their principal. Further investigation revealed that these companies had been operating even before Art and Jewelry Auction House. I also discovered that Flamingo Road was the address of a large plaza with numerous unit numbers. You could see online the location of PostalAnnex and other businesses in this plaza, although Art and Jewelry Auction House did not show up. Still, I knew it was there. The invoices for both of the forged lithographs I purchased acknowledged receipt of my payment at that address. It appeared that "Darryl McCullough" picked up the artwork from an auction house or that the auction house delivered it to him.

In either case, I was on the right trail, but we still didn't know who was behind the Art and Jewelry Auction House. We still did not have a name. I took another look at the invoices and the online paperwork of the purchases. It showed the icollector.com platform hosting the auction for an "Original Signed Lithograph by artist Marco Sassone." It showed prices and shipping charges to be paid through PayPal. Then I spotted a small line of text stating "charges will appear on your credit card statement" as "PayPal Colauction." I did not know what Colauction was or meant, but one thing was evident: this entire fraudulent enterprise comprised an enormous ring of criminal activity, auctioning forged artworks every day by hundreds of artists including Picasso, Chagall, Renoir, Miro, Dali, and Matisse—all at the expense of a general public who is less than knowledgeable about acquiring artwork. Identifying the forged signatures of dead artists has always been a challenge; art foundations usually do not like to get involved, leaving the criminals free range to produce counterfeit artworks.

I downloaded the business registration of each auction house represented by the "registered agents" in a variety of different cities in the U.S. but could find nothing regarding the registration of Art and Jewelry Auction House.

The holidays passed quickly that year, and right around January 3rd I went back to review once again the "comments and complaints" by customers on the icollector.com website. This led me to another site posting questions and answers regarding the purchase of art online. At one point, I could not believe once again what I was reading. A post published on February 4, 2009, read:

> Did you buy these pieces from an auction by 'Everything Goes' or 'Colonel's Auction House?' i used to work for this scam artist and i know mr

> coker... not sure if isen is a fraud, but the coker's sure are. Google darrel tyrone coker if you want to find out more info on these con men.

And again, still more of this extraordinary information appeared in the following post, dated June 3, 2013:

> Colonel Coker is really Darrel Coker, aka. Darrel T. Coker. He changed his first name from Darrel to his "new" name Colonel. Colonel Coker is the name he uses to cover up his illegal past. Darrel aka Colonel's past is really a mirror of what he is currently doing to abuse consumers at his auctions. He has multiple auction sites on icollector.com.com. The only difference is that he is no longer living in Florida but in Las Vegas, Nevada. Here is his mug shot from his time spent in prison for fraud and racketeering. Read more about Darrell Coker aka. Colonel Coker here:

A link was posted to mug shots of a man called Coker. I downloaded the entire history of this individual with his arrests in 1992, 1997, and 2000, showing he was sentenced on February 4, 2000, and released from prison in Florida on April 26, 2004. I found a newspaper article in the *St. Petersburg Times* by Julie Hauserman on March 18, 2006, describing the entire story of Darrell Tyrone Coker, who apparently had a criminal record stretching back to 1968. Hundreds of people across Florida had been scammed by this man, who authorities said had made as much as one million per month passing off fake art as the real thing. He lured wealthy investors to hotel ballrooms in Florida's major cities. There, he offered them wine and hors d'oeuvres and promised them a chance to bid on paintings and sculptures by Frederick Remington, Rembrandt, Picasso, and Dali. But Coker instead sold both residents and visitors cheap, virtually worthless reproductions.

In Florida he operated under the names of at least two companies: Jewelry Auction Inc. and Henry Bonnard Bronze Co., which manufactured the bronze sculptures he sold as valuable originals. In another article posted online by Mark Chervenka, Coker was said to provide buyers with fake certificates for the Remington, copies of the original Henry Bonnard Bronze Co. certificates, with a slight alteration that read: Henry Bonnard Bronze, Inc. The article also described how Coker began an auction business in Florida in 1989. Through his businesses, Jewelry Auction Inc. and Henry Bonnard Bronze, Inc., in Longwood, Florida, Coker obtained reproductions of bronzes from various manufacturers and sold them at greatly inflated prices, representing them as originals in auctions throughout the state of Florida. According to the article, Florida agents estimated sales revenue of Coker's schemes in the millions of dollars.

Now, I could put the pieces of the puzzle together: the word Colauction on the invoices was an abbreviation for Colonel Auction, and the name Darrell was used in lieu of Colonel Coker to cover up his past activities. With his name I was now able to uncover his previous companies and registrations in Las Vegas: Everything Goes Enterprises Inc., Darrel Coker Inc., and his current company, Art and Jewelry House LLC, which conveniently omitted the word "auction." Without the exact name, there is no way to search the registration of a company.

His current company's registration was filed in 2012, with an expiration date of December 31, 2015.

On January 7, 2015, I sent an email to Inspector Koenig inquiring about our meeting and letting her know that I had discovered hard evidence of the forgery. We met the next day at my home. I was ready for her. I had my package of evidence with all the pertinent information, including the documents that I had discovered online. I also provided one of the forged lithographs I had purchased, *View of Avalon,* and my three hundred page book illustrating all the other images being counterfeited. Looking through it all, Inspector Koenig told me I could have a desk in her office any time! With so much evidence delivered into the hands of the police and knowing that the individual responsible had a prior conviction of five years in prison for art fraud, I was expecting to get some results soon. Unfortunately, this turned out not to be the case. On February 24th, Inspector Koenig informed me that she had referred my complaint to the FBI, and a few days later I was happy to receive confirmation from her that the FBI was interested in my case and might contact me directly.

Another long month passed before I received a call from the FBI to schedule a phone conference for Friday, April 24th. Special agent Douglas Berndt called promptly at 1:00 p.m. He indicated that he had received only a summary of my complaint from Inspector Koenig and requested all of the information and the evidence, which I forwarded to him overnight via FedEx. I sent him the entire package of evidence that I had assembled and a copy of my book. A few days later he acknowledged receipt, but after that I did not hear from him for over a month. I decided to contact him via email on June

10th for an update on the investigation. I informed him at the same time that sales of forged Sassone lithographs were still going strong and provided him with links to liveauctioneers.com, where sixty-six items were up for sale, and icollector.com, with two hundred and eighteen items offered. Douglas Berndt replied to me the next day via an email indicating that he was prohibited from discussing details of ongoing investigations but confirmed that they were still working the case.

In July, after two weeks had passed and feeling the need to stay in touch with the FBI, I wrote Douglas an email. His short reply came the same day: "I am being transferred to Chicago in a few weeks. I'll talk to my supervisor regarding the status of your case and whether it will be reassigned and to whom." I was crushed and disappointed. I replied to Douglas's email, indicating that his assistance in getting my case reassigned to the right agent would be much appreciated. On October 27th, I sent a FedEx overnight package to FBI Special Agent in Charge Laura A. Bucheit in Las Vegas. I included correspondence, a summary of evidence, and a mug shot of Darrel Coker. But then something unexpected happened. Nothing. Ms. Bucheit never even replied. Despite earlier assurances to the contrary, the FBI came up empty.

At this point, I decided my only alternative was to pursue a civil suit. In January of 2016, I contacted my good friend and attorney Jim Niven in San Francisco for assistance. Two weeks later Jim's email read: "You hit the jackpot... I found for you a Las Vegas attorney, Dominic Gentile, and he is a Sassone collector!" That was good. Dominic took my case as a personal affront right from the start, and following several conference calls with my studio, decided to prepare a lawsuit to file in

Nevada. I began to stay in touch with his team: investigator Don Dibble, to whom I provided answers for his mounting evidence in the case, and Angelina Filippo, Dominic's intellectual *strega* (good witch), as he called her, who corresponded and deliberated on copyright laws.

I now realized I had been consumed with this entire discovery process since October of 2014, as I was determined to put a stop to the forging of my work. As a result, my studio work suffered a great deal. It was time to get back to painting. In 2013 I had been invited by Emanuele Lepri, the director of the Bata Shoe Museum in Toronto, to propose a project installation for two of their gallery spaces. The only stipulation was the project had to be site specific, meaning the exhibition had to engage in a dialogue with footwear. Shoes, I felt, combined iconography, psychology, and individual memories in a single object and also served as a marker of personal identity. They absorb the wear and tear of daily life and are an instrument of self-expression. My attraction to fashion and footwear dated back to the 1960s during my time in London and San Francisco at the height of the hippie movement.

A concept for the new project was triggered by a visit to one of the museum's then current exhibitions called *Standing Tall: A Curious History of Men in Heels.* I immediately recalled my own high-heeled snakeskin boots purchased in 1967 at Granny Takes a Trip, a boutique on King's Road in London. At the same time, I started to reflect upon the social significance of a pair of shoes. With this in mind, I plunged into the project, exploring first the paradox of the contrast between the threadbare footwear of homeless men on the street, and those fancy high heels women wear to social events.

Tim Bare Land was the first painting I completed. A play on words on the name of a leading American shoe brand Timberland, this canvas juxtaposed the brightly colored window of a storefront with a shadowy sidewalk cradling a sleeping, crumpled figure of a homeless man wearing a pair of Timberland boots. In the next painting, *Mirella and Emilia,* the shoes belonged to a different class of people—two women in a close-up view who are locked in conversation. I used Emily and our friend Mirella as models, sitting together but without showing their faces. Perhaps the most classical work in the project, this canvas featured their pretty high-heeled shoes in the foreground, dangling down from legs crossed under fancy skirts, suggesting that these women were friends and that high fashion shoes have a life of their own as objects of desire.

In *Thong Sandals,* I filled the entire canvas with the image of flip-flops, footwear increasingly worn in public and the perfect symbol of society's current fixation with fast-fashion plastic goods. To imply the superficial excitement of the object, I used bright, spontaneous brushstrokes to amplify the visual sense of motion, and to highlight the allure of the manufactured object as a symbol of carefree, sunny freedom. In another picture, I used my own old work shoes as the central subject for a large canvas called *Self Portrait.* Here, I tried to capture the worn, paint-splattered leather shoes that bear the evidence of thousands of hours of labor in the studio. Devoid of decoration, the image was rendered in a broadly suffused tonality of Venetian red to evoke the passage of time in an effort to capture an intimate inner conversation—a self-exploration that began with the 1991 canvas *We are Mannequins,* a work that remains in my personal collection and was now included as one of the ten paintings in the exhibition.

As I reflected on the snakeskin boots that traveled with me from Europe to North America, I recognized the connection with my now familiar theme of departures and arrivals—the theme I was exploring with such intensity in my concurrent series of track paintings. One of the new canvases was *Journey*, a key painting in the collection that featured a pair of my old, worn out boots on a railway track in Toronto, my new home. I saw in them an important symbol of the journey I had traveled as an artist. Concerned to elevate this simple footwear to the status of fine art, I heightened the sense of their physical presence with a highly tactile impasto. Eventually my actual boots were prominently displayed in a case adjacent to the installation of this painting as part of the exhibition *Marco Sassone: His Boots and Other Works*. The museum held an opening reception on June 8, 2016, and I was delighted both with the large public turnout and the media coverage, including an interview on CBC-National TV of Canada. The show was accompanied by a catalog written by Deirdre Kelly, art critic and journalist for Toronto's *The Globe and Mail* newspaper. "His paintings of footwear dance with meaning, ..." she noted in her essay, "they are the product of an artist wanting to understand his world by stepping into other people's shoes and deepen his understanding of self by painting what remains special to him."

Just a few days after the closing of this exhibition on September 8, 2016, my complaint was filed in the District Court of Clark County in Nevada. I was hugely relieved, and yet I couldn't help but remember how long it took to get this far. It had taken practically two years of my life to build the case for myself. Now, I finally had the chance to put an end to the ongoing production of forged artworks being marketed in my name.

However, as I would later discover, this was just the beginning of the process—an ordeal that would last for years through a series of astonishing events and lingering personal anxieties. The attorneys for Darrell Coker kept filing repeated motions in an effort to have the case dismissed on preposterous grounds, and once turned down by the District Court, they appealed the case to the Nevada Supreme Court, who again dismissed the appeals and ruled in my favor. Clyde Dewitt, the attorney assigned to my case, was responsible for fending off their motions and had won every decision thus far.

In the course of these lengthy legal maneuvers, two shocking events occurred: The shipper, Darryl McCullough of PostalAnnex, committed suicide in unexplained circumstances, and, sometime later, Darrell Coker died. As a distressing result, we lost our key witnesses for the trial, which left us to deal with the estate.

In January 2020, I flew to Las Vegas to attend a pre-trial settlement conference ordered by the court. My son, Nicola, traveled from Orange County, California, to be with me. I was excited at the prospect of seeing him for a few days, even though I was overwhelmed with anxiety about a case that appeared to be in a state of permanent limbo. My lead attorney, Dominic Gentile, called me in for a meeting prior to the conference, where he informed me that our case against the estate had weakened considerably with the deaths of two key witnesses. "If I had known what I know now, I would never have taken this case," he said, concluding that we should have no expectations of this mediation hearing; things, he thought, did not look good. It was then that I asked Dominic if I could have a few minutes to speak with the mediator, a retired judge, the Honorable Gene T. Porter.

Anticipating the challenge as things stood, I had brought along with me some items from the studio. I made sure to secure a place right next to the judge. There was silence in the room as my attorneys, the law firm's investigator, the judge, and my son all waited to hear what I had to say. I began by addressing the judge: "I would like to paint a picture," I said, "this time a picture with words." I went on to explain the importance of an artist's signature, and what it means to the artist. "The signature is what identifies his work," I said. "It's what identifies his style. In my case, that signature was developed over the fifty years of a professional career." I paused to let that sink in. "When someone steals your signature," I went on, "you feel violated in the worst way possible." Then I opened my briefcase and dumped a large stack of printed matter on the table—evidence of the sales of forgeries of my artwork, which I had personally downloaded from online auctions in 2015. "This evidence," I told the mediator, "was conveniently deleted and is no longer available online. But guess what?" I continued. "I printed every sales report, which shows that these are all images with forged signatures, along with the corresponding amount for each fake lithograph sold."

"That's 2,192 pieces that were sold!" exclaimed the judge, reviewing the tally in my notes.

"Yes," I replied. "And please note that this information was provided by the seller himself, Mr. Coker, and in his own words!" I paused. "At that time you could still just click on 'past sales' for 'artist Marco Sassone' and the information would immediately pop up in front of your eyes." My explanation seemed to have had the desired effect. You never know when a sudden intuition turns out to be the right one. The judge stood up. "It's time for me to see the defendant's team," he said and disappeared into a separate conference room. He was back in a very short while. "Mr. Sassone," he asked, "are you willing to repeat what you just told me to the lawyers for the estate?"

Dominic Gentile glanced over at me. It seemed he had never heard of such a request in his entire career. But he gave me the okay as we all stood up and walked over to meet the opposing team in a huge, elaborately decorated conference room. The mahogany-paneled walls and crown moulding gave the space an oppressive, dark feeling.

My monologue was short and to the point. The evidence indisputable. I could tell the presentation spoke volumes to Matthew Callister, the lead estate attorney, who appeared visibly surprised by the whole thing. I must admit to a sense of real satisfaction, and I thought that now, finally, the estate would want to avoid a trial and agree to a better settlement of our case.

When I think of my own form of creative expression as a painter, I feel eternally grateful for the extraordinary life it has afforded me. I cannot imagine what I would be without it. Standing at the easel with the canvas in front of me has been a profound learning experience. I have learned that your true work comes from absolute interior honesty. And yet, dishonesty infects our society and our culture in the world in which we live today. There is dishonesty even within the legal system, where the guilty party is vigorously defended by the work of advocates who are fully aware of the deception. They hide behind a smokescreen made readily available by a system in which defense attorneys indulge in their twisted dance of procrastination, with no end in sight for no better reason than their own financial gain. Would it not be possible to make the process simpler and more effective? Yet, we conspire to create this legal fog through which it is virtually impossible to travel.

Even so, this train eventually reached the end of the line, and the case was finally settled out of court. I learned about it soon after my return to Toronto. Much to my surprise, I experienced none of the overwhelming excitement or emotional aftermath that I would have expected after the news arrived. It had all taken too long. By now, I was numb. My mood was simply tranquil, pervaded by quiet feelings of relief, despite the lingering traces of distress. The case had consumed my existence for most of the past six years. My mind had too often been lost in a maze of thoughts that led nowhere. At times, it had left me feeling that even painting had become no more than a part-time hobby. It continues to amaze me that I kept up with my schedule of exhibitions through it all.

In January of 2019, I attended the opening of my traveling show *Home on the Streets* at the Columbus Centre in Toronto. This was the fourth venue following San Francisco, Los Angeles, and Florence, and it included additional works completed over the past twenty-five years. The installation filled both the upper and lower galleries and was inaugurated by the consul general of Italy. Proceeds from the event provided funding for culturally sensitive senior care. Later in November, also in Toronto, my exhibition *Urban Scapes* opened at Berenson Fine Art. It included a new series of paintings characterized, as had been my earlier work, by turbulent street perspectives. Also included were some intimate paintings that evoked the soul of Venice—a city I have long celebrated as my spiritual home.

In the world beyond the studio, it was soon to become increasingly hard for me to ignore the historical moment in which we found ourselves with the COVID-19 pandemic. It has brought me to realize the shallowness of materialistic pleasures and how every day is tarnished by the cruelty of a plague that rages around the globe. In past times, societies could accept the mortal toll of infectious diseases as a part of life, a part of their daily existence. The progress we claim to have made in recent times does not allow us to feel this way. We have learned to trust science to relieve us of a good deal of our suffering, but it appears that we have thus far little science to rely on in this pandemic. This may be its real lesson—a lesson, really, in the fragility and illusion of what we believe in as progress.

Given the chaotic state of the world at this time, I've wondered if our current predicament might offer an interesting subject for painting. Social turmoil and natural disasters have informed my work in the past: The great flood of Florence is forever imprinted on my memory, and I have long been engaged with the subject of homelessness—another true epidemic in the western world today.

Reflecting on how I might be able to approach the subject of the pandemic, it seemed to me that I could do no worse than follow the trail blazed by art and artists throughout history in response to the recurrence of similar plagues.

The COVID-19 pandemic is actually just the latest in a long series of plagues that have devastated the world over the course of many centuries. The first that comes to mind dates back to the typhoid fever outbreak, circa 430 BC, during the Peloponnesian war, a disease that decimated one fourth of the army in Athens as well as one fourth of its population in the space of a few years. Indeed, the word "pandemic" derives from the Greek *pan-demos,* meaning "all the people," suggesting a disease that spreads at extraordinary speed to multiple geographical areas and eventually threatens the entire population of the world.

During the reign of Marcus Aurelius in the Roman Empire, between 165 and 180 AD, the Antonine plague killed between five to thirty million people, according to various historical sources. While there is still some uncertainty about the nature of the disease, it is generally agreed that this plague was brought to Rome by the Roman army following the war with the Parthians between 161 to 166 AD. But it was the plague in Justinian times, from 541 to 544 AD, that reduced by half the empire's population, causing a demographic, economic, and military crisis from which the recovery would last for a couple of centuries. These examples show how the diffusion of the bacterium "Yersinia pestis" has affected the course of history. It was one of the major threats that humankind has ever had to face. The origin of the bacterium probably originated in Asia from wild rodents that developed a resistance to the virus.

Europe was later ravaged by other epidemics, including the bubonic plague that has doubtless remained the most prominent in the collective imagination, as we think of Boccaccio's *Decameron* or Peter Bruegel's *The Triumph of Death.* According to commonly agreed estimates, the death toll in Europe alone reached over twenty million people between 1347 and 1353. Again, this plague most likely originated in the Asia and spread like an oil stain throughout continental Europe, reportedly reducing the population by one third.

The plague that hit Venice in the 1500s recurred twice in less than seventy years. The city was forced to take drastic measures. The outbreak endangered the economy of the Serenissima (the Republic of Venice) as the disease claimed almost fifty thousand victims, among them Titian and Giorgione, two illustrious painters of the Venetian School during the High Renaissance.

The relationship between art and pandemics is demonstrably close, especially since art can be an effective narrative. In the face of death, artists have successfully created dramatic images, reconciling the descriptive imperative with an iconic component. One image published in 1656, for example, addressed the then current pandemic in one of the most recognizable symbols of the Black Death: *Plague Doctor*, an engraving by an unknown artist, depicts a long dark tunic, a pair of gloves, shoes, a staff, and a beak-shaped hat containing aromatic essences supposedly a filter to impede the spread of the infection.

Several other epidemics infected Europe from the 1600s onward, including the plague that spanned the period from about 1855 to 1910, starting in China and spreading throughout the world. Also in the 1900s the world experienced several pandemic waves of cholera, originally confined to India but later spread to China, Europe, Canada, and the U.S., and as far west as the Pacific coast. Russia was also hard hit by the infection, which decimated over a million human lives.

Among the prominent artists chronicling these plagues were Tintoretto, who in 1549 created a monumental piece installed in the presbytery of the church of the Scuola Grande di San Rocco in Venice; Micco Spadaro, who became a major chronicler of the plague in Naples in the 1600s, registering on canvas the gruesome images of streets and squares packed with lifeless bodies; and Gianbattista Tiepolo, who produced his greatest religious work for a monumental altarpiece in the cathedral at Este, near Padua—a painting that commemorates the devastation of the plague in 1630. Two additional artists worthy of mention are the French painter Jules-Èlie Delaunay, who addressed the plague in Rome in 1869 in an almost cinematographic canvas that is currently in the collection of the Musée d'Orsay; and Arnold Böcklin, who painted one of the most striking images inspired by the plague in 1898—the personification of death riding a winged creature flying over the empty street of a medieval town.

After the discovery of the bacteria and the production of a therapeutic serum in 1894, new epidemics became far less lethal to entire populations than those of previous centuries. The fight against pathogenic organisms continued into the twentieth century yet proved unable to prevent the millions of deaths caused by, for example, the Spanish flu pandemic that infected five hundred million people in the world between 1918 and 1920. It cost some fifty million lives and reduced global life expectancy by about twelve years. The artist Gustaf Klimt perished during this pandemic, as did Egon Schiele who wrote to his mother, "…the disease is very grave and dangerous to my life. I am preparing for the worst." Edvard Munch survived the pandemic, and in 1919 painted the splendid *Self-Portrait after the Spanish Flu* in which he manages to evoke his close brush with death in the pallid rendition of skin tones and thinning hair.

There is no scientific agreement on the spread of the Spanish flu, but it left its mark throughout the world after originating, possibly again, in China. A more recent disease that still affects people around the world is HIV, which has claimed victims since 1981. The death count currently stands at over thirty million. Among the artworks from the 1980s addressing this particular disease and the image that most readily comes to mind is the poster made by Keith Haring following his diagnosis with AIDS. The image shows three figures whose gestures mimic the old adage, "See no evil, speak no evil, hear no evil." The artist lost his struggle with the disease at the age of 31 in 1990. The other artwork that represents perhaps one of the most disturbing responses to the HIV crisis was created by David Wojnarowicz, who died from the disease in 1992. In his silver print we see a herd of buffalos careening to their death from a cliff's edge. The image evokes feelings of great suffering and despair—and draws a parallel between the AIDS crisis and the wanton massacre of buffalo in America during the nineteenth century.

In recent years, we have witnessed various forms of influenza and coronavirus pathogens that have been passed from animals to humans, including now the COVID-19 pandemic. This current epidemic presents some peculiarities that make it in some ways unique, involving both scientific and socio-cultural reasons. It is, after all, the first pandemic to have developed during the age of the internet and social media.

As I reflected on the strange experience of lockdown and how I might have imagined approaching the subject in my painting, I concluded that I had no need to address those feelings of solitude and self-isolation. Instead, I thought of the quote by the writer Fyodor Dostoevsky, who said, "Beauty will save the world," and began to visualize subjects whose beauty might help soothe the soul.

I found myself returning to my early years of en plein air painting in California and felt an unexpected pull toward those images. I roamed the studio, pulling down canvases from the racks as I sought to calm my anxieties, feeling at once restless and excited. I walked back again and again through memory, my imaginary footsteps echoing off the walls of my confinement. Everything seemed quieter, slower.

Some early evenings I found myself pacing the floor, reaching out to touch some of the objects on my painting table, picking things up and replacing them even though I had arranged them a hundred times before. The frenzy eventually sorted itself out with the time I spent working through old folders of sketches and drawings I had made on site. Without any conscious effort on my part, my attention moved on to the preparation of a series of small canvases with images that had already formulated in my mind—images I could now visualize as paintings in the manner of those long neglected landscapes—and with them came a subtle but urgent need to get back to the creative act.

As I glanced back and forth to a drawing I had made years ago in San Francisco, my brush began to sketch in rows of buildings on either side of the street—one of those steep downward slopes that are so typical of the city. I added in color indications for the dwellings and part of the sky in the far distance. The cityscape began to emerge as I worked in a muted range of color, from blue-gray ultramarine to pale ocher tones. The downhill slope was rendered with faint marks suggesting railroad tracks vanishing from the foreground into the heart of the city. Then I quietly replaced the brushes on the table and gazed at the work in progress. I had to admit I was pleased with this new piece. At first glance the canvas gave expression to some delightful descriptive qualities, reminiscent of a time of rich emotional connection with the external world.

A silent rhythm was established as I returned to the act of painting, and from the period of seclusion that followed, a new series emerged with a palette of lively colors and complementary brushwork. One of the canvases reminded me of my early work, still propped up on a nearby easel, in which a view from above created the impression of spatial breadth, suffused with warm light. The Hotel Laguna occupied the space to the right of the canvas and above it, in a spare evocation, a bank of overhanging clouds. This was the town where I once lived, Laguna Beach, a place I remembered always with affection and which I often missed. Looking at the image, I was aware of the prevalence of warm colors ranging from pale Naples yellow to peach and light orange tones, and the dashes of rust reds and sap-greens toward the water on the far right of the canvas. A number of brush marks suggested the small housing complexes and single residences on Pacific Coast Highway to the left, running up the slope and fading into a blended pattern of pale greens that evoked the hills behind.

Hours elapsed like seconds while I painted this piece. When I was done, I felt I had been able to recreate the special translucent effects of light that emanated from the simple beauty of this site-specific landscape. Such were the fleeting moments that uplifted my spirits during the pandemic.

As I recall those special moments, how could I fail to mention our Bentley rides to a deserted parking lot? These were in themselves tales of creativity and resourcefulness, a splendid performance of surviving boredom, even as the pandemic raged.

There are many takeout pizza places in Toronto, but my friends Chris and Sofia, the proud owners of seven British Classic automobiles, are also known for their predilection for a rustic pizza by Taste of Naples, a joint located out of town in a Woodbridge plaza. So every week, Emily and I dressed up for the occasion, drove out with our friends for forty-five minutes, picked up two extra-large pizzas and walked across the plaza to a patch of green grass, where we set up chairs, a table with a tablecloth, silverware, and had a wonderful time.

This unreal circumstance actually prompted my imagination to paint in words brilliant images of a Mediterranean vacation. In between bites of pepperoni pizza, it was as though we could sense the imaginary waves beyond the high wooden palisade that marked the perimeter of our surreal parking lot: the smell of the salty sea seemed to pervade the air, the blue coastline was punctuated with white sails, and the sunset promised to arrive at any moment in a panoply of magnificent color. This, and so much more, we could see and taste, along with a real Neapolitan pizza with San Marzano tomatoes and buffalo mozzarella.

* * *

In the course of my long journey as an artist, I have made recognizable images, not out of some re-established aesthetic intention, but because that is who I am. It is my natural inclination.

I have neither told stories in my pictures nor did I make art that was purely descriptive or literal in its relation to reality. Abstract art was not the course I chose because I differ fundamentally from its credo, and because my art simply did not transform or evolve into non-objective forms. As I mentioned earlier, in Chapter 11, for me the quest for any transformational originality must develop through an organic process. A good example of an artist who followed this path would be Wassily Kandinsky, who took the time to digest the lessons and values of the past before revolutionizing them in his own work. Today, many of the so-called avant-garde artists seem to think they can trash these values without knowing anything about them in the first place. They destroy what they don't know, and the result is simply a technical effect—an effect, unfortunately, passed on to the viewer.

The issue for me is not a matter of novelty or a quest for the new. Nor is it a matter of the appearance of a pleasing assortment of images that are currently flooding the marketplace. These notions address only a one-dimensional plateau of social and historical progress—a phantom metaphor of the avant-garde favored by the commercialization of art. Rather, it is a question of finding access to the "truth," our truth, the condition of being awake to the perplexing significance of our existence today.

There is a voice inside our soul that is never silent and spurs us on to keep moving forward, toward ourselves and what we must be. This voice of duty gives us little peace and undoubtedly annoys us, forcing us to never look behind but forward on a never-ending path.

As we follow our journey of discovery, when we sense the approach of some new direction in our work, we feel a confrontation between what we know and what we are about to find. And between these two areas lies a zone of conflict and anxiety. As we step away from the known—our own or the current culture's expectations of art—we may be, at first, reluctant to let go of our familiar modus operandi. If we choose to proceed, our faltering footsteps are supported by an inner mechanism, an assurance born of a concentration of visual clarity. Our instinct tells us at such moments to connect the thread of precedents in order to establish a point of reference. In doing so, we acknowledge the fertile ground of our origins as we venture onward into the now reimagined process of painting.

Over time, I began to make paintings inspired by the incessant search to discover my way, to discover what keeps me going, to reach further. I seek out visions that summon feelings in their purest moment, when they are fresh and elusive. This is the process of art, to translate this vision with paint—this wonderful, mysterious substance of sensuous, velvety consistency that captures my impulses in each and every brushstroke. As I tried to describe the act of painting earlier in this memoir, when you are in a flow and you have surrendered yourself totally to the work in progress, it feels as though you are delivering the purest expression of yourself.

The feeling of moving forward and reaching out is reflected in the latest works now in progress at my studio. These canvases feel like the focus of my existence as they come to life in a magical rhythm of succession, a flow of strokes synthesizing all the ideas taken from a myriad of sources falling into place and forming a cohesive whole.

I think of them as history paintings because they inhabit rifts, gaps, and unexplored territory. I find myself embedded in the constant dense material of painting, waiting for what the process will reveal—a process in which I act more as a witness than as a controlling agent. For me, the most important thing is to create images that capture an emotional state of being.

One painting I just completed seems to suggest where I am going. Suffused light and muted tones of ultramarine blue permeate the entire canvas. A pathway of steel rails moves from the foreground through an expanse of wasteland, vanishing as it leads toward a tiny, faint city skyline. In this languid landscape, I begin to see what feels like a significant difference from previous cycles—cycles that once communicated in a more aggressive mode, in which a fragmented worldview controlled both the imagination and the consciousness. Here, the furor has subsided, and pure pictorial emotion returns to define its own essential language. It feels as though I have drifted out along those tracks that I myself created, and I am now able to move about with ease in the unresolved state between longing and belonging, a place where I can finally find sanctuary, solace, and deliverance.

AFTERWORD

When I began making art more than fifty years ago in Florence, painting assisted me in finding a direction for my life, and provided me with the means to take control of my chaotic emotions as a way out of my crazy youth. Years later, when I moved to Southern California, I found myself in a cultural transition. My work was soon in great demand, and I was embraced by a public more loyal than I could ever imagine. My painting became an exploratory process for me. When I relocated to San Francisco a decade later, this process stimulated old memories and unearthed buried feelings that challenged me to confront my obstinate contradictions, such as my moral and social ambiguities and my perplexing doubts about personal identity. I also became acutely aware of feeling culturally displaced. I identified with the homeless. I began to notice railroad tracks everywhere, which would later become symbolic themes in my artistic journey. In my early work, I had been drawn to Venice and its many visual perspectives and became obsessed with the narrow, winding canals that lure the eye and inspire a mysterious longing to discover new and unpredictable waterways. In this sense my work is autobiographical—a journey that reveals itself in its attachment to converging lines and vanishing points. And the railroad tracks that continue to appear in my paintings keep leading me deeper into a dramatic engagement with my past, yet also offer me the prospect of moving forward in my life.

Today, my work is more direct. I have conquered distance, and my vision of distance in turn has itself become my subject. I paint in the moment, rendering spaces as they appear in my range of vision and capture images that are tangible manifestation of my universe. My themes have become simpler, yet essential: visions of images in forward motion along narrowing paths, frustrations with growing older, acceptance of mortality, and anticipation of the final arrival, as portrayed in my painting *Terminus*. As I approach the culmination of my American journey, the future awaits, where nothing is definite except that everything has been transformed.

ACKNOWLEDGMENTS

First I wish to acknowledge my friend Peter Clothier, who planted in me the original seed to write *American Journey* more than twenty years ago. Collaborating with me on a subject matter so intimate and at times painful, Peter's keen writer's instincts showed me how to follow the story and develop the narrative.

I am particularly grateful to Donelson Hoopes for his insightful text for the monograph, *Sassone,* published in 1980. It was his writing at the time that set the stage for a new plateau of creation in my ongoing painting process; and to Peter Selz for his incisive introduction in the catalog, *Master & Pupil: Oskar Kokoschka, Silvio Loffredo, Marco Sassone*, published in 2001.

I wish to extend my profound gratitude to my art teachers: first, my father, for the greatest gift of all: he believed in my art from the very start; Ottone Rosai, whose instructions in *plein air* Florence are forever imprinted in my memory; Ugo Maturo, who instilled in me early on the art and affection for chiaroscuro; Silvio Loffredo, who transformed the entire direction of my life by the living example of his freedom of expression; and Guy Maccoy, the father of serigraphy, who instructed me in the art of handmade silk screening.

I am grateful for all the art dealers, agents, collectors, curators, writers, and critics who have promoted my work and nurtured my career, and especially those who have provided unfailing support during the various peregrinations of my life.

I particularly want to thank the following people for their generous support: Sylvia Bello, Adolfo Nodal, Angela Alioto, Pasquale Iannetti, Roberto Pucci, Ilaria Bonuccelli, Janet Dominik, Deirdre Kelly, Pierluigi Bacci, Robert A. Whyte, Jonathan Goodman, Maria Porges, Sharon Fitzsimons, Gianni Fassio, Amy Selwyn, Massimo Bertozzi, Diane Nelson, Emanuele Lepri, Odon Wagner, Laura Adreani, Carlo Eletti, Jennifer Stucker, Valentina Fogher, Andon Yanev and Lidia Yaneva, Rhonda Carano, Enzo Coniglio, Amelia Antonucci, Peter Falk, Franco Piras, Josef Vykydal, Ron Segal, Antonio Miniaci, Don Piragoff and Carole Brown.

I also wish to acknowledge friends who are no longer here to read my tribute to their place in my life: Bruno Galeotti, Oliviero Comparini, Elaine and Jill Stucker, Cliff Abbey, Armen Gasparian, Felix Bernard, Guy Maccoy, Tom Enman, Wally Findlay, Phyllis Barton, Tom Bradley, Sheila Woodworth, Sergio Franchi, Silvio Loffredo, Tommaso Paloscia, Donelson Hoopes, Don Carano, Lorenzo Petroni, John Wilson; and especially, of course, my parents, Anna and Nicola Sassone, whose love and affection had no limits.

I am indebted to my assistants, Annie Cormier and Sarah Burton, for their excellent work in locating and organizing materials for this memoir.

Dulcis in fundo, my profound love and gratitude goes to my beautiful wife and art dealer, Emilia Ianeva, whose inspiration filled my life when it was needed the most. I wish to thank her for her valuable insights and patient observations on the manuscript as it progressed; and especially for embracing my absence at those all-too-frequent moments when she caught me deep in thought, lost in some distant corner of my *American Journey*.

INDEX

C

D

E

F

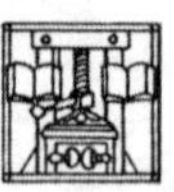

This book was designed
and produced in the U.S.A. in July 2022.

The monochromatic image depicted on the end sheets was created
by reproducing in duo-tone the oil painting *Ca'di Cecco*
by Marco Sassone.

Composed by AuthorImprints.,
Carlsbad, California
Printed and bound by Sheridan Books, Inc.,
Chelsea, Michigan

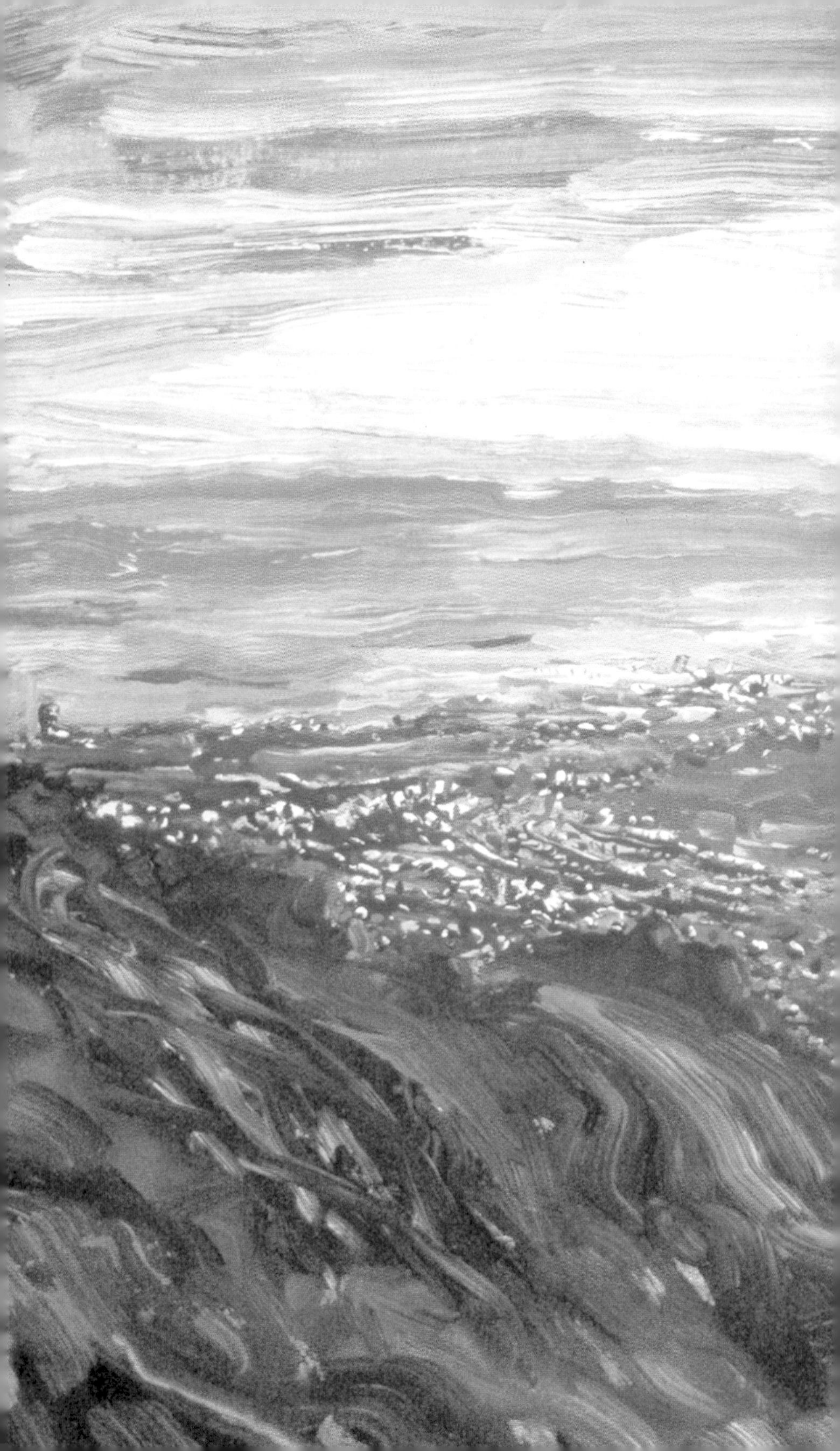